Up Against the W

Also by Peter Laufer

Dreaming in Turtle: A Journey through the Passion, Profit, and Peril of Our Most Coveted Prehistoric Creatures

Organic: A Journalist's Quest to Discover the Truth behind Food Labeling

The Elusive State of Jefferson: A Journey through the 51st State

Interviewing: The Oregon Method (editor)

Slow News: A Manifesto for the Critical News Consumer

No Animals Were Harmed: The Controversial Line between Entertainment and Abuse

Forbidden Creatures: Inside the World of Animal Smuggling and Exotic Pets

The Dangerous World of Butterflies: The Startling Subculture of Criminals, Collectors and Conservationists

Neon Nevada (with Sheila Swan Laufer)

¡Calexico! True Lives of the Borderlands

Hope Is a Tattered Flag (with Markos Kounalakis)

Mission Rejected: U.S. Soldiers Who Say No to Iraq

Exodus to Berlin: The Return of the Jews to Germany

Highlights of a Lowlife: The Autobiography of Milan Melvin (editor)

Shock and Awe: Responses to War (editor)

¡See You Later, Amigo! An American Border Tale (illustrated by Susan L. Roth)

Made in Mexico/Hecho en México (illustrated by Susan L. Roth)

Wireless Etiquette: A Guide to the Changing World of Instant Communication

Safety and Security for Women Who Travel (with Sheila Swan Laufer)

Inside Talk Radio: America's Voice or Just Hot Air

A Question of Consent: Innocence and Complicity in the Glen Ridge Rape Case

Nightmare Abroad: Stories of Americans Imprisoned in Foreign Lands

Iron Curtain Rising: A Personal Journey through the Changing Landscape of Eastern Europe

Up Against the Wall

THE CASE FOR OPENING THE MEXICAN-AMERICAN BORDER

PETER LAUFER, PhD

Anthem Press
An imprint of Wimbledon Publishing Company
www.anthempress.com

This edition first published in UK and USA 2022
by ANTHEM PRESS
75–76 Blackfriars Road, London SE1 8HA, UK
or PO Box 9779, London SW19 7ZG, UK
and
244 Madison Ave #116, New York, NY 10016, USA

First published in the UK and USA by Anthem Press in 2020

British Library Cataloguing-in-Publication Data
A catalogue record for this book is available from the British Library.

Library of Congress Control Number: 2020940396

ISBN-13: 978-1-83998-576-8 (Pbk)
ISBN-10: 1-83998-576-3 (Pbk)

This title is also available as an e-book.

Photographs and maps by the author.

para Sheila
con aprecio profundamente
y amor infinito

CONTENTS

ILLUSTRATIONS

PREFACE: BIENVENIDOS, AMIGOS

I am prejudiced to favor immigrants. How can I not be? My father came through Ellis Island. I have the page from the logbook where his arrival was recorded by the immigration officer on duty. He answered all the questions to the satisfaction of the inspector.

"Whether a polygamist?"
"No."
"Whether an anarchist?"
"No."

And Question 24:

Whether a person believes in or advocates the overthrow by force or violence of the Government of the United States or of all forms of law, or who disbelieves in or is opposed to organized government, or who advocates the assassination of public officials, or who advocates or teaches the unlawful destruction of property, or is a member of or affiliated with any organization entertaining and teaching disbelief in or opposition to organized government or which teaches the unlawful destruction of property, or who advocates or teaches the duty, necessity, or propriety of the unlawful assaulting or killing of any officer or officers, either of specific individuals or of officers in general, of the Government of the United States or of any other organized government because of his or their official character?

"No," my father answered. It was 1923 and America was still more worried about immigrating anarchists from Middle Europe than Mexicans coming north.

"You're an American by birth," my father repeatedly reminded me. "I'm an American by choice."

Years ago, my wife Sheila and I spent days searching the bowels of the La Porte County courthouse in Indiana, finally finding her grandfather's naturalization papers.

"It is my bona fide intention," he swore to the clerk of the La Porte County Court in 1913, "to renounce forever all allegiance and fidelity to any foreign prince, potentate, state, or sovereignty, and particularly to Franz Josef, Emperor of Austria and Apostolic King of Hungary."

We secured the address of the house in what used to be called the Poletown section of La Porte where her mother lived before immigrating to California. Poletown was still on the wrong side of the tracks. The railroad bisects La Porte. South of the ornate courthouse, gracious Victorian mansions line Michigan Avenue under a canopy of well-established trees. But east of downtown and north across the tracks the boxy houses are humble, packed into the rusting factory and warehouse district. The wrong side of the tracks is the usual entry point in an American city for immigrants. And in La Porte, Poletown was filling up with Mexicans (along with other immigrants from south of the Rio Grande), Mexican restaurants and Mexican grocery stores.

Radical Change

In the summer of 2001, just weeks before the September 11 attacks, I wrote the following essay for the *San Francisco Chronicle*, a strident call to open the southern U.S. border to Mexicans who wish to come north:

We Americans work hard to keep Mexicans out of the United States, Mexicans who want to wash our dishes and pick our crops. Those crops need picking and those dishes need washing, so workers come north despite our best efforts. America ought to open and demilitarize our southern border immediately, welcome our Mexican neighbors to come and go with the ease of Canadian travelers to this country, and finally put an end to a sordid and shameful chapter in our national history. Not only is such a change in policy the proper moral and logical course of action for us to take, there will be no negative effects to the lives of most Americans.

The current border, from its Berlin Wall-like ghastliness against cities such as Tijuana, to the equally harsh deserts to the east, doesn't keep Mexicans from coming north and working here illegally. The heavily armed Border Patrol, equipped with the latest hi-tech magic, can't stop this surge of money-motivated migration. We all know that. Just look in the kitchen of your favorite restaurant, or along the roadside at one of the ad hoc hiring stations where desperate manual laborers congregate around all over the United States. Mexican workers are everywhere north of the border, especially in California. The only Mexicans who choose to come north illegally and don't are the unlucky who get caught. And many of them just try again moments after they are deported.

Since the passage of the 1996 Illegal Immigration Reform and Immigrant Responsibility Act, the U.S. Border Patrol has grown into the nation's largest law enforcement agency, with nearly ten thousand officers. Nonetheless, our southern border remains porous.

A friend of mine who works in gardens and construction in Marin County commutes—illegally—from his home in Sinaloa. He's practiced at the journey, telling me jumping the border at Nogales, hitchhiking up to Tucson, and grabbing a Southwest flight to Oakland is just a necessary part of his work routine. Another friend simply walked into the United States past overworked border guards at a bridge between Ciudad Juárez and El Paso. Once on the U.S. side, she piled her hair up high on her head, made up her face, and with her short shorts and entitled attitude, she sashayed to the airport for a flight further north, sure no one would mistake her for a desperate Mexican peasant. She was right, and she's lived in rural California ever since, raising a family of U.S.-born children.

I have traveled the artificial line between our two countries with Border Patrol officers, and many have acknowledged that they cannot keep determined Mexicans from crossing north.

It's time to try a new approach.

Let's begin by opening the border to all Mexicans who wish to travel north. Supporters of guns, guards and fences argue that if the border were open, the United States would be smothered by Mexicans escaping their poverty-stricken homeland. Yet there is no restriction on immigrants coming to California from Mississippi or West Virginia, and California is not inundated with a parade of workers from those poorer states. They cannot afford to live here without working and they apparently don't want the jobs that are available. As long as those agriculture, construction, restaurant and other positions are vacant, workers will come north. But that's good. We need the help. Our economy depends on its Mexican work force. Economically driven immigration ultimately is self-regulating. When and if enough migrants fill the jobs U.S. citizens refuse to take, there will be little motivation for Mexicans to leave home. There is no restriction on the movement of labor within the European Community. When the German economy was humming, the Portuguese, for example, moved north to better paying jobs from Stuttgart to Berlin. When stagnating growth then created high unemployment in Germany, the Portuguese went home or sought jobs elsewhere.

Critics argue that unrestricted traffic north from Mexico will result in increased demands on schools, health care and welfare. But that's also a fatuous worry. Few workers from Mexico who do not qualify legally for such benefits attempt to secure the services. They are afraid of being caught. And if a worker earns a living up here and does qualify for benefits, it does our social services systems no harm for them to collect.

Historically there is no basis for keeping Mexicans south of the frontier. Aside from the fact that much of the West was once half of their country, there were no restrictions on the movement of Mexicans back and forth across the current border until relatively recently. Controls were first placed at the border in the late nineteenth century to keep out Europeans and Asians who were denied legal access to the United States. Well into the twentieth century Mexicans continued to enjoy free passage back and forth from their country to ours. U.S. authorities found that most of these border crossers traveled for work and they were treated as commuters.

Restrictions began to be enforced during the Mexican revolution when Mexicans were forced to pass a literacy test and pay a one-time eight-dollar fee to cross legally into the United States.

Today Mexicans are treated as a threat, and futile attempts continue to keep them on their side of the line. Some proponents of a closed border fear problems associated with over population. Others worry that an open border will encourage employers to pay even less for entry-level jobs because of a growing and anxious labor pool.

Perhaps these concerns could be rationalized if our border controls worked. But in addition to the fact that most any determined Mexican eventually can get north and find a job, the borderlands have become a tragic gauntlet for them to run. Violent robbers, cheating *coyotes*, murderous desert heat, and cruel vigilantes all compete to victimize those crossing the border illegally. For many, the border patrol is the least of their problems and its officers may end up providing life-saving rescue from the other threats.

Yet despite these miserable conditions, a Mexican who really want to come north, comes north. Most just want to come work, make some money, and go home. After the Berlin Wall fell back in 1989, there was an initial rush of East Germans west. Then they went home. They did not enjoy the West German culture, they missed their families and friends. They went home.

So let's stop this deadly nonsense—at least as a test—and replace the failed barrier we've erected with a banner reading *Bienvenidos*. Let's make it as easy for a Mexican to come north as it is for a Canadian to come south. (July 12, 2001: A22)

Timing is critical. Shortly after my call to open the border was published in the *Chronicle*, the World Trade Center and the Pentagon were attacked. Immediately following those tragedies there were few takers for the idea of opening the southern frontier to Mexicans. But as the years pass since the 9/11 events, the validity of eliminating the futile attempts at keeping Mexicans out of the United States only seems greater. Not only would such free passage for Mexicans end a deadly charade along the borderline, it would make it much easier for the United States to secure its southern border against aliens who are real threats to its security.

Consider these points. The current border policy is a fraud. Mexicans come north despite U.S. law restricting their migration, despite the stretches of ludicrously expensive, Trump-promoted wall built after he became president. The U.S. government spends further enormous amounts of money and human resources chasing millions of Mexicans already in the United States. If these migrants crossed into the United States in an orderly fashion, unafraid of deportation, the numbers of people trying to cross into the United States illegally would be dramatically reduced. The Border Patrol would be in a much better position to apprehend those undocumented OTMs (other than Mexicans, to use the Border Patrol's parlance) who may pose a much greater potential threat to national security than do most Mexicans who eventually get across to the other side despite efforts to keep them out. Fringe benefits to such a policy would include a radical drop in the abuse of Mexican labor by U.S. employers. They could no longer easily take advantage of Mexican workers afraid to stand up for a fair wage and decent working conditions. Predatory *coyotes* would be out of business.

The best arguments for eliminating attempts to control Mexican migration are that such a policy is counterproductive to attempt and impossible to achieve. Instead, open the border to Mexicans. These neighbors are coming north despite U.S. laws. Open the border to Mexican workers so that the bad guys cannot hide in their shadows as they sneak across the border. Open the border to Mexicans the United States wants and needs, and then the Border Patrol can direct its vast resources against OTMs trying to break into the United States—the ones in the tunnels, those running across the desert and jumping the fences—among them without doubt some real villains. Open the border to Mexicans, a significant fuel for the U.S. economy, and make it easier for the Border Patrol to keep out the drug traffickers and the terrorists, and make it easier for the United States to efficiently process those desperate migrants from other countries seeking needed asylum.

To find fact, opinion and experience to bolster my argument, over several years I've visited and studied borders worldwide. I've traveled the serpentine U.S.-Mexican border, meeting with the victims and the perpetrators of U.S. government immigration policy. I've been contemplating alternatives to the status quo. I'm a journalist, so I've looked at the border wars through the prism of news and news reporting. Stories related here of my Mexican colleagues, journalists fighting bribery—a plague long institutionalized as a tool to manipulate Mexican journalism—offer glimpses into the rot in the Mexican economy, rot that emboldens frustrated workers to look to Gringolandia for a better life. I've wandered deep into Mexico to observe, experience and record the poverty and hopelessness that drive migrants to leave their homes and risk their lives on the long journey north. I've talked with undocumented immigrants living the American Dream and walked the beat with cops frustrated by unenforceable immigration laws. I've added to the mix stories from immigration lawyers and from those ultimately responsible for enticing Mexicans north: their employers in *El Norte*. On my journey, I've avoided the obvious border trip, that crooked line from San Diego and Tijuana east to Matamoros and Brownsville, the line that marks the artificial national frontier separating Mexico and the United States. Instead, I've traveled the extended border, crisscrossing our melded cultures from Niagara Falls to Chiapas, from Mexico City to Washington, DC, studying the borders that exist in our heads and hearts, searching for sane and humane solutions to the problems and conflicts plaguing our two countries.

FOREWORD BY FORMER PRESIDENT OF MEXICO, VICENTE FOX

When talk turns to borders and walls, I speak from experience. My grandfather left his native Ohio and crossed the border when he migrated into Mexico in 1895. He worked hard and eventually bought the hacienda that's now home for my Fox Presidential Library. Around his land he built a wall because my grandfather wanted to protect his property from Pancho Villa and his revolutionaries. He needed a high wall for the job. And the wall worked.

That wall still protects our hacienda from unwanted intruders. But its role is completely different from walls that attempt to stop migration. I like to quote from Ezekiel and the biblical dismissal of such walls. "When anyone builds a wall," Ezekiel teaches, "I will tear down the wall which you plastered over with whitewash and bring it down to the ground, so that its foundation is laid bare; and when it falls, you will be consumed in its midst. And you will know that I am the Lord." And I appreciate the observations of the Dalai Lama who reminds us that nations belong to their citizens. Not to the leaders. Not to the presidents, not to the prime ministers.

As I write in my book, *Let's Move On: Beyond Fear & False Prophets*, what good are walls around nations now when airplanes and drones can fly over them? People get very creative when faced with walls. Homemade bombs put holes in walls. Those seeking refuge or reunification with their families slip through the holes or tunnel under the walls or risk their lives on barbed wire to get over those walls.

When I was the president of Mexico we were working toward trying to abolish the concept of borders. What prevented us from doing it? Selfish nationalists who think that the rest of the world is no good. So they decide to build walls. Walls are for the fearful. You do not start building walls in the Land of the Free. The United States doesn't keep its people behind concrete and barbed wire.

In *Up Against the Wall*, journalist Peter Laufer makes use of his longtime experiences studying borders and barriers to help us recognize the differences between personal walls such as those around my grandfather's home and those like Donald Trump's "impenetrable" wall along the Mexico-United States borderlands. Laufer reports on failed border walls turned into tourist attractions like the Great Wall of China, Hadrian's Wall and the Berlin Wall. He shows readers new walls built on national borders since the Berlin Wall came down. He traces human migration as an unstoppable force when it's driven by survival. And he documents stories of those who want to stay home and migrants who want to return to their friends and families and customs. Why should you trade enchiladas and tacos for hot dogs and hamburgers?

Up Against the Wall puts contemporary walls into historical context. It's a guide for both policymakers and those thinking about migrating. And it's a primary text for those who seek to understand the history, the philosophy and the psychology of borders and walls.

In one of my infamous videos posted on YouTube I showed a simple drawing to the camera and spoke directly to Trump. "It's a ladder, Einstein," I said about the picture. "You're going to build a $25 billion wall that can be defeated by a twenty-five-dollar ladder?"[1] In the following pages Peter Laufer climbs up a metaphorical ladder and looks out over our walls—the ones we may need, the nonsensical ones and the evil ones. We meet the characters who build them and those who break them down. Laufer doesn't only present the problems, he offers creative solutions. And we come away from his book, I hope, with a better understanding of what the Dalai Lama and I talked about when we met: We eight billion people own this world. It doesn't belong to one person or to nations, but to everybody.

Our family hacienda is now a boutique hotel; its profits help us fund the development work of Centro Fox—aiding those in need. The hotel is filled with reminders of our family's and our nation's past including a stark undated and uncaptioned black-and-white photograph taken on the hacienda grounds probably during the dark days of the Mexican revolution. Uniformed men with rifles are waiting for an order from their commanding officer to shoot, his sword raised high about to make the deadly signal. The guns are aimed at a man in civilian clothes, his hat doffed and held by his side, his eyes open and stolidly meeting the aim of his executioners.

The image is a sober reminder of what it means to be *Up Against the Wall.*

Guanajuato

2020

INTRODUCTION

How often do we Americans need to be reminded that almost all of us are daughters and sons of immigrants, that ours is a nation of immigrants?

I am beginning this introduction to the paperback edition of *Up Against the Wall* at the desk of my Hotel Denver room in Glenwood Springs, Colorado, twenty years after the 9/11 attacks. At 9 a.m. on September 11, 2001, I was in a meeting at the National Geographic Society in Washington, DC, where I was launching a talk radio program. The meeting adjourned, of course, as soon as we learned that planes hit the World Trade Center and the Pentagon. On the walk back to my hotel I passed hushed onlookers watching smoke from the attack rise above the Potomac, and I watched as National Guard troops took up positions in Georgetown. A few days later, with return flights to the West Coast still grounded, I rented a big Buick and headed home, rolling across a stunned America, an America understandably fixated on the devastation in New York and Washington. I sped across the country, stopping for talks with Americans living far from Manhattan and DC.

Ten years after 9/11, in the summer of 2011 and in a newer Buick, I retraced my journey. I wanted to hear Americans talk from what I hoped would be points of view of – to use President Obama's campaign slogan – hope and change. I wanted to learn how places changed over the time that had passed. And I wanted to hear how the same types of people I talked with that first post-attack week (and some of the very same people) viewed 9/11 from the decade later vantage point. Developing an understanding of the solidarity, patriotism, hate, fear, lust for revenge, and – at times – compassion that were displayed on that first trip would, I wagered, benefit from being put into perspective by this new series of conversations. I decided that the decade unit of measure would be the appropriate amount of time to let pass before I rented that second Buick and rolled back across the States, pulling off Interstates, seeking the crossroads. I revisited the places where I stopped in 2001, captured more pictures and asked new questions in 2011.

For 2021 I am completing the project, hitting the road through America's Heartland once again for this 20-year retrospective of the nation's trajectory – from the 9/11 attacks through the turn-of-the-century Obama years to the post-Trump and Covid-pandemic era. I'm trying to look toward the future by taking to heart the Shakespearian "past is prologue" guidance inscribed on the façade of the National Archives in Washington. I'm seeking the story told from the perspective of people and places between Washington and the West Coast, a story that analyzes our changes from the 2001 headline in *Le Monde*, "We Are All Americans," to our starkly divided Red and Blue America of one generation later.

I've traveled American roads since my childhood, crisscrossing the Midwest, tagging along on family business trips. My first trip to the West Coast was via the two-lanes of U.S. Highway 36, and that ride was followed up by countless coast-to-coast expeditions. When the relentless wintertime cloud cover finally seemed too much to bear while I was living in Berlin, I told a German friend I was driving south until I found the sun (Italy!). "How American," was his response. Indeed. We are, as Kerouac titles his vivid American guidebook, an on the road people.

Before I left on that pre-iPhone 2001 cross-country sprint, I bought a video camera. From Washington to San Francisco, during the traumatic week after 9/11, I engaged dazed, angry, confused, and thoughtful Americans who were wrestling with their responses to the attacks, and I recorded their reactions. I also secured audio and video documentation of moments in a time that could not be replicated: snippets of live radio reports recounting encounters with unfolding events following the devastation; ad hoc displays expressing grief and sorrow, patriotism and national resolve; and evidence of stoic Americans continuing to go about their daily business that needed to be done even as they reeled from shock, grief and loss.

When I looked at the material once I arrived at my studio in San Francisco, I realized its growing value. The footage captured the immediate and visceral response of Americans far from the spotlight of what became known as Ground Zero. Were these interviews conducted even one week later, the responses from my interlocutors would have been tempered (or exacerbated) by the passage of time, and they would have been influenced by the continuing reactions of American political and other social leaders along with my subjects' interpretations of reactions occurring in the world community. The landscape – dominated by the sudden appearance of American flags and solidarity statements on marquees – soon would revert to a more passive look. My intent in 2001 was to let the footage age. My belief was that over time, as the distance from 9/11 increased, these interviews would develop as Cartier-Bresson-like decisive moments and thus become of historical value – documents for study that aid in the understanding of a pivotal period. 9/11 and its immediate aftermath forced Americans to reevaluate their status quo attitudes towards their own identity and borders, to rethink their opinions regarding migration into the United States and their feelings about the diasporas that live within our borders.

The American road trip continues to be a common carrier with which we view ourselves. From de Tocqueville to Huck Finn to *On the Road* and *Travels with Charley*, the list is long because the concept works. We Americans often try to define and understand ourselves by getting out on a road (or river). Equally rich is the oral history literary tradition. Studs Terkel nurtured Chicagoans to make *Division Street America* come alive with their distinctive voices and William Least Heat-Moon circumnavigated the States in *Blue Highways* and convinced those he encountered to share their all-American life stories for posterity.

Feeling kinship with those storytellers who blazed the cross-America trail before me, I am transiting the country once more. Which brings me to this Hotel Denver desk. For 2021 the rules of engagement are radically changed. Covid-era travel is no longer the casual jump-in-the-Buick affair it was back in relatively recent 2001 and 2011. Nonetheless, with a satchel full of face masks and hand sanitizer along with three Moderna vaccine jabs in my left arm, I chose to hit some American roads for some in-person brief encounters with people and places. Zoom, as we teachers and students learned, is a great tool but screen-to-screen cannot equal face-to-face. So I am making this third – and final – cross-country post-9/11 quest with socially and physically distanced encounters, parachuting into select Heartland spots as I wrap up the research and finalize these three distinct yet intertwined engagements with changing America and Americans. These journeys and their stories build a fascinating linked narrative that, I am convinced, can help us cope with our foundering nationhood.

Consider the woman I talked with at a Greyhound station in Effingham, Illinois. "I want revenge," she told me immediately after 9/11, "for all the innocent people who died."

"What should that revenge be?" I asked.

"I feel that the whole country that started this should be wiped out," she said, looking at me through her John Lennon glasses with no sign of irony as she climbed aboard the bus.

"What will that revenge accomplish?" I wondered.

"I don't really know," she acknowledged, "it's just a good feeling, knowing we won."

Or consider the man at a Georgetown, Colorado, coffee shop who worried in 2001, his voice and eyes vehement, "It's all about retaliation and blowing everybody else up, instead of trying to find out why exactly this happened and what we can do to stop it from happening again."

"It's beyond me to even fathom what the United States is going to be like after this," a National Guardsman lamented to me from his post on

M Street in Washington before I headed west, his eyes hidden behind mirrored sunglasses. "Why would we be so despised so that so many innocent lives would be wasted?" he rhetorically asked while knowing he had no answer. "It's a deep emotional question that will take many years for me to come to grips with."

These points of view – and the myriad opinions, questions and diatribes that I collected from sea to shining sea – are framed in my 20-year adventure by intense close-up portraiture and character studies of the Americans stating them, while the late-summer American countryside and urban scenes play counterpoint. The cityscape adds editorial content, sometimes with cries for understanding combined with advertising. Regular gas for $1.59 offered an Indiana gas station in 2001, with a footnote on the sign pleading, "Please God Bless America."

America plods into the new millennium engaged in what often feels like wars of all types without end. The on-the-road analyses of our predicaments and circumstances that I'm making are made far from the loci of financial and political power: Manhattan and DC. They were captured immediately after 9/11 and after the passage of enough time for interviewees to refine their thinking. Hence they offer us, I argue, valuable insight into our status as a nation and serve as a lasting, consequential and impossible-to-replicate humanities document. It's story that freezes instructive moments in time. From the time of immediate and unexpected national unity in 2001 to today's starkly cleaved America, talking with each other can help us make sense of ourselves and our times while we're trying to figure out what we might do to repair at least some of the divisive damage we're suffering. We must not shy from rejoicing in the continuing good fortunes of this American experiment we live. And hitting the road is both a joy and an academy. "O, highway!" wrote Whitman in appreciation of road trips, "you express me better than I can express myself!"

It was late August 2021 when I flew over some flyover states and rented still a third Hertz Buick in Salt Lake City for a sprint to Denver. At SFO the announcements were incessant: face masks were mandatory. The United crew welcomed us on board with a packet of hand sanitizer and reminded us multiple times as we crossed over California, Nevada and Utah to keep our masks on even between "bites of food and sips of drinks." We flew over apocalyptic smoke from Sierra Nevada wildfires and landed to tragic news from the Kabul airport as the U.S. government ended its 20-year war in Afghanistan.

Immigration proved a back story as I wandered along the wide Salt Lake streets encountering sources. A woman with Maltese heritage mused about the cultural affinities of Afghanistan and Malta. An India-born American recalled his grandfather waking him at their Delhi home just after 9/11 to warn him of war because of the fraught relationships between India, Pakistan and Afghanistan. The next day I stopped at a melon stand in Green River, Utah, and the grower noted that his wife is from the Philippines as he compared America's war there with its Afghanistan experience. Lunch was a burrito from the family owned El Mexicano restaurant. The family came north from Michoacán but the American-born daughter who took my order has yet to visit south of the border; her father forbids it, calling his homeland too dangerous. The eastbound I-70 sign at Green River ominously warns: no services for 107 miles; the speed limit is an Autobahn-like 80 miles per hour. The soaring desert buttes and massive rockpiles and vast emptiness are otherworldly but also a reminder that America's birthrate is declining and there's plenty of room from sea to shining sea. At a rest stop between Green River and the Colorado border I joined a couple of truckers as we took postcard pictures and selfies of the barren beauty, their dreadlocks framed by the stark-white southern Utah sands.

Back on the road I sped on, the vast, seemingly empty enormity of the visual solitude in harsh counterpoint to the satellite radio booming BBC voices to the Buick, voices describing the crowds at Kabul airport desperate to immigrate to America. East from the Colorado border the freeway traced the route through the Rockies forged by the Colorado River and here the cragged steep canyon walls became decorated with evergreens and their companion foliage. The climb up toward Loveland Pass exposed the broad reach of the range until the dramatic landscape disappeared and the freeway tunneled me under the Continental Divide.

It was two lovely road days speeding though Western majesties, interrupted only rarely by exit signs promising meals homogenized by McDonald's and its ilk.

At Denver my solitude was thwarted at the airport by the crowd crush at the TSA checkpoint and on the jammed airport train to the departure gate. Double-masked and triple-inoculated, I suppressed my Covid paranoia by remembering my time through security was measured in only a few minutes as was my time on board the train. A quick flight to Omaha and a good night's sleep after a Beyond Beef burger (in beefland!) prepared me for the sprint over the Missouri River and on to an August Iowa. I rolled through Walnut admiring the wrap-around porches of gracious old frame homes. "Welcome to our front porch," invited a sign adorning one. "Don't blame me/I voted for Trump," a flag flying from another announced. "Note the cornfields," my seatmate on the flight from Denver had advised. "At this time of year the corn is still tall and green, and when there's a breeze it looks like flowing water." Indeed, I embraced those glorious not-yet-amber waves of grain just south of one-block Walnut downtown. At Winterset I took a quick tour of the John Wayne birthplace museum – such typical Americana. Not on display was a notorious Wayne immigration quote. "I don't feel we did wrong in taking this great country away from them if that's what you're asking," he told *Playboy* magazine in 1971 when he was queried about the negative portrayal of Native Americans in his hit Westerns. "Our so-called stealing of this country from them was just a matter of survival. There were great numbers of people who needed new land, and the Indians were selfishly trying to keep it for themselves."

I crossed the Mississippi into Illinois just north of Davenport and sped past the opportunity to visit Ronald Reagan's birthplace and his boyhood home. John Wayne was enough for this trip of that Hollywood era and for the politics of those two stars. I pulled into the Chicago suburbs at dusk, treated myself to a room at the Palmer House and a grilled branzino. Just strolling from the hotel two blocks to the restaurant was a visual immigration treat. Multicultural Chicago: the world is packed into the Windy City.

Pushed off the frontpages by the pandemic, by the wildfires and by Afghanistan is the continuing trauma for immigrants heading north from Mexico. President Biden stopped the federal government's construction of Trump's border wall. But the Supreme Court ordered Biden to continue the so-called "remain in Mexico" Trump policy that forces asylum seekers to wait south of the border – often in dangerous and squalid ad hoc campsites – until their immigration court hearing dates. And when the Biden administration took office, a Trump order expediting deportation of migrants caught illegally crossing the order was left untouched. Public health in the Covid era is the rationale for deporting such asylum seekers. But overall, President Biden's policies and proposals radically differ from his predecessor's. As soon as he took office Biden authorized admittance of more refugees, preservation of temporary legal status for migrants who came to the United States as children and reinstatement of the immigrant visa program – reversals of Trump's anti-immigrant stance. Biden's immigration bill – still pending as I write this – proposes citizenship opportunities for residents who came to the United States without proper documentation and an increase in residency visas that can lead to citizenship.

On my Hotel Denver desk was a folder titled "A Colorful Past" – it's a timeline of the hotel's storied history and a further reminder of how immigration permeates our history. In 1884, the brochure notes, one of the hotel's founders, Henry Bosco, landed in America. "Coming to New York from Italy with just 30 cents, he made his way to Colorado at age 16." And I can attest to the fact that immigrant Bosco built a lovely hotel. His success story reminds me of a favorite Mexican restaurant in Berkeley, Taqueria Talavera. Printed on the receipts is this message: "You were served today by an immigrant."

Peter Laufer
Chicago, 2021

Chapter 1

UP AGAINST THE WALL (EXPLETIVE)

The author and poet Jonah Raskin[1] was mopping up his soup and salad dinner at the Casino bistro in Bodega—the Sonoma County village where scenes from Hitchcock's "The Birds" were shot, a county once part of Mexico and these days filled with immigrants from Jalisco, immigrants documented and otherwise. We've been friends since he served as chair of the Communications Studies department at Sonoma State University—where I briefly taught.

We were talking about President Trump's Mexico border wall, my study of walls worldwide and the research I was conducting into the origin of the phrase: Up against the wall.

"Did I tell you about the time," Raskin queried me, "that I shouted, 'Up against the wall, motherfucker' at a production of Joseph Heller's play, 'We Bombed in New Haven,' and Heller added that line to the play and that it's in the published text?" Raskin seemed pleased with his role as a literary footnote even though he added, "I didn't get any credit."

In fact, author Heller noted Raskin's audience participation moment when the Columbia University student newspaper *Spectator* interviewed him in 1968 about his anti-war play. "As the actors came out for a curtain call," the author of *Catch 22* remembered, "a man stood up in the last row of the orchestra and yelled out, 'Up against the war [*sic*], mother-fucker!' We were stunned," Heller told the paper, "because we didn't know who he was talking to. When we finally met the man, he explained what he meant to say was that we should take to the barricades—that we should be out fighting, rather than just sitting watching a play."[2]

So what was it that Raskin advocated being up against? The war or the wall? Both? Vietnam was a shooting war and a societal wall. When I checked in with him, his answer across the years from the 1960s was unambiguous, despite Heller's contemporaneous memory of the moment. "I yelled from the back of the theater, 'Up against the *wall*, motherfucker!'" Raskin told me, adding that the performance was a fundraiser for the National Lawyers Guild, "the old lefty organiza-tion that revived in the 1960s because of young lefty lawyers like my friend Bernardine Dohrn and my wife Eleanor Raskin." He insisted he would not have even considered substituting "war" for "wall" when he disrupted the curtain call. "I don't mess with classics of street slang. Didn't then, don't now." And a classic of street slang it is.

Perhaps the phrase originated in the poem by LeRoi Jones, "Black People," in which the text instructs: "All the stores will open if you say the magic words. The magic words are: Up against the wall, mother-fucker, this is a stick up!" During the 1967 Newark, New Jersey, riots (which he identified as "rebellion"), Jones was charged with resisting arrest and carrying an illegal weapon. At his trial later that year, Judge Leon W. Kapp read from the poem. Jones was found guilty and sentenced to three years in state prison, a sentence overturned when an appeals court ruled that Judge Kapp's recitation prejudiced the jury.[3] In a 1991 interview, Jones (by then he called himself Amiri Baraka)[4] said Judge Kapp "decided to prove I had caused the riots by reading from a poem [...] [a poem] not even published until after the riots were over. I objected that I was being tried for possession of two poems, and I was right."[5] Or perhaps Jones wasn't the original author of the call to action but incorporated the line into his poem because Newark police were apt to use it when arresting black citizens.[6] Whatever its origin, from the Lower East Side to Columbia University and thence across the continent, the phrase became common currency for rebellion. A posse of self-styled revolutionaries headquartered Downtown in New York City adopted it for their moniker and Mark Rudd, a leader of the 1968 student strike at Columbia, incorporated it into his open letter to the university's president, Grayson Kirk, and credited it to LeRoi Jones ("whom I'm sure you don't like a whole lot," he added as an aside). The call became a rallying cry of the strike. And a year after Raskin's yell, in 1969 on their *Volunteers* album, the Jefferson Airplane sang out, "Up against the wall, motherfucker!" for the chorus of their anthem "We Can Be Together."

The call, without the oath, dates to ca. 1910, according to the British lexicographer Jonathon Green. It originated as military jargon meaning serious problems, according to Green's research, "reinforced by the 1960s radical slogan, 'Up against the wall, mother-fucker!'"[7] And the military jargon originated with the reality that firing squad victims often are literally up against the wall.[8] And up against the wall were piles of corpses during the murderous days of the Mexican Revolution when Pancho Villa, Emilio Zapata and the *federales* shot each other down with ease and glee, as civil war bled the country between 1910 and 1920.

Up against the wall, motherfucker: Patty Hearst apparently used the line when she famously participated in a bank robbery and called the cry out while cradling a machine gun—although it seems the coopted newspaper heiress dropped her voice at least for the final word of the order; lip readers working for federal prosecutors reconstructed the full sentence.[9] I probably heard it—of course not for the first time—but repeated as Hearst's quote during testimony at her 1976 trial, a bizarre show I covered as a correspondent for NBC News.

Even without the expletive, the up against the wall imagery is clear: stuck, nowhere to go (except—with luck—through it, under it or over it). Language, especially slang, mirrors reality. Balls to the wall. Hitting a wall. Breaking through the wall. Climbing the walls. Off the wall. Back to the wall. Banging your (my?) head against the wall. "Walls have an aroma of betrayal and death about them," is Professor Raskin's point of view. He tracks his awareness of walls to the short story "The Wall"—the 1939 Jean-Paul Sartre existential study focuses on firing squad executions, the victims up against a wall. "I'll think about how I'd like to get inside the wall, I'll push against it with my back [...] with every ounce of strength I have," one of the condemned tells others in his cell, "but the wall will stay, like in a nightmare."[10] Intriguing: my Casino rendezvous with Jonah Raskin in Bodega occurs proximate to Christo and Jeanne-Claude's "Running Fence" site—the artists' 1976 installation of an 18-foot-high and 24.5-mile-long fence made of nylon. The piece ran from U.S. Highway 101 to the Pacific across Marin and Sonoma counties. This too was no impenetrable wall. The design allowed for cars and trucks, livestock and wildlife to cross the fence path.[11]

Good fences make good neighbors? Robert Frost takes on the aphorism in his classic 1914 poem "Mending Wall." Working with his neighbor to fix their common stone wall he muses the now-classic wall critique, "Before I built a wall I'd ask to know / What was I walling in or walling out, / And to whom was I like to give offence." And then he knocks down the concept of walls with his coup de grâce. "Something there is that doesn't love a wall, / That wants it down." And yet walls remain ubiquitous—the metaphoric, the exclusionary and the confining.

Encountering Borderlines

The first time I encountered an obstacle separating my home state California and our southern neighbor Mexico was back in my high school days. Two chums and I were on a road trip in a rattletrap VW Beetle, vagabonding along the Pacific for a summer adventure. Just below Ensenada we were stopped at a roadblock by *federales* who demanded travel documents. They looked at our papers and ordered us to turn back toward the States. Gringos under the age of 18, they informed us, were forbidden to drive further down the Baja coast without a letter from their parents authorizing the trip. In those pre-Internet days we couldn't send an instant text missive back home for the required permission slip.

These days of course it is the U.S. government working overtime controlling the border with Mexico.

"I will build a great, beautiful wall on our southern border," thundered Donald Trump, first as a candidate and then as president, and his followers bellow back, "Build the wall! Build the wall!" On the east side of San Diego, just over the border from dusty Tijuana shanties, test prototypes were built in 2017 to show the world how that wall might look: monoliths of steel and concrete launched skyward. The Trump wall samples stood tall as political threats, reminiscent of the bloody gash the Iron Curtain made across Europe.

But along much of the Mexican-U.S. border—a sprawling land mass where the First and Third Worlds meet—there's been a hefty impediment preventing easy access into most of California, Arizona, New Mexico and Texas since not long after my underage friends and I were kept out of Mexico. For some miles it's a fence, in other places poles stuck close together. Harsh weather and landscape do the job for long stretches of the boundary. And in especially well-traveled urban zones it already was a wall long before Trump grabbed the border as a cause célèbre. Not that any of those variations along the dividing line keep the hearty and determined from crossing the frontier.

"They use a ladder." I met U.S. Border Patrol officer Eduardo Olmos at a place where the borderline is a steel wall. A seasoned expert in border security work, he was matter-of-fact about the simple tools and techniques used by border jumpers to get over the existing wall. "They put a carpet or a blanket on top of the concertina wire, and then they'll have a rope ladder on the other side." Olmos explained defeating walls with the same simplicity employed by Vicente Fox. A hop, skip and a jump from Mexico into California.

We humans have been building walls—physical and conceptual—since Adam and Eve were forced across the line out of Eden. Not all walls are of the brutal Berlin Wall-type, designed to keep us in or out against our will. Consider the front door of a home or the bathroom door inside it—just pragmatic, not necessarily exclusionary. Walls originally created for tribal protection eventually become curious relics, even tourist attractions. Think of the Great Wall of China, Hadrian's Wall against the "barbarians" and medieval European city walls. Consider the Maginot Line—some 200 miles of fortifications built by France—a failed attempt to stop Hitler's invasion. And the Ringstrasse now serves as Vienna's hub, encircling its old city where protective walls stood until they were deemed obsolete. Austrian-Hungarian Emperor Franz Josef replaced the ramparts with broad boulevards; the city grew and prospered (Figures 1.1 and 1.2).

Walls serve as stereotypical backdrops for executions—both in real life and cartoons: the condemned are literally up against the wall. A drawing by Dan Reilly for the *New Yorker* magazine is a prime example of the firing squad wall used for a joke. The victim is tied up and blindfolded as the officer in charge tells him, "I'm sorry, we've had to drop the traditional last cigarette, on account of complaints from the firing squad about secondhand smoke." Franz Joseph's younger brother, the Archduke Ferdinand Maximilian, sailed to America from the security of his walled Miramare Castle redoubt in Trieste and declared himself Emperor of Mexico. Mexicans decided otherwise and a firing squad executed him up against a wall, a finale memorialized in a series of captivating Manet paintings.

Figure 1.1 A bleak winter scene along the failed Maginot Line where upended rails were placed along the border with Germany to stop Hitler's invading tanks. The Panzers simply went around the blockade.

Figure 1.2 Modern life can be as quotidian as a bus ride alongside a two-millennia-old Roman wall in Rimini—a wall designed to protect the city from invaders that now attracts tourists.

Perishable Walls

After extraordinarily heavy rains in Tuscany, a 65-foot section of the San Gimignano city wall—built some 800 years ago—collapsed. A few days later I met with the town's mayor.

"In the Middle Ages," Giacomo Bassi told me when we met in his city hall office, "walls could have a real function. Without them there was death and destruction." The city walls provided protection. "But walls built today," he said, "have another meaning. Exclusion."

It's a message President Reagan understood when he pointed at the Berlin Wall and preached, "Mr. Gorbachev, tear down this wall!" I lived in Berlin when it was divided, when East German soldiers armed with rifles and shoot-to-kill orders cordoned off West Berlin. And I returned to join the throngs that chipped away at the concrete after the wall was breached—pieces of it I brought back to America remain in my office as reminders. Today a few preserved lengths of the wall lure busloads of the curious, visitors anxious to understand how the divided city coped. I listened as a smiling tour guide enthusiastically informed his clients, "Here you can actually see a part of the Berlin Wall!" And while the tourists took their selfies it was easy to imagine how even today's harshest fortifications will eventually devolve into educational delights complete with nearby ice cream and T-shirt stands.

Tuscany's graceful old walls, alive with flowers blooming between stones, now shade visitors at *gelaterias* and *osterias,* upscale leatherwork shops and haute couture outlets. Repairing the wall damage was Mayor Bassi's priority when we talked. Visitors to San Gimignano's walls fuel the little city's economy. "We are going back in history," Mayor Bassi said, worried about the worldwide resurgence of obstacles. "We no longer need walls." Travelers and migrants, he insisted, should be free to cross borders. It's an appropriate attitude for an official whose city lies on a pilgrimage route from England to Rome.

Yet we are living at a time when a new generation of walls separates us. The Hungarian border fence along its line at Serbia, created to stop refugee traffic from Syria and Afghanistan. The Israeli underground wall, designed to prevent tunneling under the wall that already exists on its 40-mile border with Gaza. The Indian wall of barbed wire along its border with Bangladesh, strung to keep out unwanted migrants. Morocco's sand and land mine wall against incursions from Western Sahara. The ugly concrete wall in Lima, Peru, built by a wealthy neighborhood fearful of the poor folks from across the street (pocked with doors to allow maids and cooks and gardeners access to their jobs on the rich side). The list is long and global. The Canadian border with the Lower 48, touted as the longest international border in the world free of a military defense, is hardened with police, various types of bulwarks and mandated formal border crossing points where official documents must be shown by cross-border travelers—even those who live in villages that straddle the border with no physical barrier face a conceptual wall delineated by signposted warnings that they must cross their own town only at official control points.

Walls Surround Us

Some walls are metaphoric and transcend a physical barrier. After the Berlin Wall came down Berliners on both sides of the destroyed barrier noted the "wall in the head" because of the east-west cultural divide that developed during the years the city was separated, a divide that did not disappear with end of the wall. We create walls of silence when we socially shun others. We build invisible walls based on our expectations of personal space in crowds or when we meet others. In some cultures, at least prior to the Covid-19 pandemic, friends and acquaintances kiss their hellos and are almost lip-to-lip in conversations, while in others folks maintain a judicious distance when talking and rarely touch each other unless their relationships are intimate.

Venice is a walled city, walled off by nature: water. The Grand Canal and its tributaries protected its Roman settlers from the marauding Attila the Hun. Other walls we build in our relentless attempt to control nature. The seawall at the destroyed Fukushima Daiichi nuclear power plant in Japan, for example—a failed barrier designed to hold back tsunamis. The Netherlands and Singapore hope seawalls keep rising waters from inundating their cities. Nature again reminds us who is boss with walls of flames such as the devastating fire in my home California county of Sonoma, fire walls that destroyed thousands of homes in just one deadly night. Surly homeowners create spite fences, walls of trees and bushes planted to block the views of neighbors they dislike. The paranoid and worried among us build walls around themselves, living in gated communities where the houses are equipped with panic rooms—hardened interior walls—in case those gates fail.

Walls can be art. On the west side of divided Berlin—where access to the wall was not restricted by the well-armed guards, ferocious guard dogs and automated machine guns of East Germany—the concrete barrier became a miles-long canvas for painters, the politics of control a common theme. Likewise, the Palestinian side of the West Bank barrier built by Israel is fabulously graffitied by Banksy—particularly arresting is his "Girl Frisking a Soldier" imagery. Sculptor Andy Goldsworthy created his long, meandering stone wall installation in upstate New York countryside. Graffitists and muralists find opportunities for their work on urban walls worldwide. Decorated sound walls muffle highway noise. Phil Spector produced his Wall of Sound to back up singers with his trademark cacophony and the Grateful Dead built the group's wall of sound, the massive array of amplifiers and speakers the band required to blast its music to huge crowds of fans. Pink Floyd's "The Wall" offers an operatic ode to desperation. Libraries and bookshops show off their colorful walls of books. Walls figure in jargon and slang: "Throw it at the wall and see what sticks," which also describes a folk technique for testing when spaghetti is properly cooked.

"We construct borders, literally and figuratively," Frances Stonor Saunders explained in a 2016 lecture at the British Museum (before Brexit recreated a border), "to fortify our sense of who we are. And we cross them," said the journalist and historian, "in search of who we might become."[12]

All this wall thought brings me back to the Mexican border with California and the slabs of steel and concrete soaring into the desert air as examples of a future American dream wall—the Hollywood stage set of samples built in 2017 to show the world examples of what Trump envisioned for his dream of a fortress America. Or an American nightmare, depending on one's point of view. "These prototypes," Border Patrol officer Olmos told me approvingly as we stood in their shadow, "are going to make our job efficient." His piercing eyes glinted against the bright sunlight as he looked along the border wall toward where it disappears into the Pacific. Much of the pre-Trump wall is made from surplus Vietnam War-era landing mats—steel mesh that's relatively easy to compromise with a Sawzall or an axe. "They use whatever tools they can get their hands on," Olmos said about his nemeses who break through the barrier. The risk of capture is worth taking because the wall crashers know Eduardo Olmos and his patrolling colleagues—despite their fast trucks and sophisticated surveillance tools—cannot be everywhere. The wall is vulnerable.

"We humans are resourceful," I suggested to the patrolman, "especially if we're trying to get somewhere."

"Very resourceful," he agreed. "We have video of a smuggler making a cut in the wall with an axe in a minute and twenty seconds."

Barely Touching through the Wall

We drove in the patrol wagon along the north side of the wall down toward the Pacific and Friendship Park. There, for a few hours on weekends, family and friends separated by the border can meet and communicate through the wall that separates the Tijuana and San Diego sides of the park. The wire mesh is too tight to touch anything other than finger tips.

Figure 1.3 Making do—friends and family visit through the border wall at Friendship Park under the ever-watching eyes of the Border Patrol.

At the gathering place I met Sergio Bautista. Smiling, he was talking through the tiny holes in the wall with a woman on the Mexican side, a woman who appeared only as a shadowy outline through the dense mesh barrier between them. Bautista had flown across the States from Chicago to spend just over an hour with his friend, their first visit in thirteen years. The park opening hours are severely restricted on the California side by U.S. border authorities. I did not want to infringe on their limited time together, but after their visit Bautista and I talked. "It's just so difficult," his emotions were mixed: happy for their time together, frustrated by the strained circumstances. "It's pretty hard just to be able to touch the tips of your fingers, your little fingers" (Figure 1.3).

Heading back to the airport for his flight home, Bautista was conflicted. There are problems in Mexico he's happy to keep far from Chicago. "Drugs and cartels and all the killing." But not his friends and family. "We just want to be with the ones we love." His brilliant smile flashed and his brown eyes sparkled, despite the dire circumstances.

Don't Fence Me In—or Out

Across cultures and time, we humans have built barriers in vain attempts to keep the Other away from us. The good news is that such fortifications eventually fail. Survival often requires migration. And in today's world of easy jet travel and the Internet jumping borders it's increasingly difficult for arbitrary authorities to wall us off from one another.

Looking back at the wall on the Mexican border as I drove north I found myself singing the old Cole Porter song that speaks to a mythos of the Wild West, legends all but lost in densely urbanized and fearful Southern California.

"Oh, give me land, lots of land under starry skies above/Don't fence me in!"

Trump's dream of a wall is a monstrosity that never will be built from the Pacific to the Gulf, if for no other reason than its ludicrous expense.

"Let me ride through the wide-open country that I love/Don't fence me in!"

Instead of a wall, billboards facing south should line the border calling out "*¡Bienvenidos!*" because the U.S. southern border, like San Gimignano in Italy, is on a pilgrimage route. Pilgrims head north seeking asylum from crime and failed states. They head north hoping for a better life. They find safety and security. They find good jobs with good pay, jobs that need workers.

So it's always been, as it always should be. And so it will be in the future, regardless of walls—or no walls.

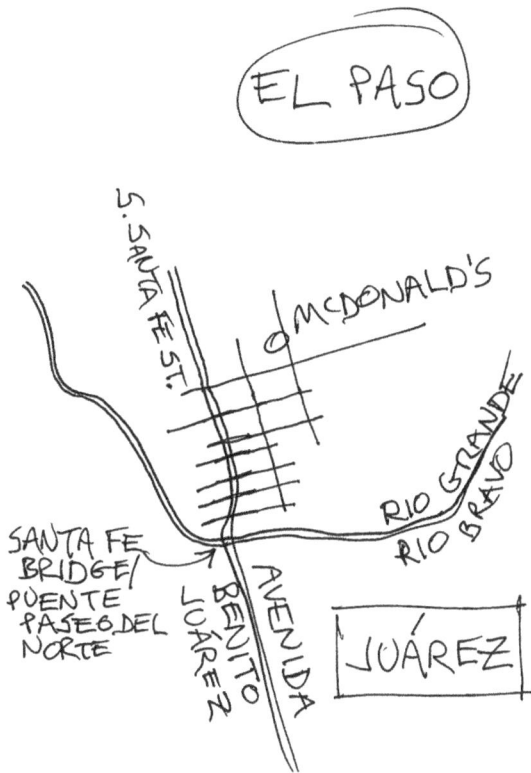

EL PASO

S. SANTA FE ST.

MCDONALD'S

RIO GRANDE
RIO BRAVO

SANTA FE
BRIDGE/
PUENTE
PASEO DEL
NORTE

AVENIDA
BENITO
JUAREZ

JUÁREZ

Chapter 2

ILLEGAL ALIEN OR CLEVER NEW AMERICAN

L et me introduce you to that friend of mine who crossed into the United States from Ciudad Juárez over to El Paso. When she recounts her migration story to me, Juana María is a bright and bubbly woman in her late thirties. Her toddler daughter is in the living room learning English from a television program when we sit down in her kitchen to talk about her trip across the border over thirteen years before. Her two boys are in school. She offers me a cup of tea.

"Do you have anything decaffeinated?" I ask.

She does. Her bi-cultural kitchen cupboards include *mola*, tortillas and decaffeinated mint tea. I've heard Juana María's[1] border crossing story often, but in bits and pieces. Today she's taking time out of her schedule to recount it from start to finish.

It was 1990 when Juana María first came to the United States. She had waited patiently in line at the U.S. Consulate in Guadalajara and applied for a tourist visa, which she received. Eight months earlier her husband had crossed into California, looking for work. A hardworking mechanic, he found a job easily—on a ranch where his pay included living quarters in an old mobile home.

She remembers all the dates precisely. "I came on May 27th in 1990. That's the first time I came to the United States." Juana María speaks English with a thick Mexican accent, and only rarely drops a Spanish word into the conversation. Her English vocabulary is more than adequate for her story. She's spent the last several years studying English, working with a volunteer tutor, and her boys bring English home from school and into the household. "I flew from Guadalajara here to California." In addition to her 3-month-old first son, she traveled north with her mother-in-law and her 13-year-old brother. She was 23. Stamped into her Mexican passport was her prized tourist visa.

When she reached the immigration officer at the airport she was asked a few key questions. "He asked, 'How much money do you have to spend in the United States?' I had only five hundred dollars. My mother-in-law didn't have anything. He said, 'That is not enough money for three people to visit the United States for two months.'" The Immigration and Naturalization Service officer asked the next crucial question, and she now knows her honest answer doomed her trip. "He asked, 'Why are you coming here?' And I told the truth, 'I come to visit my husband. I want to stay with my husband and I want my child to grow up with his father.'" Despite the valid visa, Juana María and her family were refused entry. It was obvious she was no tourist; she was an immigrant.

"We stayed all night, like we were arrested. We didn't go to jail because we had two little boys. But we stayed all night in one room in the airport." A generation later the Trump administration's Immigration and Customs Enforcement (ICE) radically changed U.S. policy: children were torn from their migrating parents' arms and jailed in appalling conditions.

The immigration officer was Latino, Juana María says, and told her, "Oh, I'm so sorry. I feel so bad about what I'm doing." She says she remembers the moment vividly when he took her cash. "He bought a ticket. The next day we flew back to Mexico on another airplane. One officer went with us into the airplane and made sure we were sitting down in the airplane. And he never gave me my money back. He bought that ticket with my money."

A month later Juana María was shopping for a *coyote*. "I didn't want to stay in Mexico. My husband was here." Her older brother convinced her to avoid the Tijuana crossing into San Diego, scaring her with stories of rape, robbery, abandonment and murder in the hills along *la frontera*, the border. She decided on a crossing from Ciudad Juárez into El Paso. She bundled up her baby, and once again accompanied by her mother-in-law, she flew from Guadalajara to Juárez. This time she didn't tell her husband of her travel plans. "I didn't tell him because if something happened he would have worried about me and my boy. I wanted to give him a surprise."

Her brother confirmed arrangements with the *coyote*, secured an address of a house for the rendezvous with the guide. Juana María took a cab at the Juárez airport, but when the three travelers arrived at the Juárez house, they were unable to find their contact. And they quickly realized that they had left a suitcase in the cab. "We were missing in the big city," she says. "In the suitcase we had diapers and formula." Luck was with the migrating trio. The taxi company insisted on buying formula for the baby; when the company found the missing baggage, it delivered to the hotel where they had booked a room.

Juana María called her brother. He contacted the *coyote* and sent him to the hotel and there they made their border-crossing plans. "I was nervous, but he told me to relax." In those pre-9/11 and pre-Trump days, Mexicans routinely crossed the bridge into El Paso to shop. The crowds were so great and the traffic so important to the local economy that immigration officers only spot-checked border crossers walking north. Juana María was told to dress like a typical Mexican housewife, carry a shopping bag, and act confident. "We looked like people from Mexico who are shopping and going back home." They agreed to make the crossing during the noon rush hour. The *coyote* figured inspectors would be eating lunch and that the throngs crossing the bridge would camouflage his clients.

The next morning a car came to the hotel for Juana María. She was dropped near the border and walked north. "We crossed, walking"— Juana María, the baby, her mother-in-law, and the *coyote*. "I was wearing a dress to look like a Mexican shopper. We crossed at the border and we didn't go far. We walked for maybe ten or fifteen minutes into El Paso." As the migrants strolled north, homeless coconspirators living on the street kept the *coyote* informed that the path was free of *Migra* (Spanish slang at the time for the INS, the Immigration and Naturalization Service—the government agency that became a unit of ICE). The coconspirators were tipped a dollar for the intelligence. "Finally, we stopped at a McDonald's, because it was 104 degrees."

She ate her first American meal in the cool of the McDonald's—a hamburger of course, and the *coyote* called a taxi. They drove to a house where a friend of her brother lived, and there they spent the night. The easy part of the journey was over. Now the job was to get Juana María out of the borderlands and up into the interior and onward to join her husband in California. A further masquerade was needed. She no longer had to look like a Mexican housewife; she had to look like a Mexican-American.

That's when they made me look like a teenager. They put me in shorts with a lot of flowers. They put me in a blouse—phosphorescent orange. And they put my hair up, like a *chola*![2] They colored my eyes black, and red lipstick! Oh, my goodness.

Juana María is a pretty woman, but her wardrobe is conservative and she wears only minimal makeup. She was happy to play dress-up "because I needed to look like the girls from El Paso. The teenagers in El Paso look different from the teenagers in Mexico. That's why they changed my looks."

They flew to Dallas with no trouble, the baby disguised as an El Paso infant, sporting a Hawaiian shirt. Her mother-in-law was still with them, not worried in "a dress like a North American" because her hair is blonde. "I felt nervous," Juana María admits, but more than just nervous. "I felt embarrassed to look like that, when I looked at myself in the mirror I said, 'Oh, my God. No!' But I needed to relax and look normal, like all the other people in the airport."

When they arrived at the Dallas-Ft. Worth airport they waited for another brother to pick them up. "He passed me three times, and he didn't recognize me." Finally she said to him, "Hi, honey! I'm Juana María." He was shocked at her appearance.

> Well, I looked like a *chola*! He told me, "If your husband sees you looking like that, immediately he will divorce you." We left the airport, and the first stop was Sears to buy make-up and a dress, to wash my face and change clothes. We went to my brother's house and then we called up my husband and I said, "Honey, I'm here!" He said, "No, you are joking." I told him I was serious and that I had another surprise—I had his mother with me.

The mother-in-law had told her husband she would only go as far as Ciudad Juárez, but she went across into the United States, says María Juana, on a lark. "The *coyote* said, 'It's fun. You can cross. It's not dangerous.' So she crossed to have one more adventure in her life. My brother paid only five hundred dollars for all three people. Very cheap."

The date of her arrival in *El Norte*[3] is fixed in her mind. "I crossed the border June 24, 1990." After a week visiting her brother, she flew to California for a reunion with her husband. It was July 1, just in time for the Fourth of July festivities at the ranch where he worked. "My husband told me I needed to buy clothes for the celebrations. I got blue jeans and a red-and-white blouse, because those are the three colors of the American flag."

Juana María's parrot is chirping. Her daughter takes a break from the television to listen, eat some corn chips and make a mess on the counter trying to pour some 7-Up into a glass. Outside cattle are feeding at the trough. Her blue heelers periodically bark. Through her kitchen windows I see the bucolic California hills that surround her home. "I haven't been back to Mexico for thirteen years." She looks pensive when I ask her why. "Because I don't have a Green Card and now I am worried about crossing the border. I hear a lot of bad stories. It costs $2,500 for each person." That early year 2000 price tag looks like a bargain a generation later.

Living without proper documentation for 13 years was nothing much more than an annoyance for Juana María. "I don't do anything illegal. I live a good life and take care of my kids." Immigration officers rarely show up in her rural neighborhood, and when they do patrol places she frequents in the nearby urban district, she says she's warned and just avoids them. "When the INS[4] is around here they say on the [Spanish language] radio station: don't go out to Wal-Mart or Sears or whatever shopping center because the INS is around. So I don't go there. After one or two days, they're gone."

I ask Juana María what she would do if an immigration agent approached her. "If he asks me for a Green Card, I can't do anything," she says about this perpetual threat to her domestic tranquility.

If you don't have the Green Card, they only arrest. They say, "You have a right to call a relative, but you're going to jail." If I don't have a Green Card, they'll deport me to my country, to Mexico. That's what they do. They don't ask for identification, they ask for a Green Card, or your permission to stay in the United States, like a passport. If I don't have anything with me, they'll arrest me, and they'll take me out to the border.

But life was more uncertain for her when Pete Wilson was governor of California and he rallied voters to pass Proposition 187, the referendum that limited the rights of undocumented migrants and was ultimately struck down by the courts. During the anti-immigrant climate of those years in the mid-1990s, just picking the kids up at school was cause for concern. "The INS came to the schools and they arrested parents. For more than a week, we didn't send our boy to the school, when I heard that the INS was here in my county."

Juana María figures about 70 percent of her Latino friends in California are in the state illegally. When we talked, Juana María still held out hope for legalizing her status. Meanwhile, she and her family thrived. She worked hard at the local PTA, organizing fund-raising dinners of rich Mexican food. Her daughter was christened at the local Catholic church in a Spanish-language ceremony, followed by a block party crowded with friends and relatives, food and music. Her husband went off to work each day; she worked part time. They paid their taxes: Americans by every definition except for paperwork.

A few days after we talked at her home, it was Mexican Lunch Day at the local elementary school. Juana María brought together a group of the Latino mothers to prepare burritos. The women were lined up in the kitchen, the first ladling out the rice, the next passing out a tortilla, the third the beans. The burritos were topped off with lettuce and cream and salsa. The money raised was used to provide childcare for Latino mothers who were taking classes to earn a high school equivalency certificate.

Despite the all-American lifestyle, Juana María suffers because of her illegal status in the United States.

I feel sad because I cannot go to Mexico and come back again. I cannot visit my relatives. My friends who have Green Cards, they do that every year or every other year. I want to go to Mexico. But how can I cross? Maybe I'd be lucky, and not have any problems, like the first time. Or maybe I'd have a lot of problems.

She has reason to worry; she's heard the horror stories. "I have friends who came two months after I came here to the United States. Two years later they went to Mexico." The return trip was a disaster. "One of the ladies," she says it with a combination of sadness and a matter-of-fact reporting of the news, "the *coyote* killed her. With a screwdriver. In Tijuana. I say no. I'm not going. I love my relatives. But my life is first, and my kids."

Nonetheless when Juana María's father-in-law was dying, her husband chose to take the chance on a trip back to Mexico. In just over ten years, the price of a *coyote* had increased fivefold. He paid the $2,500 for help crossing from Tijuana to San Diego. The costs for help crossing illegally continue to soar. As the Trump administration focused political capital and dollars on the border, *coyote* fees—along with the bribes to authorities and bandits on the route north—tallied as much as ten thousand dollars.

Juana-María's husband crossed with a false Green Card—not a counterfeit, but stolen. *Coyotes* prowl border nightclubs, Juana María explains, looking for drunk Latinos with legitimate identification papers. They steal their Green Cards. Her husband sat down at a table with a *coyote* who displayed a stack of stolen Green Cards. Together they searched through the cards for a picture of a Mexican who looked enough like her husband to satisfy a border guard. He crossed the border with someone else's Green Card. The system isn't perfect. He crossed successfully three times. She tells me,

> But the last time the officer said, "You don't look like him!" They arrested him and sent him back to Mexico. He called me from Rosarita and said, "I am here because they caught me and sent me back to Mexico." I called the *coyote* and said, "You promised me my husband would come to California safely. If my husband is not here in my house, I will not pay you anything." The *coyote* went to get my husband at Rosarita and he crossed again at Tijuana with the same stolen Green Card. That day was lucky.

"Sometimes the *coyotes* have business with the immigration officer," she said, "and they give him money under the table. My husband flew home from San Diego. When he was on the airplane, I sent the money by Western Union to the *coyote*."

That's Juana María's theory, that the *coyote* bribed the guard. It's hard to imagine a U.S. immigration officer jeopardizing his career and pension—not to mention risking prison time—for a cut of a $2,500 *coyote* fee. Hard to imagine, but certainly possible. U.S. officials along the border have been arrested for conspiring with smugglers. Corruption is not limited to the Mexican side of the border.

Crooked Cops

The Border Action Network is an Arizona-based group founded in 1999 that documents charges of abuse against the Border Patrol and other government agencies involved with securing the Mexican border. The list they post on their website of charges against Border Patrol agents gives credence to Juana María's theory. Here are a few excerpts from that list from the era when she recounted her story:

> Off-duty Border Patrol agent William Varas faces charges that he lied to authorities in July 2002 when he claimed that he fired his gun at immigrants only after they had first shot at him. Agent Matthew Hemmer was arrested in August 2000 on state charges of kidnapping, sexual assault and sexual abuse. A criminal complaint said Hemmer took an undocumented woman, then 21, to a remote location and sexually assaulted her before allowing her to return to Mexico. Agent Dennis Johnson, a former supervisor, was sentenced to seven years in prison for sexual assault and five years (concurrent) for kidnapping in connection with a September 28, 2000 incident. Johnson sexually assaulted a 23-year old El Salvadoran woman who was in custody, naked and handcuffed. Agent Charles Brown, a 23-year veteran, was arrested in November 2003 for allegedly selling classified information to a drug cartel. Brown worked in the agency's intelligence unit.[5]

Juana María's Solution

The Bush Administration's 2004 election year proposal offering temporary worker status to Mexicans in the United States illegally was no solution to the border wars from Juana María's point of view. Offering Green Cards is all well and good, she says, "but I feel bad that he wants to give permission for three years to work here, and then after three years you go back to your country." She looks puzzled and disgusted by the suggestion. "You're living your life here, you work so hard," she points out with hurt pride, "now, go back? No. This is not an option."

What is the solution for Juana María and the millions of other Mexicans living without documentation in the United States? "Amnesty for good persons," she says. "So many persons come here for work, to have the best life."

But why should someone who broke the law be given amnesty and the opportunity legally to pursue the American dream? Her answer comes immediately and without hesitation. "Because we work hard and we are important to the country, to help the country grow. And we grow too, because we have the best life."

And the long-term solution? Should any determined Mexican who wants to come to the United States be greeted with a warm *bienvenitos*?

"No problem," she agrees, "they can come."

Does she favor an open border?

"Yes. Open the border."

Her reasons are clear and come from personal experience.

"No business for the *coyote*. No people dead along the border. Then people in Mexico can come here and work, and the United States has cheap workers. That's simple. Open the border and you have no problems. Then Mexican people can feel free to come here, like the Americans go to Mexico."

If the border were open, where would Juana María prefer to live, Mexico or California?

"I love the life in California, but I miss my family," she says, sounding a little dreamy.

Especially Christmas time, or New Year, when we make family parties. The traditions are so different comparing here to there. In Mexico we eat beans and cheese and tortillas, but every family is together. Here we have turkeys with everything, but I don't feel happy. […] I mean, I feel happy because my kids have the best school, and we stay together with my husband. But I have a heart, and my heart is in Mexico.

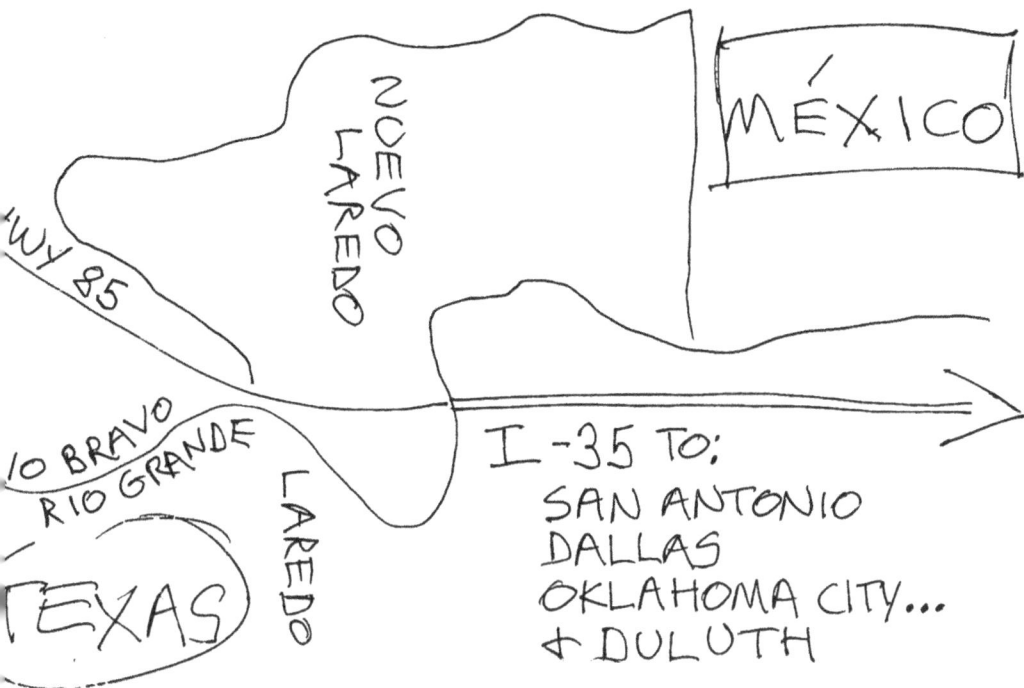

Chapter 3

STILL LIFE ON THE BORDER

On the crime-ridden, violent streets of Nuevo Laredo, some huddled masses listen to mariachis and wait for nighttime as they plot how to cross without documents from Mexico into Texas.

"I'm not worried about the *Migra*," says one worker poised to cross the Rio Grande. "Cuando el estómago tiene hambre, no piensa en dificultades." When the stomach is hungry, you don't think of difficulties. The men eat sardines from tins, sip orange soda and trade stories.

"I usually go to Florida with the tobacco, or North Carolina for the tomato."

How many times have you crossed?

"Well, I've crossed a lot of times. Maybe fifty or sixty." A laugh.

On the Day of the Migrant for years local Catholics led processions in Nuevo Laredo from the central park—where many migrants gather before making the crossing—across town to the International Bridge. They walk in silence and carry white crosses to commemorate the Mexicans who have died trying to get into the United States. Nuevo Laredo Priest Leonardo López calls the deaths "executions by unemployment, the economy, and the persecutions of migrants."[1] Advocates for migrants' rights blame U.S. border policies and the unsuccessful Mexican economy for the desperation that drives them to cross the border illicitly. "These immigrants that have died are not only victims of a dream but also of their desire to get ahead, of the frustration of not having money or stability," says López.

Trump-era orders added to the desperation in Nuevo Laredo and other Mexican borderland cities. Under the dismissive so-called Remain in Mexico policy, migrants traversing Mexico seeking asylum in the United States were forced to stay on the south side of the frontier until their number was called for a hearing—and wait for weeks that stretched into months, a dangerous and deplorable limbo that for most ended with asylum denied. The vicious, inhumane policy led desperate families to send their children across the border alone because U.S. law obligated officials to accept into *El Norte* unaccompanied minors applying for asylum.

Pueblos along the migrant trail make *migradollars* as staging points for the trek north. Places such as Altar, 160 miles southwest of Tucson, fill with travelers as the U.S. Border Patrol tightened border security at urban crossing points. From Altar north into the United States there is nothing much more than desert, bandits and bribe-taking cops. In addition to merchants selling food and water in Altar, organized smuggling gangs are at work, providing temporary housing in marginal *casas de huéspedes*—guesthouses—and offering onward guided trips into the United States at prices that increase as the United States make the border more difficult to cross. Deadly cartels expand their brands from drugs to guns to people smuggling.

It is not against Mexican law to cross from Mexico into the United States, but it is against the law to smuggle undocumented foreigners. Consequently Mexican law enforcement officials could chase the smugglers since plenty of their clients come from countries south of Mexico's border—but the cartels can outgun the cops. The former Mexico interior minister, Santiago Creel, watched the smuggling business grow fast after the United States instituted its Southwest Border Strategy in 1994, a strategy that forces undocumented migrants from hardened border cities into the wild desert. "We are talking about international mafias of extremely dangerous groups that have caused great pain to many families," Creel said of the smuggling operations. "The great problem we face is a humanitarian one," agreed the head of the Organized Crime Unit of the Mexican attorney general's office at the time, José Luis Vasconcelos.[2]

Travelers too poor to afford the guesthouses and the smugglers' fees camp outdoors. The Catholic church at Altar tries to help the indigent migrants. There, Father René Castañeda Castro presides over a dormitory for scores of the overexposed, and a kitchen to feed them. He and his crew try to convince the desperate migrants to turn back, telling them stories and showing them videos of the dangers ahead. "It's not a desert anymore," he tells them, "it's a cemetery."[3]

A Legit Business Opportunity

The free market adapts to change quickly on the Tijuana-San Diego border. Immediately after the 9/11 attacks, legal border crossers were faced with extraordinary delays as U.S. agents carefully checked documents and searched cars. Those walking across the border also were subject to increased scrutiny, their papers checked thoroughly and their possessions sent through airport-style inspection machines. The wait was hours long. But there was a third option. In addition to motor vehicles and pedestrians, there was a unique line for bicyclists. And very few border crossers were heading north by bicycle. There was virtually no waiting in the bicycle line.

Thus a group of Mexican entrepreneurs set up shop just south of the border with a haphazard collection of bicycles, offering them for rent to anyone standing in the hot sun waiting to pass the U.S. control point. I was in that line and jumped at the opportunity to speed up my passage, happy to rent a bicycle ludicrously too small for me. Riding was not an option. I couldn't fit on it. I gave the new businessman five bucks and took temporary custody of the bike. He instructed me to push the bike up to the crossing point, passing the hundreds of pedestrians sweltering in the sun.

"What do I do with it once I'm on the other side?" I asked him.

He smiled. "There's another *bandito* at the other end who will take the bike."

And indeed there was. As soon as I cleared U.S. immigration minutes later, his partner grabbed my bicycle and sent it south to earn another five dollars.

Striptease Interlude

My wife and I were en route to Dallas and made a typical tourist stop along the border. We parked the car in the shade in El Paso, and left a window cracked open and plenty of water for our dog, Amigo. Then we walked over to Juárez just to see it, before the long drive across Texas. (As a popular postcard says, "The sun is riz, the sun is set, and we ain't out of Texas yet.")

We were strolling down the streets of Juárez, just walking around looking at the sleazy honky-tonk joints that hug the border, and Sheila said, "Why don't we go into this one?" She'd never been in a strip club before. Inside were Formica tables lined up theater-like in front of a stage. The place was empty; it was still early in the afternoon. We sat down and ordered a couple of beers, asking for Carta Blanca. "Okay," nodded the waiter. He disappeared into a back room and returned with a couple of bottles of beer with labels identical in design to the Carta Blanca trademark. Except they said, Carta Cruz. It tasted terrible, watery. He charged us top dollar, which we paid, because the floor show was included.

We nursed the beers, waiting. Finally the waiter climbed up on the stage and announced, "And now," dramatic pause, "the world famous Miss Lola Brigetta!" From the wing stage left, Miss Lola slouched out on the boards. She was wearing a green-sequined dress that looked a little worn out, as did she.

On the stage, perched on a stool, was an old portable record player. Wires trailed across the floor to speakers set up on the edge of the stage, facing the audience: just the two of us. Miss Lola turned on the record player, plopped the needle onto the spinning vinyl, and began walking around the stage, more or less in time to the burlesque music. She made it abundantly clear that she was not just disinterested, but utterly bored. Quickly she claimed center stage and began unzipping her dress, not as a stripper, but as if she were getting ready for bed and no one was watching. Underneath were her bra and panties. The music bumped and ground. She pranced around in her underwear. Then she took off her bra and dropped it on the stage next to her dress. She meandered around some more in her pasties and panties, stopped and looked at her watch. She called off into the wing what we only figured must have been a message to the manager, something like, "I've been out here long enough, okay?" He must have said okay, because she quickly pulled off the panties, giving us a look at her thong while she tapped her foot waiting for the record to end. Then she picked up her clothes and walked off the stage. The whole affair lasted the amount of time it would take to smoke a cigarette.

Yesteryear's Borderless Border

Sent to cover the Mexican Revolution by *Metropolitan* magazine and the *New York World* newspaper, journalist John Reed traveled with Pancho Villa and reported from the front lines in 1913 and 1914. He went to Nogales to interview the future Mexican president Venustiano

Carranza—described by Reed as "a slightly senile old man, tired and irritated." The Nogales he found was nothing like the armed camp that divides the contemporary border. "Nogales, Arizona, and Nogales, Mexico really form one big straggling town," he wrote.

> The international boundary runs along the middle of the street, and at a small customshouse lounge a few ragged Mexican sentries, smoking interminable cigarettes, and eventually interfering with nobody, except to collect export taxes from everything that passes to the American side. The inhabitants of the American town go across the line to get good things to eat, to gamble, to dance, and to feel free; the Mexicans cross to the American side when somebody is after them.[4]

No meandering back and forth between this Nogales and that Nogales any longer. In 2018, the U.S. Army was ordered by its commander-in-chief Trump to line the 20-foot post-9/11 wall through Nogales on the American side with coils and coils of concertina wire—a bloody trap for border jumpers and a photo-op for the White House. "This is not right, what they're doing," was the response of Nogales, Arizona, Mayor Arturo Garino. "This should not be happening to our community."[5] On the Mexico side, white wooden crosses hung on the Nogales wall in memory of those who died crossing the border that John Reed saw as "one big straggling town."

Freelance Gringo *Coyotes*

Over fifty thousand cars, trucks and busses roll through the main crossing point between Tijuana and San Diego every day. The Department of Homeland Security admits it only stops and searches a fraction of them. Because of these odds, plenty of migrants take a gamble and just come north through the official crossing point, hidden casually under sleeping bags and baggage or carefully stashed in secret compartments.

This type of human smuggling caught the fancy of freelance gringo *coyotes*—students and other cash-strapped San Diegans who discovered that a quick trip over the border and back can earn them *mucho* tax-free dollars. And the risks are minimal—even if the penalties can be severe for those who are caught. But prosecutors acknowledge that they rarely pursue these ad hoc smugglers if their human cargo is not mistreated and if they are not dealing with more than a few migrants.

"The number of cases exceeds the available resources in the criminal justice system," is how Adele Fasano, then the San Diego director of Customs and Border Protection, reacted when the gringo scheme made news. "We prioritize and prosecute the most egregious ones."[6]

These gringo *coyotes*, often high school students, don't necessarily need to arrange for their cargo in advance. Savvy Mexicans solicit the gringos where they're frolicking at Tijuana bars and dance clubs.

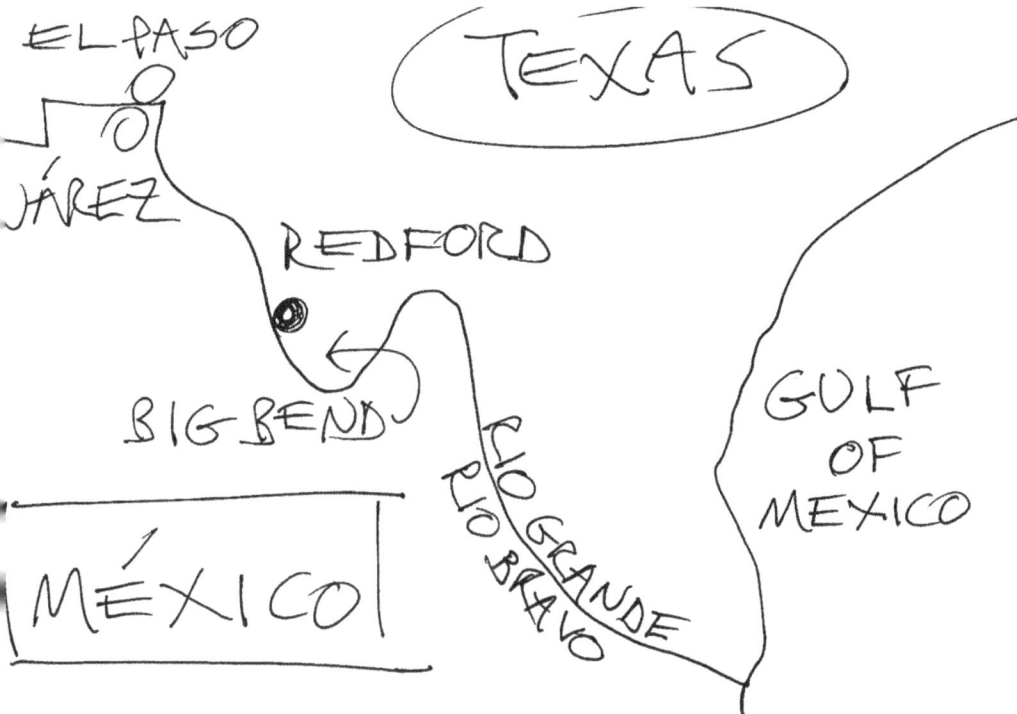

EL PASO
JÁREZ
TEXAS
REDFORD
BIG BEND
MÉXICO
RIO GRANDE
RIO BRAVO
GULF OF MEXICO

Chapter 4

ON GUARD

In 1993, the U.S. government imposed what it called Operation Gatekeeper along the border at San Diego. A high gash of concrete replaced ad hoc and sometimes minimal fencing while the Border Patrol bloated with new hires. But Operation Gatekeeper did not keep Mexicans out of the United States, it simply pushed them from the urban crossing point at Tijuana east to the rural deserts of California and Arizona. The Immigration and Naturalization Service (INS) claimed it was not surprised that the migrants moved to the more dangerous deserts and continued to cross. "Our national strategy calls for shutting down the San Diego sector first, maintaining control there, then controlling the Tucson and South Texas corridors," explained INS spokeswoman at the time, Virginia Kice. "We recognize that traffic will increase in other sectors, but we need to control the major corridors

Figure 4.1 Marking division from sea to shining sea, the starkly differentiated Mexican-American borderline drops into the Pacific between San Diego and Tijuana.

first."[1] It was a failed policy. Traffic across the borderline only grew, with deadly results (Figure 4.1).[2]

In the first few years of Operation Gatekeeper, and the similar Operation Hold the Line at El Paso, the number of Mexicans who died en route north increased markedly. The University of Houston Center for Immigration Research, citing what it called conservative estimates, reported that well over a thousand undocumented immigrants died trying to cross the border from 1993 to 1996. "For every body found there is certainly one that isn't," said the center's codirector, Nestor Rodriguez.[3]

"It's a shocking number of deaths," was the response from the late Roberto Martínez, then the director of the U.S.-Mexico Border Program for the American Friends Service Committee. "It sets us back on the human rights issue. It can't be ignored by the governments on both sides of the border."[4] Yet in the years since, the border remained heavily fortified at San Diego and other urban centers and the death toll in the deserts keeps climbing. By 2020, the official body count was closing in on ten thousand, with the wilds of the desert undoubtedly providing the final resting place for scores more unclaimed and uncounted.

A report in 2001 by the U.S. General Accounting Office (GAO) had already condemned the Southwest Border Strategy, the name used by the Border Patrol for its scheme to dissuade illegal crossings by hardening urban ports of entry. By that time the Border Patrol had doubled its agent roster over a period of some seven years and had seen its annual budget multiply four times to well over $6 billion dollars. The result? "The primary discernable effect," stated the GAO, was simply a "shifting of the illegal alien traffic."[5] And the deaths of over two thousand migrants.

The Southwest Border Strategy was the brainchild of former El Paso Representative Silvestre Reyes. Reyes held unique credentials for his job. He was the first member of Congress with working experience as a Border Patrolman. He retired after 26 years with the Immigration and Naturalization Service, 13 of them as Border Patrol chief in Texas. "The chaos of illegal immigration, uncontrolled and unaddressed, as it existed before I implemented Hold the Line in El Paso, was unacceptable," Reyes testified. "It was unacceptable to the officers and it was unacceptable to the community." Even as the deaths mounted in the deserts far from El Paso, Reyes expressed pride and confidence in the strategy.

> I have first-hand knowledge of not only the difficulties and struggles we face on the border, but also of the success we have had with initiatives such as Operation Hold the Line and Operation Gatekeeper. While our Border Patrol has made progress, we all agree that we have a long way to go before we establish control of our 2,000-mile border with Mexico.[6]

The Border Patrol requires its agents speak enough Spanish to pass the agency's language tests. That prerequisite is at least partially responsible for the fact that many of the agents are Latino. Some were born in Mexico and became U.S. citizens; some were born in the United States and have lived in Mexico. Others have parents or grandparents who came across the border without proper documents. Veteran agent Marco Ramirez was raised in Mexico, but says he does not let his heritage interfere with his work. "The way I see it," he explains, "you carry the badge in one hand, and in the other hand, you carry your heart."[7]

Immigration invaded presidential politics during the 1996 campaign, with both political parties inciting fear. First Bob Dole blanketed television with ads accusing Bill Clinton of being soft on undocumented immigrants. The pictures accompanying the aggressive narration were of migrants clandestinely crossing into California. Clinton was on the air in retaliation with pictures of a brown-skinned man handcuffed by the Border Patrol, inflammatory images that were punctuated by text claiming a 40 percent increase to the Border Patrol ranks during Clinton's first term, along with record numbers of deportees.[8]

Shot Dead

More Border Patrolmen on the frontier, of course, resulted in increased encounters between them and Mexicans trying to cross into the United States. Over a weekend in late September 1998, Border Patrol agents twice reacted with guns to what they said were threats from Mexicans who were armed with rocks and refused orders to stop. Agents shot both migrants dead. The official Border Patrol explanation was terse, impersonal and clinical: "Fearing for his life, [the agent] brings out the weapon and shoots this person, striking the person in the torso area," said Border Patrol spokeswoman Gloria Chavez about one of the shootings. Her colleague, Border Patrol spokesman Mario Villarreal said about the other, "The agent ordered him to drop the rock and stop. [The man] went on in an aggressive manner. The agent discharged his service firearm in self-defense, striking the individual in the torso."[9]

"Something is going wrong," was the response of the Mexican consul general in San Diego, Luis Herrera-Lasso, who explained that rock throwing is commonplace along the border and that the Border Patrol need not use deadly force to combat it.[10]

In 1989, the U.S. government sent regular army troops back to the Mexican border, this time with the rationale of fighting drug traffickers. On July 30, 1997, it suspended those border operations, two months after a Marine corporal shot and killed 18-year-old Esequiel Hernandez Jr. as the high school student was herding goats near his hometown of Redford, Texas.

Redford, understandably, was shocked.

"The only thing we know is that a good kid is dead who shouldn't be," said Hernandez's English teacher Kevin Stahnke immediately after the killing.[11]

The teacher and the rest of Redford—the population in 1997 was 107—soon learned that Esequiel was herding his family's goats down near the Rio Grande, as usual, the afternoon of the day he was killed. He was carrying his grandfather's 1910 rifle, as usual, to protect the goats from a pack of wild dogs.[12] He apparently shot a few rounds in the direction of brown shapes moving near his goats.

Those shapes were four Marines, covered in brush for camouflage, their faces blackened. They were deployed on the border for surveillance duty, assigned to track suspected drug smugglers and report on the traffickers' whereabouts to the Border Patrol. These Marines were a unit of something called Joint Task Force Six, a Federal agency set-up to coordinate operations between the military and the Border Patrol. The U.S. military is proscribed by law from performing domestic police work. That prohibition was established in 1878 with the passage of the Posse Comitatus Act. But in 1981, federal law was changed to allow for cooperation between the military and civilian police, specifically for the purpose of stopping illegal drugs at the border.

Joint Task Force Six, known as JTF-6, was the work of then Secretary of Defense Dick Cheney, who—along with Joint Chiefs of Staff Chairman Colin Powell—chose to militarize the border, an escalation of the so-called War on Drugs. Part of their strategy was to deploy the Marines without telling local townspeople. Since Esequiel and the rest of Redford were not informed of the patrol, they also could not know the orders for the Marines' tour in their neighborhood. Unlike domestic police, the Marines were not to identify themselves. They were not to fire warning shots. And if they felt threatened, they were expected to shoot to kill.[13] These were their "rules of engagement." As the months passed following young Esequiel's death, that term, "rules of engagement," infuriated the citizens of Redford.

"What are these 'rules of engagement?'" questioned a neighbor of the Hernandez family, Diana Valenzuela. "We had no idea we were being engaged in the first place. I was amazed when I heard that the military was walking around the hills in our backyard."

Another Redford schoolteacher, Leonel Ceniceros, agreed. "It seems crazy to me now that they were even here. When you think about it, these are young Marines brought in here from out of state. They've probably been told there are drug dealers all over the place, you're in enemy territory, protect yourself. But the result is, this good young man is dead."[14]

"They say they are trained to kill," Esequiel Hernandez's older brother said about the Marines. "They should kill in war, not in towns."

The Marines essentially said the same thing in their initial official response to the killing. Marine Colonel Thomas Kelley told a news conference, "If you reach the point where you fire for fear of your lives, then you usually fire to kill."

After Hernandez fired his grandfather's old rifle, the Marines radioed to their Border Patrol associates that they were the targets of his shots. They tracked Hernandez and say he again raised his rifle and aimed at them. That's when 22-year-old Corporal Clemente Bañuelos fired a single round from his M-16 and saw Hernandez fall. The Border Patrol recovered his body over twenty minutes later. The Marines did not try to save his life after he was shot; their orders did not require such follow-up. According to the autopsy, Hernandez bled to death.

"These people had no right to be here," said retired Episcopal priest Melvin La Follete about the Marines. A friend of the Hernandez family, La Follete organized Redford citizens to fight against the militarization of their border town. "The Marines left their observation post, they stalked him, they came onto private property. And then they killed him. We were going blithely about our business, not knowing that Congress had handed away the civil rights of people on the border."

Eventually the Hernandez family received $1.9 million dollars from the federal government in compensation for their loss of Esequiel. In return the government admitted no fault.

"This was a tragedy, not a criminal act," said Jack Zimmermann, a lawyer for the shooter, Corporal Bañuelos. But the Texas Rangers were not convinced. After a review of the record, Ranger Sergeant David Duncan said, "The federal government came in and stifled the investigation. It's really depressing."

Esequiel Hernandez Jr. dreamed of a career in law enforcement. On his bedroom wall hung a U.S. Marine Corps recruiting poster.

Months before Hernandez was killed, the JTF-6 troops reported their first Mexican casualty. A Green Beret on duty east of Brownsville, Texas, took aim at a figure climbing out of the Rio Grande. Eleven shots later Cesario Vásquez, en route to Houston to look for a job, was dying.

Despite these tragedies, during the 2003 debate in Congress prior to the Iraq war, Colorado Congressman Tom Tancredo, a longtime proponent of militarizing the border, told his colleagues the United States was already fighting a home-front war. "Our borders are war zones," he told them.[15] "There is a war going on on our borders. People are being killed on our borders. Troops are needed on our borders. Our homeland needs to be defended."

President Trump temporarily deployed the U.S. military to the border in 2018. Photo-ops included soldiers stringing razor wire along the existing barrier. Trump, with typical hyperbole, threatened a massive troop presence if Congress refused to spend the billions he was demanding for construction of his wall. "We will build a Human Wall if necessary," he typed on Twitter.[16]

One of those Marines Trump sent to the Arizona border was Adam Woodward, who described his tour of borderlands duty as an exercise in boredom: just observing the desert, punctuated by rare police work. "One day we spotted these two individuals probably seven, eight miles out," Woodward and his partner watched for an hour while "these guys are getting closer and closer." The Border Patrol unit the Marines called had not arrived by the time the two hikers reached the Marine post. "They finally got up close enough where I could yell at them." He ordered them to lie down. "They laid down where they were at." The Marines and their detainees waited until the Border Patrol arrived to take over the case. And that was the climax of Woodward's tedious role in Trump's publicity campaign.[17]

Chaos Reigns

As Mexicans continued to die along the border from attacks by the U.S. military and the Border Patrol, at the hands of bandits and cheating *coyotes*, and from the extreme heat and cold of the desert, the United States continued its efforts at slowing the flow of migrants. In 1998, the Arizona border became the path into the United States with the greatest number of illegal crossings, according to the Border Patrol, outstripping Tijuana where the extensive patrols and the expanding wall convinced migrants that the Arizona desert was a better risk. The next year the Border Patrol caught nearly half a million undocumented migrants in Arizona, a doubling of their caseload in just five years.[18] By the year 2000, the radical wall along the Tijuana-San Diego line was replicated in the Arizona desert at Douglas, across from Agua Prieta. But five miles of floodlights and cameras, sheet metal and iron were unable to do anything but complicate the crossing and make it more expensive and dangerous for illicit travelers, pushing them away from the urbanized Douglas–Agua Prieta twin cities and into the unforgiving wilds of the desert.

Agua Prieta *presidente municipal* Daniel Fierros could see from the changes in his city how futile the Southwest Border Strategy and its new strip of wall in the desert north of his town were to U.S. goals of securing the border. "People who didn't have income rent [rooms in] their houses," he said about the economic boom new migrants brought to his part of the border. "People sell fast food and things to cook with. Taxis get more business. And the *coyotes* do very well. We don't con-done it, but it's a business as lucrative as drug trafficking, without the risks."[19] By 2000, hundreds of guest houses—just homes with rooms to rent—were operating in Agua Prieta, catering to border crossers waiting for the right moment to head north.[20]

In 1994, there were 58 Border Patrol agents working out of the Douglas station. By 2000, their ranks soared toward six hundred, by 2020 close to four thousand agents were on patrol just along the Arizona line. And still the trail north filled with migrants on the move.

The people-smuggling business thrived as the border became harder to cross. *Coyotes* upped the prices for a guided crossing; they fought with each other for the lucrative human cargo. Warfare between smuggling syndicates spread from Mexico and the border further north into U.S. cities. More expensive and sophisticated smugglers promised to get migrants far from the border into safe houses where they could rest and make onward plans before disappearing into American crowds. Again, the U.S. government responded with force, doubling the number of immigration agents in Phoenix, for example, to one hundred. "We're dealing with ruthless individuals who view human life as nothing more than cargo for profit," said Michael Garcia, acting assistant secretary for Immigration and Customs Enforcement.[21] "Smuggling-related violence in the Phoenix area has reached epidemic proportions," Garcia said about the need for more officers.

Phoenix police reported instances of rival traffickers kidnapping migrants from each other and holding them for ransom. Day laborer Anna Roblero said she was one of those kidnap victims when she arrived in Phoenix after paying a *coyote* four hundred dollars for passage across the border. "We walked for three days and three nights through the desert," she told National Public Radio during an interview on a Phoenix street. "When we got across the desert, the smugglers told us to wait for some men to pick us up, but they never came. We didn't know where we were." Different smugglers then took custody of the group and demanded more money. Roblero said she called a cousin, who was able to raise the money, but it took over a week, a week she spent confined in a house. "I just cried and cried. I thought I was never going to see my kids again. They had guns and I thought they were going to kill us. Thank God my cousin came and gave them the money."[22]

Since a conviction for people smuggling usually results in a much less severe jail sentence than a conviction for drug smuggling, experienced criminals from the drug trade saw a business opportunity with human cargo and moved into trafficking in human beings.

Chapter 5

DEATH ALONG FOR THE RIDE

Texas summers bake. I know; when we lived in a stuffy Dallas bungalow, my wife and I periodically treated ourselves to relief from the heat and humidity with the company car. We'd just sit in the driveway, air conditioner cranked up high, listen to the radio and cool off. WFAA Radio bought the gasoline and somehow we rationalized the exhaust.

On a hot May 13, 2003, well before summer, down by the Mexico border near Harlingen, smugglers guided as many as a hundred immigrants into a freight trailer. They had just crossed the border illegally, wading across the Rio Grande as so many millions of Mexicans and others had done before that hot night. The doors to the long van swung shut, and the truck headed north through the night toward its destination, Houston.

Not three hours later, just outside Victoria at a Harris County gas station, the driver stopped his rig, opened the back doors of the trailer and abandoned it and its devastated cargo.[1] Nineteen of his hundred or so passengers were dead or dying, killed by heat stroke and dehydration, greed and incompetence, desperation for a better life and unenforceable U.S. immigration laws. One of the dead was a 5-year-old Mexican boy.

"No Sheriff likes to be called at two o'clock in the morning to be told he has multiple deceased people in his community," Sheriff Mike Ratcliff says when he recalls that miserable night.

"Upon arrival at the location we discovered there were multiple victims on the ground. Then, of course, we had to deal with the victims who had dissipated into the woodlands surrounding the area—snake-infested terrain—that we had to worry about." Sheriff Ratcliff tends to speak in official-sounding jargon, with words such as "dissipated" and "co-victims." But after just a few minutes discussing with him then the worst case of human smuggling in U.S. history, his compassion is obvious.

"We had some witnesses, co-victims, if you will, who described the number of people in the vehicle. We could estimate that as many as 60 to 90 people were on the ground in our community. We had to deal with that problem as well."

While Customs and Border Protection, with a special ICE investigative team, raced to Victoria to take over the federalized investigation, Ratcliff's detectives hunted down the truck driver, Tyrone Powers, finding him a few hours after he ran from the tragedy.

The sheriff is still shaken six months later when he retells the story of that dreadful night. His deputies called him to come quickly, which was no problem. His home is just a mile and a half from the crime scene. He feels no mercy for the ring of smugglers and their driver.

"It's difficult for me as a 26-year veteran of law enforcement to consider that a person doesn't know the cargo in his van," he says about Powers' initial defense tactic. "Human cargo is unacceptable. The thought of human beings trapped, encapsulated in that trailer and brought to our country, or taken anywhere in 100 degree weather is totally …" his voice trails off for a few seconds. "Well, it's just unacceptable."

What's the correct penalty for such a crime?

"Should a person be put to death for the death of nineteen people?" He considers the question. "I would tell you in my estimation, if they did it one time, they could do it again because greed seemed to premise everything. If greed allowed them to do it that one time to nineteen people, and that little boy, then the opportunity for them to do it again would not be changed by anything but death."

Driver Powers did finally open the trailer door. Was that an act of humanity? No, says the Sheriff, it was a result of stupidity.

> His stupidity ran out when his human resources came into play and he decided to buy water for some of the victims and he opened the doors to the trailer. That was when stupidity was overcome by human nature. But the one factor to be considered is that if he did this one time, there is the potential that he could do this again. And the world can't stand that loss of life. Our community will not overcome that tragedy. We are now the site of the most tragic immigrant loss of lives in our nation's history.

Oil and cattle were the magic that made Victoria famous during its booming past. Back in the 1930s ranchers around Victoria began discovering oil and natural gas under their rangeland. By the 1950s Victoria boasted more millionaires per capita than any other American city. Today memories of those times are enhanced by the stately Victorian homes still scattered throughout the city. The Sheriff's office is in the heart of the old downtown, a modern concrete and glass building just off the old city square. Sheriff Ratcliff clearly wishes a truckload of dead immigrants had not replaced oil and cattle as his city's reason for notoriety.

"As sheriff of the county, I will do whatever I can to ensure that our community and our state and our nation never have to undergo that type of tragedy again. We are a caring people. We love fellow human beings. If they come to the country illegally, we will deal with them under the appropriate law."

But Ratcliff is convinced the laws need to be changed. "We need to come up with laws that would help these people. We need to create the legal method for people to enter our country to work or go to school or do other things that they feel they need to do to help their families and themselves."[2]

Buried Alive

Inside that trailer coffin, suffocating with his brother, was Guillermo Cabrera from Veracruz, Mexico. He was on his way to the rolling hills of south-central Kentucky, promised work on a dairy farm.

"The heat started about eleven, really by nine," he says about the ride north. "By eleven, twelve you can really feel it. Hot. Some people were already fainted, six or seven. Some friends in there started to faint. And like that: very strong heat, like in Hell, an inferno."

Cabrera and I are sitting at a plastic table in what he calls *la tiendita*, the little store, Paul's Minute Market at the Key Stop gas station in Temple Hill, Kentucky. Cabrera survived the inferno; his brother died.

> We were both there, but I never saw my brother during the whole crisis. I never saw him again. I couldn't find him. Where was he? When they opened the door, there were a lot of people lying on the floor of the trailer because it was really hot inside, very hot. But I do not know how I got out of there. Many of us have no idea how we got out of there. We realized that we were alive because God is great.

Guillermo Cabrera's eyes tear. He looks away, but keeps telling his story.

"Later, seven days later, I learned that my brother had died. I was in the hospital. I was there for four days, almost dying. I was really sick. I didn't know what was going on. Everything was erased."

Cabrera is wearing a baseball cap announcing, "Branson, Mo. The Ozarks." His T-shirt is more specific. It's a rendition of the Liberty Bell featuring the words, "America" and "Let Freedom Ring." He drove up to the

Minute Market in an old faded red Ford Ranger pickup. We met at seven in the morning. Three old-timers were nursing their coffee behind a sign in the window announcing, "We sell and recommend Coon Hunter's Pride."

"Is it okay to talk here?" I asked him, quietly in Spanish, not knowing his immigration status.

He assured me it would be no problems and he casually greeted the regulars. Cabrera is one of the lucky ones. Not only did he survive the inferno but the U.S. government also rewarded his trauma by granting him the legal right to stay north of the border.

Whose fault was the disaster, I ask him.

"Well, you pay for them to bring you here safe and alive," he says about the smugglers. "But they don't know how you are going to arrive. If they are going to put you into a trailer, they should give you fresh air. Since everything is closed, you don't know what is going to happen in there."

He soon knew something was very wrong.

With all the heat, your head is not working well. Many things start going on in your head. I thought of God, my family, everybody. Many of us survived. We tried to take apart a piece of the wooden door. My brother was one of those who were taking apart the door, because he was really desperate. His hands were all destroyed from that.

Once the doors opened, Cabrera headed over dead bodies to the fresh air.

I walked over many people and got down. And then I just collapsed. The ambulance came and they took me to the hospital. I was there for four days, and then they took me to jail for six days. They worked on the permits to allow us to stay in this country legally. They gave me one of those after the accident.

I suggested a solution so others need not fear sharing his fate in the future: an open border between the two countries so workers could travel north freely. His answer surprised me.

"No, that would not be possible. All of Mexico would be here."

Particularly grating for the sheriff is that the trailer tragedy did not put a dent in the abuse of migrants on the road.

> Nineteen people perished on May 14th and on May 15th eighteen people were stopped approximately ten miles north of that point, and of those eighteen people who had stopped at a roadside park, two had to be carried into a hospital—just two days later! They were compacted into a trailer that could not sustain them. They were taken to a local hospital and kept overnight for dehydration.

Washington Post reporters Kevin Sullivan and Mary Jordan noted that in the same week as the trailer tragedy, at least eleven other people died trying to cross the border—died without the headlines accorded to the trailer deaths because the eleven others were part of the now-routine tally of loss of life on the frontier. Sullivan and Jordan recorded drownings in the Rio Grande and heat exhaustion in the deserts of Texas and Arizona, deaths that occurred one or two at a time, quietly, without much notice.[3]

Sheriff Ratcliff expresses no patience with the standard anti-immigrant lines.

> The borders are being screened for drugs and weapons. Certainly I want our country rid of drugs and weapons. But look at what is going on, adverse to what our nation is all about. To me, optimum consideration should be given to the presence of human beings in those very cargo vehicles that travel our nation daily. When we lose sight of that, we lose sight of a lot of very important matters. I thought about it several times that day in our command center. I think the intensity of what is perceived as a threat really doesn't exist.

He says it is an illusion that Mexicans take jobs from Americans. He is disgusted with the argument that immigrants abuse the social services available in the United States. "And who wouldn't want to? That's my answer. Who wouldn't want to come to the most wonderful country in the world? Can you blame them?"

Change the laws, insists the sheriff, to encourage migrants to pay taxes. Of course, migrants without papers already pay plenty of taxes. They pay sales tax. They pay indirect property tax when they pay rent. Those who use fake Social Security numbers lose salary to money withheld that they can never collect, money that helps fund the overall Social Security System from which legal residents profit. It's difficult for the undocumented to use Medicare and other services both because of the registration process and because of their fear of the discovery of their illegal status.

Opportunity is what America is all about, says the sheriff, again invoking the memory of the lost 5-year-old boy.

What would he have done in our country? Who could he have become? These people came to our country looking for opportunity. You can talk about the Statue of Liberty and what it represents all day long, or you can say that it's a hill of beans. But it's true! These people come into our country looking for opportunity. One word. Opportunity.

The law needs to be changed, says the sheriff, to reflect reality. "Use history. Approach the current day with what America lives upon and should: its own history. Examine what we have done in the past. Look at and give weight to the open arms of the east coast," he says about the welcome offered to migrants from Europe. "Carry the Statue of Liberty to the borders of Mexico and Canada and create laws that identify with what the French gave to America. You can't open the doors to a country by etching in stone alone the words that welcome you. You have to create law that represents what's etched in stone."

And Mexico, he says, shares the responsibility.

We need to eliminate human cargo. We need to insure this does not happen again. [Former] President Fox needs to educate his folks as to what is legal. These people come to our country not knowing what is appropriate and what is not. And they pay $2,000 for a ride in a conveyance that cattle wouldn't be carried in. Because they don't know any better. If we welcome people to our country, let's do so legally and let's make sure they can be educated on how to get to our country legally. Two thousand dollars would have bought somebody a Green Card all the way in. But they don't know that.

CALIFORNIA

NEW MEXICO

ARIZONA

1,954 MILES

MÉXICO

TEXAS

GULF OF MEXICO

Chapter 6

A WEARY LAWYER'S VIEW

As the case against the Victoria smugglers developed, Texas-based immigration lawyer Barbara Hines was surprised to find herself representing one of the migrants who was packed into the truck trailer Sheriff Ratcliff was disgusted to learn headed north with a load of human cargo just the day after the Victoria disaster. Hines went to law school specifically motivated to work for social justice. After passing the bar in the mid-1970s, she expected to join the cadre of lawyers inspired by the women's movement and engage women's rights issues. She remembers drifting into immigration law by chance.

"I showed up at a legal aid office in 1975 and someone said, 'Do you speak Spanish?' and they handed me twenty immigration cases. At that time, there were no immigration courses. There were very few people practicing immigration law and people used to say, 'You're a *what* kind of lawyer? What in the world do immigration lawyers do?' "

It turns out that immigration lawyers fall into two basic categories: those who help people coming to the United States legally and those who help people already in the United States who are facing problems with the authorities. It's the latter type of law that Barbara Hines practices, a specialty known as family-based immigration and deportation law. Her clients are trying to legalize their status in the United States. They're seeking work permits, temporary visas or the precious Green Card—the ticket that denotes a legal permanent resident, and is a first step toward U.S. citizenship. Often she deals with crises. She represents Green Card holders facing deportation for a crime or a bureaucratic misstep. And she works with asylum seekers, those who escape to the United States fearing persecution at home.

Over her long years of practice, she sees increased enforcement of increasingly restrictive immigration laws. "In an ironic way, it's decreased our work because there's so little we can do for people."

In addition to her private immigration law practice, Barbara Hines teaches law at the University of Texas in Austin where she founded the Immigration Clinic. The clinic represents clients without funds and otherwise without access to legal representation. Work at the clinic is particularly focused on the needs of immigrants facing deportation and those seeking political asylum. Clients include battered immigrant women.

"I think it's really all about the haves and the have nots," she says about migration into the United States.

I even had an immigration judge come to my class and say, "You know, if I were in the same situation as most of these people, I'd come too." If you're starving or even if you're in search of a better life, why wouldn't

you move? Everybody moves. It's the historical phenomenon of migration. Why do people migrate? They migrate because they want something better. People don't voluntarily leave their home surroundings
unless there is some push factor.

Airplanes and the Internet only make the global population more
mobile. "Twenty years ago," Hines said in the early 2000s,

> the only people that could get to the United States were the Mexicans
> and the stowaways and the people that could get tourist visas, because
> how were you going get to the United States from China? Now, because
> of more sophisticated smugglers, people from China can get on the boat
> and then they can beach the boat in Mexico and they can come up the
> exact same way that the Mexicans have come for years. People are more
> aware that it's a possibility that you might be able to get here from Eastern
> Europe and China. You have to pay a lot of money, but now there's some-
> body that's able to get you here.

Hines and her students visit Texas lockups where undocumented
migrants are held during deportation proceedings. They look for
prisoners who might benefit from legal representation and they offer
their services. It's a scatter-shot approach to social work, looking for the
mostly destitute migrants picked up by the Border Patrol and other law
enforcement agencies. But it's better than nothing in a judicial system
packed with potential clients where only a few independent lawyers are
available to represent them pro bono.

"If people happened to be brought in that day and their luck was
good, they would get us as their lawyers," Hines says about her periodic
visits to jails and prisons.

> Just by chance we happened to find someone who was on that truck
> trailer. What was really shocking to me was that it was discovered just
> after the one in Victoria. The second one was called Operation Pick Axe

by investigators. I said to my client, "Didn't you hear about the truck before? How could you have gotten on this truck?" My client told me one of the smugglers said, "Don't worry. Here's a pick axe. If there are any problems, just bang on the cab and I'll hear you." That's why investigators named it Operation Pick Axe.

Hines's client, intent on finding work north of the border, climbed aboard. "It's very sobering to me to think about how desperate people are."

Over her long career Hines has watched as people smuggling along the Mexican border has become big sophisticated business. Much of it used to be informal. An experienced border crosser would help his friends and family cross to *El Norte* and maybe take some money for his trouble. When others in his village heard of the successful trip, they'd ask for help and offer to pay him a fee. Today, the smuggling is professional and expensive. "All of a sudden it got taken over by the cartels, the gangs," says Hines.

In Arizona immigrants are being held as hostage between one warring smuggling gang and the other. In the 1980s it was unheard of that that would be going on. It's like drug wars—trafficking in persons—and it is very, very lucrative. That's the reason it's moved into boxcars and trucks. There's just so much more human smuggling on a much larger scale. There's just been a really notable shift in the way people come. It used to be you just paid some little smuggler right at the border a couple hundred bucks. But it's not like that anymore.

Hines worked to get her trailer victim legal status in the United States based on the suffering experienced crossing the border and then being herded into another potential death truck. The U.S. government does allow for sanctuary as a humanitarian gesture when a border crosser suffers extreme trauma en route. License to stay in the United States is also offered when prosecutors feel confident that the migrant can offer valuable testimony against traffickers.

Working with undocumented migrants, teaching law, living along the extended border—all add to Barbara Hines's conviction that the current immigration laws are a travesty. "Unless we're going to put up the Berlin Wall," she said long before Donald Trump's campaign to do so,

> and as long as people are starving and can't feed their kids and want a better life, people are going to keep coming. All these really, really strict immigration laws do is just create a population of more and more undocumented people. One of the ironic things about 9/11 is that there is a much stronger argument now to say why would you want this entire population that's underground? Aren't we supposed to know who's here so we can be looking for the real terrorists? The policy is a failure. Increased enforcement on the border hasn't stopped the flow. All it's done is made the price much higher, because what happens now is immigrants are pushed out into the desert because of the increased enforcement in the urban areas. So there's a greater risk to life—but it hasn't stopped people from coming.

Hines believes the United States must at least adopt some sort of temporary worker program to cover the millions of undocumented laborers north of the border.

> We make you risk your life to get over here. You may die in the desert. But once you get here, we'd love to have you. That's what's so ridiculous about this policy. It's not that once you get across the desert nobody will hire you. People are dying to hire you. I don't think there's any workable solution unless we look at why people immigrate.

Most people come north from Mexico for work and family. Until the 1986 immigration law was passed by Congress it was not against the law to hire undocumented immigrants. But after 1986 employers were subject to fines for failing to determine the legal status of their workers. That policy is a failure. Authorities cannot begin to check all places of employment, and workers are clever about obtaining false documents once they are safely north of the border. Barbara Hines says pressure from industry put a stop to initial attempts to enforce the new law targeting employers.

"There was a lot of political pressure," Hines says about Immigration and Naturalization Service (INS) raids on the meatpacking industry in the Midwest back in the early 1990s. "The meatpacking industry and their senators and representatives put a lot of pressure on the government to stop doing this. They said, 'We need people. Leave us alone.' The authorities backed off on employer sanctions." She says the raids, and the threat of more that exists as long as the employer sanctions law remains on the books, merely developed a new industry. "It spawned an interest in fake documents. You just go to a flea market and, for fifteen dollars you buy your fake Green Card. Employers are not an immigration expert. They can't know whether this is a fake card or a real card."

Workplace raids returned with a vengeance during the publicity-seeking Trump administration. These periodic police actions grabbed headlines while traumatizing families, businesses and communities. But such raids are a policy failure: the vast number of undocumented workers fueling the American economy means authorities wear pragmatic blinders.

Any improvement would please Barbara Hines. "I don't like to have to tell my clients, 'No, you cannot go to your father's funeral. No, you cannot go home to see your mother before she dies […]. Well, you can go home—but you can't get back.' I'm sure my clients would be willing to have any temporary worker permit that would allow them to cross the border and not have to come back through the desert or the river."

"Right now, you're spending all of your resources patrolling the borders for most people who have absolutely nothing to do with terrorism. Sometimes I feel sorry for this agency," she says about the Department of Homeland Security and their impossible task of securing the border. "Although I have spent most of my life suing this agency, I kind of feel sorry for them."

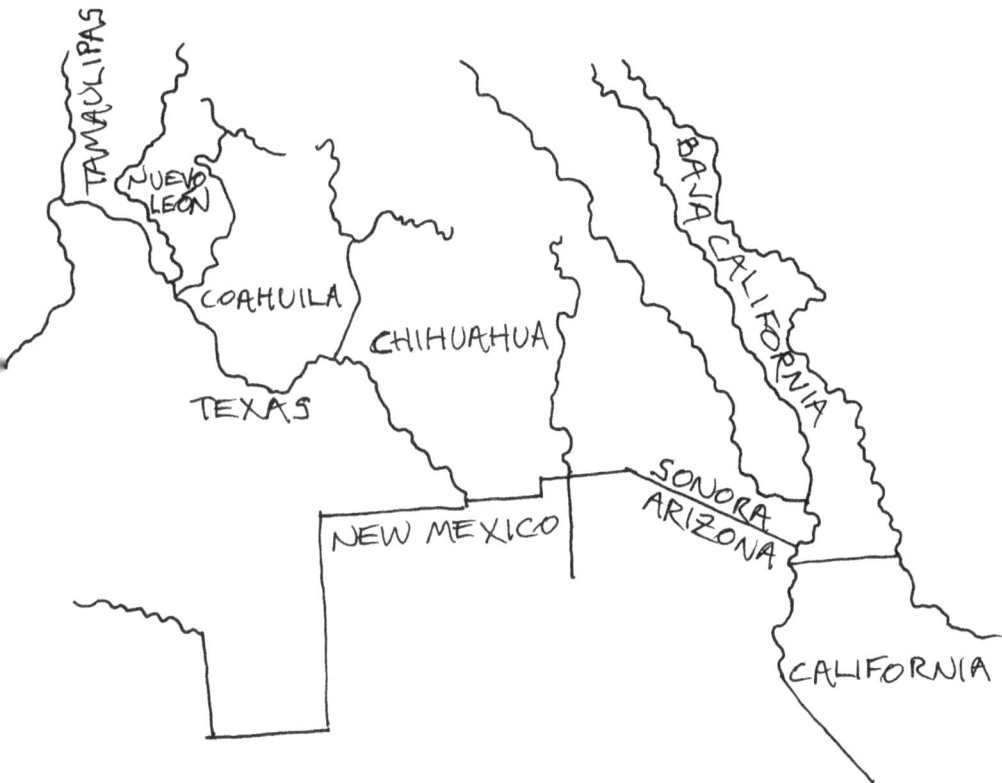

Inspired by Torres-García

Chapter 7

WHAT IS A BORDER?

G et up in the morning and stumble to the bathroom. There probably is a door on that bathroom. Do you close it? That probably depends on who is in the house with you. If you've been sleeping with a friend or a lover, or just sharing a bed for convenience, you've faced a border before the bathroom. "Get back on your side of the bed," you may have mumbled if your companion disturbed your sleep. Or, "You've got all the covers!"

We are surrounded by borders. They provide us with security and comfort, limits and definitions.

Once in the bathroom, perhaps you decide to close the door. You might want some privacy while you go about your morning routine. Or maybe you don't want to disturb your companion with the noise you make, so closing the door creates some sound barrier. If the door is equipped with a lock, you face another decision.

There are plenty of other borders in your home. "Stay out of my room," you may instruct your kids. Perhaps you've got some secrets in the dresser or you just don't want them sitting on your clean sheets with their dirty jeans. The kids may want to keep you out of their rooms, too. House rules create borders without walls and doors. You may not allow food in the living room, or you may forbid skateboards on the rugs. A particularly unruly friend of one of your kids might be barred from spending the night in the family home or even forbidden from visiting under any circumstances.

Of course if your own child is a taste mischievous, he may let that blacklisted friend in through his bedroom window in the middle of the night and shove him out at dawn. You might never know that the troublemaker was in your house. And while you're at work, someone might be watching TV in the living room, eating a peanut butter and grape jelly sandwich, in violation of your house rules. As long as there are no crumbs on the floor, or purple stains on the carpet, you might never know that it was transformed into an after-school snack room.

Is there a fence around your house? If so, why is it there? Perhaps it keeps your dog in your yard. Perhaps it keeps other dogs out of your yard. Maybe you built it just to define the border of your property, to give you a sense of what is yours and how far into the distance that ownership extends. Or your fence may block a view you don't want to look at: the neighbors' turquoise house, or their '67 Dodge Charger up on blocks. Your fence may provide a sequestered playground for your children, a safety zone from which they can't escape if they're still toddlers.

Is there a lock on your gate? Is there a lock on your front door? If you live in a metropolis, there may be several different types of locks on your door: a spring lock, a couple of deadbolts and a chain to allow for some restricted communication or exchange of goods without actual entry. This crucial border between your sanctuary and the rest of the world may be equipped with a peephole to check on the identity of visitors, along with all the locks. Apartments in rough neighborhoods often are equipped with

Figure 7.1 In Rosario, Argentina, this smiling convenience store owner protects himself and his stock against bandits by doing business from inside the walls of his cage.

a steel bar that fits into a hole in the floor and braces against the front door, creating an obstacle to those who, frustrated by the locks, may attempt to break down the door and cross the border—uninvited—into your place.

Where else are there borders—protected and unprotected—in your daily routine? (Figure 7.1) If you drive to work or school, you create a rolling castle with your car, its borders the obvious and rigid exterior steel. But unlike your house, you can't hide very well in your car. The borders you count on for protection and privacy do not include visual borders. On the contrary, especially as the driver, you are highly visible to an enormous number of anonymous other people. You may count on the steel and glass to protect you from this horde. In worrisome neighborhoods, you probably hope the engine doesn't fail and that you don't run out of gas, forcing you to abandon your car and cross its border into a world you were expecting just to pass through. We drive along streets with the windows down, enjoying the breeze, with an expectation that no one is going to reach into the car at a stop light and throttle us. Yet it's common to flick the automatic door locks for an extra sense of security.

At work and at school, there are more borders. Metal detectors at the doors. Identity cards to allow passage past guards into buildings. Codes to punch into door lock keypads (keypads that record for some authority your entry and egress). Old-fashioned keys to offices. Areas off limits to the unauthorized. Cops and guards and cameras patrol these borders. Even at play we deal with barriers. Rope lines patrolled by bouncers keep us out of nightclubs if we don't meet standards of fashion and attitude.

Many of these borders at home, at work and at play need no enforcers. As a society we accept each other's signals, and respect and obey them. Few of us want to barge into a bathroom and disturb a friend or relative engaged in behavior they would prefer to keep private. We appreciate the signpost of the closed door, just as the housekeeper in a hotel walks on past the rooms where a Do Not Disturb sign is hanging.

Public transport is a maze of borders. Without paying the fare, you can't get on the bus. Or at least you're not supposed to get on the bus. The driver often is the enforcer, demanding cash (exact change only, another barrier to entry) or a transfer or to see a pre-paid pass. If a passenger attempts to ride without paying, the driver must decide whether to attempt to eject the freeloader.

These familiar borders all around us usually are respected, their rules enforced by our ethics and honesty, our fear of the consequences if we violate them, and our continuing contract with a supposedly polite and civilized society.

We create borders to define our personal space, and we devise techniques to patrol and enforce them. How close do we stand to others in a line? Where do we keep our hands in a crowded subway car? Do we kiss or shake hands meeting someone or bow from 6-feet distant and say, "Namaste," in deference to Covid-19? All these decisions mark borders.

San Diego Union reporter Sandra Dibble, who covers the U.S.-Mexico border beat for the paper, tells a personal border story that echoes my own childhood: how she and her brother fought for space in the back seat of the family car. I recall my sister and I drew an imaginary line across the back seat of our family's 1957 Oldsmobile on long car trips. Dibble says of Mexicans and Americans who live along the border, "We're stuck in the back seat of this car that someone else is driving, and we're annoying each other."

More Borderlines

I arrive at Schipol Airport in Amsterdam and am intrigued to see the billboards not just at the airport, but all over Holland, sultry ads for Peter Stuyvesant cigarettes. The graphics are dark and mysterious, featuring what appears to be a buxom woman showing off almost everything but her nipples as she stands half turned from a row of urinals. She's looking with a smirk into the middle distance, cigarette in hand. The headline announces, "There are no borders."

"Excuse me, can I have something to eat?" I watched as the panhandler solicited a couple at a Berlin sidewalk cafe. "Some of the cheese perhaps?"

Polite—not a stumbling drunk, not drooling—he was inoffensive except for the interruption. He dressed for the hot day in shorts and a shirt that looked clean enough.

No question the scrubbed couple was finished eating before he made his request. He had already made one pass by their table, slowly inspecting the possibilities, before he edged back toward them, imposing on their lazy Sunday morning. He saw the basket still filled with bread and the barely tasted jam waiting in a silver dish. There was plenty of butter, and on her plate she had ignored several tomato wedges, apple slices, a handful of cherries and much of the main course: various cheeses and meats.

The couple had been murmuring at each other, shaded from the direct sun under the cafe's umbrella. The silence between their words was accompanied by languid satiated looks. And she would run her hands through the perfectly cut bristle of hair on the back of his head. They would kiss and smile and kiss again. She wore a silver hoop earring in one ear and in the other, a wire ornament that balanced horizontally and moved as if it were a mobile.

"No," she told the interloper and dismissed him with her hand.

He moved off and they prodded at the food that they had forgotten until his intrusion. Another bite of cheese, a few cherries. They kissed some more.

But breakfast was over and she pushed her plate away, still full of cheese, just a minute or two after the passerby made his request. She reached into her bag, pulled out a Gauloises Blondes, and lit it. He continued to pick at the leavings on his plate and stroked her hair a couple of times. They were distracted now. A cop paced slowly past the cafe. The traffic was noisy; brakes shrieked.

Why did she say no to the hungry passerby? He was not disgusting, not stinking from drink or filth. But his was a dirty intrusion, with two or three days of beard, leaning over her varnished wooden table, leering over her breakfast, violating her border. Why should she have said yes?

The couple no longer talked much and the kissing stopped. About ten minutes after the bum asked for the cheese, the waiter cleared their plates from the table. They paid their bill and headed into the summer Sunday.

Borders in the bed, the bedroom, the bathroom, the home. Borders around the yard or at the lobby door of the apartment building. Borders in the car or around your body on the subway. Borders at the office and the school, at the restaurant keeping hungry beggars from the leftovers. All these personal borders lead to state-created and state-controlled borders. In some cases—prisons and East Germany come to mind—state borders are created to keep us from escaping. But most state borders are designed to keep others—those we consider bums—away from us.

When the Chernobyl nuclear power plant in Ukraine spewed radiation, the prevailing winds blew the worst of it north into Belarus. There were no nuclear power plants in Belarus. Ivan Kenik, the government official in charge of dealing with the problems the incident caused Belarus, observed, "The Chernobyl disaster taught us there are no borders to the modern world."[1]

"A border," defined journalist Ambrose Bierce, "is an imaginary line between two nations separating the imaginary rights of one from the imaginary rights of the other." The caustic social critic disappeared in 1913—presumably bound to report on Pancho Villa and the Mexican Revolution—after filing a dispatch that still can resonate for adventurers: "Goodbye—if you hear of my being stood up against a Mexican stone wall and shot to rags, please know that I think that a pretty good way to depart this life. It beats old age, disease, or falling down the cellar stairs. To be a Gringo in Mexico—ah, that is euthanasia."

Chapter 8

FAILED BORDERS

I'm at the foot of La Rambla in Barcelona, circling the Mirador de Colon, the monument to Christopher Columbus. He stands on a column, high above a traffic circle at the old port, pointing out to sea. The monument was built in 1888 and displays the architectural flourishes of the era. Columbus is guarded at the base of his column by regal-looking lions, and the column is decorated with filigree, angels and anchors. A band around it near the top announces Gloria Colón. The man himself is gigantic, pointing not west to the hemisphere he claimed for Spain, but south out to the Mediterranean Sea and Africa. Columbus sailed back to Barcelona on his first voyage to and from the New World, a land with no fixed borders until the European settlers who followed Columbus carved it into colonies. He arrived in 1493 and showed Ferdinand and Isabella the loot he brought back from

America: gold, spices, strange animals and a sampling of the natives he caught and subjugated. "Good work," said the king and queen, who sent him off on two more trips to explore and settle, or plunder and conquer, depending on your point of view.

The pointing Columbus statue made me think of California artist Yolanda Lopez's poster of a Native American in an Aztec headdress pointing an accusing finger. The image is captioned, "Who's the illegal immigrant, pilgrim?"

Borders Crossed

Spain and Morocco are separated by 10 miles of the Strait of Gibraltar and by their status as First and Third World countries. Desperate Africans brave the waters of the Strait, trying to smuggle themselves into Spain and the rest of job-rich Europe. People-smugglers offer expensive and dangerous rides across in overcrowded and barely seaworthy boats. Those who don't drown en route may well get caught by the Spanish Civil Guard. But enough migrants make it safely to shore to convince others desperate for a better life to take a chance. "You don't want to know what I went through to reach this city," said a young Moroccan who managed to get to Barcelona. "Do you know how many people die every day trying to cross the Straits? Why do we come here? We come because we want to work, to send money back home."[1]

Tunisians sail north and land illegally in Sicily. Undocumented African immigrants complain of prejudice in a Europe where they often live as second-class citizens. Many Europeans consider the Africans and the culture they bring with them a threat. The story is replicated wherever a poor country is within reach of a rich one where cheap labor is needed. In today's world of efficient travel, that match can come from across the globe.

Dover, England, is an example. I was there in the summer of 2000, just after a truck full of tomatoes arrived on a ferry from the Netherlands. Customs inspectors decided to check the cargo. They pulled open the rear doors and found bodies. The truck had been hired by smugglers to bring a load of migrants from China into the United Kingdom. Behind the crates of tomatoes they found more dead, a total of 58 asphyxiated in the refrigerator truck. The sole air vent had been closed for unknown reasons. Two of the migrants miraculously survived.

"Those two have been fortunate because as people are dying there is that person's air to breathe," Dover Coroner Grahame Perrin explained their macabre good fortune. "Those two have been very lucky."[2]

I walked up the Folkestone Road from the docks where the death truck was opened and I stopped for a drink at a seedy pub called The Engineer. The jukebox was blasting in competition with the loud television. The tables were messy with overflowing ashtrays and dirty beer glasses. It was late afternoon. A woman was feeding a slot machine while her boyfriend chatted with the barkeep. I sat outside, nursed a Guinness and watched the street parade. Stark white Englishmen and women were coming home from work, pouring out of buses. Darker people shared the neighborhood, many of them asylum seekers who managed to get to the English shores and were waiting in Dover while their cases were adjudicated. Two were in a nearby phone box, studying official-looking papers and talking on the phone. A glazier was busy repairing the broken front plate glass window of a kebab shop. Dover is another border city dealing with the push of immigration from South to North.

"We're not rednecks," Dover mayor Gordon Cowan found it necessary to announce after the *London Times* followed up its reports of the Chinese immigrants' deaths with a story charging that Dover was filled with racists and bootleggers. The local paper *Express* responded with a picture postcard photo of Dover Castle, the sub-headline, "MAGNIFICENT!" and an interview with the mayor who insisted, "Dover is a very pleasant, safe place in which to live, work and visit. We love our town and we are very proud of its national and international importance."[3]

I left The Engineer as the Beatles' "Michelle" blasted out of the jukebox, mixed with the equally loud strains of Middle Eastern music coming out of the open window of an upstairs flat across Folkestone Road.

Come with me to Cairo, Egypt, teeming with over twenty million people in the greater Cairo region. Jammed streets, deafening traffic noise, perpetual horn honking. Dirty. Filthy. A devastated infrastructure: rusting, cracked, crumbling, broken, shattered. Most buildings and roads in desperate need of repair. I'm here working on a journalists' exchange program funded by the U.S. Agency for International Development. We're bringing Egyptian journalists to the United States for intensive training in American-style journalism.

It's the fall of 2003, two years after the 9/11 attacks.

I hail a cab from my oasis at the Marriott Palace in Zamalik along the Nile. I jam myself into the tiny and ancient Fiat taxi that's been repainted so many times it appears the car body is made out of enamel, not metal. We head out to the fashionable suburb Maazir. The USAID fortress is up a blocked road in Maazir, looming like a cross between a Hyatt Regency and a maximum-security prison. Behind the barriers, the U.S. bureaucracy labors. The Cairo mission dishes out half a billion dollars in aid to Egypt each year, more than goes to any other country in the world, save Israel.

I give up my passport, step through airport-like security and make my way to a meeting with the administrators of the journalism training program. We have a problem. Only 15 of the 25 students we picked to bring to the United States were granted visas by the U.S. consul, and 13 of the 15 were women, creating a gender imbalance in the classroom. A few months earlier, when we submitted the 25 names for clearance, young and unmarried Moslem men were being flagged for detailed background checks by the U.S. embassy in Cairo—on instructions from the State Department—and the lag time for visas was interminable for most of the men in our group while they were investigated. Washington said it was trying to make sure no terrorists were granted visas, and this was two presidential administrations before the Trump-ordered ban on visas for visitors from several Muslim-majority countries.

There was no such trouble for the women in our group; all but one received a visa promptly. When the cohort presented their Egyptian passports at O'Hare airport in Chicago, the women all sallied through the gates with a cheery, "Welcome to the United States" from immigration officers. The two men were pulled from the line, ushered away for mug shots and fingerprinting, hours of questioning and extra paperwork.

Shortly after our first students arrived in the United States, the Middle East was plagued with a series of suicide bombs perpetrated by women. "Don't expect it to be easy for the women either this time," a USAID staffer tells me about our second group. Since the 9/11 attacks, she says, the rules are constantly changing as Washington scrambles, trying to figure out how to control U.S. borders. "Sometimes we issue visas in the morning and we have to hold the passports because the rules change before the Egyptians come to pick them up in the afternoon."

The U.S. government wants to control the country's borders and choose who enters. Yet because of the dysfunctional attempts at control on the U.S.-Mexico frontier, efforts overseas are of questionable value. Those screened out in Cairo could go to Mexico and walk into the United States with the farm workers and cooks, maids and mechanics. Many Middle Easterners could pass as Mexicans, blending into the swarthy, dark-haired crowd pushing north.

If the United States really wants to secure a post-9/11 border, fixing the U.S.-Mexico boundary is a much more constructive goal than denying male journalists with jobs and close family connections at home in Egypt a two-month stay at an American university.

More Borders

I'm sitting on the steps from the lobby down to the basement restaurant in my hotel in Athens, the Hotel Divani Palace Acropolis. The hotel is just a few blocks from the Acropolis; when I sit out on my balcony I can glance up from my newspaper to see the Parthenon. In the early morning it magically appears through the fog. At night it's lit like the jewel it is.

But here on the basement steps where I'm writing now, I'm looking at the remains of the Themistocles Wall. The hotel foundation is built around portions of the wall. These remnants were carefully preserved and are displayed behind a glass wall adjacent to the steps.

The Themistocles Wall is an early example of how hard it is to keep the Other out. It dates to 479 BC, built by the Athenian military strategist Themistocles, designed to protect Athens from invasion threatened by Sparta. Despite it, the Spartans jumped the wall and attacked.

The section I'm looking at is made up of rows of block—formidable looking—several yards wide. Almost 2,500 years later the remainder lie here: solid and substantial, but worthless then and now as a barrier.

While I'm gazing at these ancient ruins, CNN and the *International Herald Tribune* are full of the latest attempts to wall people off from one another, Israel's stark barrier inside the West Bank. Panoramic television pictures cannot help but conjure up memories of the Berlin Wall. The scar of concrete is so similar (although much higher), as is the cleared no-man's-land. In the newspaper, the human scale of the wall is made clear in a photograph of a Palestinian man, stereotypically showing stubble on his chin, peering—is it furtively? or with despair?—through a narrow gap in the wall at an Israeli soldier. The contrast is clear. The clean-shaven soldier sports a sharp military haircut. He's wearing aviator-style sunglasses, the wires of his walkie-talkie are obvious on his crisp uniform. The Palestinian is wearing a rumpled keffiyeh. The architect of the Israeli wall is Dany Tirza, who says of the barrier, "It gives order to space."[4]

"Good fences make good neighbors" is a cliché overused when attempts are made to rationalize barriers. The prestige of Robert Frost is often invoked along with mantra. That line comes from his poem "Mending Wall," and the suggestion when using the quote is that Frost endorsed such borders. Ariel Sharon cited the Frost line when he was first attempting to explain away the barrier separating the West Bank from Israel.

In fact Frost's poem is a meditation on that day he was working with his neighbor, the two of them repairing that stone wall on their property line. As they labor, it is the other man who insisted, "Good fences make good neighbors." It was then Frost who reacted, "Before I built a wall I'd ask to know what was I walling in or walling out, and to whom

I was like to give offense. Something there is that doesn't like a wall, that wants it down."

Panic Attack

Now the scene is a ludicrously luxurious villa under construction not long after the 2008 housing market collapse in San Francisco's exclusive Sea Cliff neighborhood. The view wraps around from the Pacific Ocean to the graceful span of the Golden Gate Bridge and on eastward across the bay to the City's skyline. Starter homes in this neighborhood can easily sticker shock most of us by beginning at $10 million dollars. Blueprints for the villa reveal an inside shelter. The home with an interior barricade is the plaything of a Silicon Valley billionaire. Cost is not a factor. But security is an issue.

The billionaire wants his villa equipped with a panic room—a place he can hide if his castle is attacked, a place where he's convinced he'll remain safe no matter what until help arrives to rescue him. No expense is spared. High-powered weapons are brought to Sea Cliff to test the sanctity of the panic room. Windows, doors and walls are subject to assault.

The interior borders hold against the war games.

Panic room philosophies are replicated with panic communities. Gated housing developments span the globe. Guarded by rent-a-cops, these enclaves give the paranoid wealthy a sense of security. I remember that back in the early 1970s, with a certain amount of not-so-latent arrogance and hubris, I often drove my battered 1947 Chevy up to the guardhouse at the movie star enclave, the Malibu Colony. "Kiewit," I would say, my unruly long hair barely held out of my face by an inefficient tie, wisps of it hanging in my face. The guard would check his roster and— sure enough—my name was on the list as a guest of that family. The barrier across the road would rise and my jalopy and I would head through the Colony wall even though my friend Johnny's neighbors probably looked at me and thought I was exactly what they were trying to keep out of their exclusive beach community (Figure 8.1).

Figure 8.1 Portugal's Guimarães Castle, built over a thousand years ago, needed no panic room. It is a panic room: windowless. All walls.

Why I Have a Stasi File

At Checkpoint Charlie in 1987, I was locked in a holding cell for several hours one day as I was returning to West Berlin from East Berlin. I was working on a report about the origin of a story that AIDS was the result of a runaway CIA experiment. I had traced the story back to what appeared to be its source, a conspiracy-addled East German university professor living out his retirement in a high-rise apartment near the east side of the Wall.

With my satchel full of notes from the interview with the professor and a tape recorder, I walked back toward the border crossing. The guardhouse sat like some sort of misguided, oversized tollbooth on the line that separated East and West. The passport officer sat up above waiting travelers, looking down through a glass window from his cage. A solid, locked door blocked entrance into West Berlin. The area was lit up brightly with irritating fluorescent tubes. A mirror placed at a 45-degree angle above the guard made it possible for him to see the back pockets of waiting travelers.

The drill was always stern—no smiles or casual exchanges. The guard took your passport, looked at the visa and your picture, then studied your face to make sure you were you. Then the procedure was repeated, to make really sure. If all your papers were in order, the solid metal imitation wood door buzzed. The lock was now open and you passed into the customs inspection zone. On this trip, the customs officer decided to take a look in my bag.

When he found the tape recorder, I was charged with practicing journalism without a proper permit and led into the holding room. My bag and papers were taken, the door was locked, and I was left alone.

The room was empty except for a desk and a couple of chairs. Periodically, one guard or another would come back with some scrap from my papers and we'd converse briefly.

"What's this?"
  "A credit card receipt for gasoline."
  And he'd be gone again.

Finally my stuff was returned intact, and I was allowed through to the West after being cautioned to get approval before I attempted another reporting job in the East. The fact that the professor I had interviewed on my forbidden tape recorder was part of East Germany's propaganda machine probably speeded my release.

The other crossing point for Westerners into East Berlin was the Friedrichstrasse train station. I was stopped by an East German border guard at Friedrichstrasse on one of my trips to the East because I was carrying that day's edition of the *International Herald Tribune*. He walked me over to a garbage can and told me to dump it, making an overt public display indicating that he was not just confiscating it to take home for himself.

Then I was escorted to a windowless cubicle and told to empty my pockets.

"What's this, hashish or heroin?" The guard was fingering pocket lint that clung to my wallet. Again, credit card slips were fascinating to the inspector. This time the delay was only a few irritating minutes (Figure 8.2).

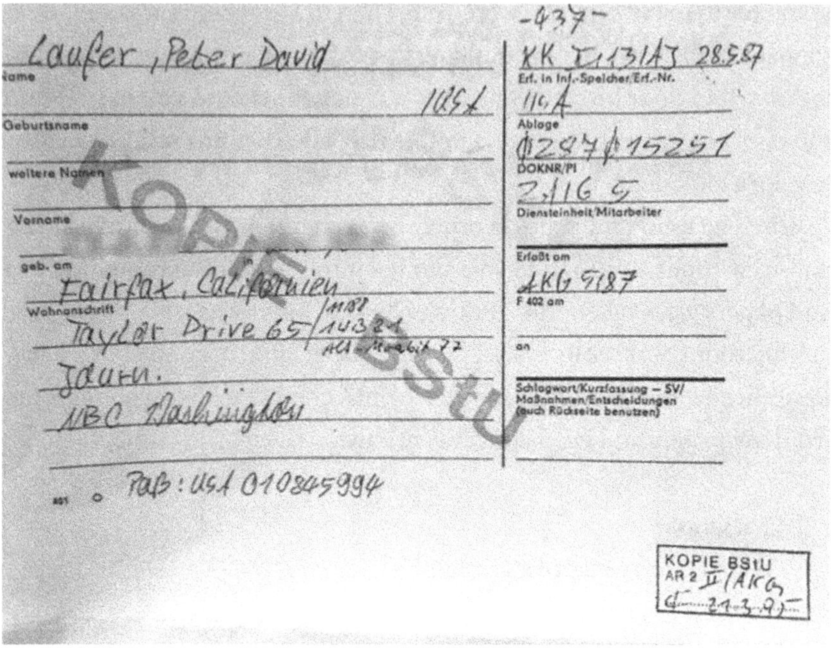
-437-
Laufer, Peter David
Name
Erf. in Inf.-Speicher/Erf.-Nr.
116 A
Ablage
Geburtsname
0287/15251
DOKNR/PI
weitere Namen
Diensteinheit/Mitarbeiter
Vorname
Erfaßt am
geb. am
in
Fairfax, Californien
F 402 am
Wohnanschrift
Taylor Drive 65
an
Journ.
NBC Washington
Schlagwort/Kurzfassung – SV/ Maßnahmen/Entscheidungen (auch Rückseite benutzen)
PaB: USA 010845994
KOPIE BStU
AR 2

Figure 8.2 The cover sheet for the author's Ministerium für Staatsicherheit (Stasi) file.

But even the strict East German border failed to keep Germans from crossing, and eventually it failed completely.

Not long after the Wall collapsed I visited Checkpoint Charlie, and there was meager evidence left of the vicious concrete barrier that divided East and West. A guard tower remained on the site, as a souvenir. One of the familiar four-language border signs was still posted: "You are entering the American Sector." Both the tower and the sign now are owned by the Checkpoint Charlie Museum.

Looking down at the sidewalk and street, searching for the actual line of the old frontier, I wander between parked cars and find a red line on the sidewalk. That must mark the wall route. A Ford is parked over it, but I follow it out to Friedrichstrasse and look over to where the guard tower sits. Yes, this unceremonious red (who chose the color?) strip clearly is the line. Now I'm on the east side. I take a step. Now I'm on the west side. The murder and misery the Berlin Wall caused is erased from daily routine, except at the T-shirt shop just over the west side of the line that offers Berlin Wall posters, Coca-Cola, Häagen-Daz

("America's No. 1 super premium ice cream"), and, of course, alleged pieces of the Wall encased in plastic for 9.90 deutsche marks (small) up to 29.90 marks—depending on the size.

Post-Berlin Walls

Despite the failure of border walls over the centuries, in the first years of the twenty-first century, the United States certainly wasn't the only country trying to protect its interests with a physical barrier.

India looked at its 1,800-mile border with Pakistan and decided a fence might help keep out militants seeking to solve the Kashmir crisis with violence. The Demilitarized Zone in Korea separated the North and South, lined with 148 miles of barbed wire and other barriers. When I visited the DMZ in the 1980s the barbed wire was fresh and shiny, the paint on the guard's posts fresh and sparkling, all spiffed up for an upcoming visit by President Ronald Reagan, who famously said in Berlin "tear down this wall!" not long after the Korea visit. Cyprus was bisected by a 112-mile fence keeping the Turkish and the Greek Cypriots apart.[5]

Eventually these barriers open. In the spring of 2003, for example, Turkish Cypriots allowed day trips across the line between the two Cypriot political entities for the first time since 1974. In those first few days after the checkpoints were opened, thousands of Greeks and Turks took advantage of the breach in the fortifications between them to check out the other side of the island. At one border crossing point a Turkish Cypriot looked at the long lines on both sides waiting to cross and observed, "People are like rivers; you can't stop them"[6] (Figure 8.3).

Nicosia in 2020 remained the last divided city in Europe. I walk along the barrier—the 55-gallon drums topped with barbed wire, the boarded-up abandoned homes and shops—and then walk through the passport checkpoints. Later I journey north from Larnaca with Kendeas Yiannaki toward the village he fled as a teenager in 1974 when Turkish troops invaded the island. He now lives in London but returns once a year to look longingly at what was home. We stop at the crumbling road that leads toward his abandoned family house. The path is blocked by

Figure 8.3 The abandoned Green Zone in Nicosia, keeping the Turkish Cypriots and the Greek Cypriots apart in the last walled city of Europe.

concrete and steel barricades. "I will never forget," he ruefully tells me, yet he looks resigned as he adds, "I will never forgive, and I will always come back here and look." The Turkish army occupies his hometown. "I'm absolutely furious, fuming," he responds when I asked him how it feels to look down that barricaded road, now overgrown with weeds. Yiannaki refuses to accept the Green Line as a permanent wall. "I was born there. It's my house and I want it back. I can't say, 'Okay, they took it. It's forty years ago. Let it go.' It doesn't work like that." His face is lined with grief and frustration as we head back into territory on the south side of the UN Buffer Zone, Greek Cypriot territory (Figure 8.4).

"We've wasted forty years!" my cousin lamented about her life in the post-war years behind the Iron Curtain. Her soft voice only sounds sadder with her lilting, musical Hungarian accent. There is a softness built into the intonations of Hungarian that makes it difficult to sound shrill or angry. Even the newscasts on the radio take on an imploring tone. Routine conversations—business in a store, a casual chat— transmit a warmth. We were talking over coffee, looking out from the Buda hills across the Danube to the flat reaches of Pest. Hungary played

Figure 8.4 The Cyprus Green Line is a ghost-town swath across the island, a scar leaving echoes of emptiness since 1974.

a key role in the revolutions that overthrew the Soviet puppet states in Eastern Europe. Its government listened carefully when the Soviet Union announced that it no longer would manipulate its client states as it did when it sent tanks to suppress the 1956 Magyar revolt, a revolt against authoritarian rule disguised as communism.

The result: "Vacationers" from East Germany pointed their rickety, smog-belching little Trabants toward Budapest and an ongoing road trip to West Germany. Hungary looked the other way as masses of Trabbies putt-putted through the Hungarian rip in the Iron Curtain. The cars were notoriously unreliable. Joke of the era: Why is there a rear window defroster on a Trabbie? To keep your hands warm when you push it! But the convoys chugged along and made it to a warm welcome in Austria, and freedom.

Yet the stink of paranoid nationalism and the hate of latent—and not so latent—anti-Semitism both rebounded with a disconcerting flurry in Hungary when the Iron Curtain was breached in 1989. My cousin's father recommends she change her last name so she need not worry about anti-Semitic discrimination. She dismisses his concern. But he remembers his brother, shot by fascists during World War II and dumped dead into the Danube.

By the time refugees from the wars in Afghanistan and Syria began their mass exodus into Europe, Hungary's government-fueled propaganda machinery added Muslims to its enemies list. The purveyors of the goulash Communism that poked the holes in the Iron Curtain that helped lead to its demise decided they could embrace walls after all—walls that kept the Other out. In a surge of efficient construction activity Hungary threw together an electrified, razor wire-topped fence stretching 10 feet toward what must be a confused heaven. And not just one. Two such fences running parallel along its border with Serbia. "I hope it inspires the Americans," boasted Lazlo Toroczkai, the mayor of a Ásotthalom as he strolled along the newly militarized borderline looking like an undercover border patrolman in his dark suit, dark tie and dark glasses. "It saved my town. Calmness has returned."[7] The new iron curtain stretches across the 100-mile border between the two countries, a gash marking where fortress Europe begins.

"You see a wall," Thomas Wolfe writes in *You Can't Go Home Again*, "you look at it so much and so hard that one day you see clear through it. Then, of course, it's not just one wall any longer. It's every wall that ever was" (Figure 8.5).

Graffiti on brick walls can be as expressive as the role of walls in literature. Unofficial markings leave little to the imagination on the Palestine side of the barricade that Israel built in an attempt to protect its territory from unwanted intrusion. One arresting image is a hyperrealistic rendering of Donald Trump seeming to embrace an actual watchtower on the wall. Paintings attributed to Banksy act as faux holes in the wall, the images depicted as if through the concrete are both idyllic and bucolic peaceful scenes of beaches and mountains or pragmatic drawings of ladders rising to the top of the wall.

Where to stay? Perhaps at the Banksy-inspired Walled Off Hotel which features what it calls "the ugliest view in the world." Windows look out at a section of the 125-mile-long wall, a wall towering over twice the height of Trump's dream wall: 25 feet. Next door is a store

Figure 8.5 A police dummy at work on the highway outside Addis Ababa, alongside a makeshift wall of corrugated metal.

called the Wallmart. There activists can buy paint and rent ladders to aid their own redecoration of the concrete swath.

Come on up to what's fondly referred to as the world's longest undefended border, the place where Canada meets the United States. Of course, it's not undefended. It's just absent armies facing off against each other. But policing authorities check papers and it is a violation of the law in both countries to cross without official approval—especially since the 9/11 attacks.

Yet desperate refugees from Africa, worried about their asylum status in the United States, trek through brutal North Dakota winters, around the walls at formal crossing points, and into Manitoba, hoping for a welcoming atmosphere in Canada. "He dropped us," one refugee said about his cab driver, "and he said, 'See those lights over there? That is Canada. You just walk up.'"

Taxi driver as immigration counselor. In the first three months of the Trump presidency, over three hundred Africans arrived in the Canadian border town Emerson after evading U.S. border patrols and crossing the line into what they hoped is a safe sanctuary. Some, unfamiliar with the frigid winters, wore flimsy summer clothing and lost fingers and toes to frostbite. "The wind is blowing in all directions," said a refugee from the safety of a house in Emerson. "It was really painful. I sat down and said to myself, 'I can't keep going,' because I was so, so weak." But he forced himself to get up and continue walking north "because I just wanted to get out of America. I didn't want to be deported home."[8] Weather as a border wall.

There is no physical barrier separating Blaine, Washington, and British Columbia where the Peace Arch Park welcomes picnickers from both sides to comingle. South of the park and from the Pacific to the Atlantic—signs spotted along the international boundary warn the curious or the intrepid not to cross without "presenting yourself to an Immigration Officer" and announce "violators subject to fine and/or prosecution." I hailed a fellow parkgoer to take my picture at the arch, posing next to its legend, "May these gates never be closed." Signs as walls.

There are other walls along the relatively porous Canada-U.S. line. Standing on the Whirlpool Rapids Bridge just downstream over the Niagara River from Niagara Falls, I'm looking through the girders of the railroad bridge next to me. I can see the falls in the distance. It is a gorgeous midsummer day, clear blue sky except for a few puffy clouds. Now I'm at the railing, resting my notebook high over the gorge, and there is just enough gusting wind to activate some vertigo. I see a metal plaque announcing "International Boundary Line" and it exhibits an actual line with "United States" written on one side in raised steel lettering, and "Canada" on the other. I'm on the Canadian side.

A few cars are backed up waiting to clear border formalities. But no little farouche Canadian kids are trying to sell me Chiclets.

The rushing Niagara River is a much more formidable river than the Rio Grande. But there is no barbed wire separating these countries, and no crowds waiting to cross from one to the other. I head over to the immigration officer's hut.

"*Buenas noches*." I'm sure that's what the guard said to me. I expected a "Howdy" or maybe a "*Bon nuit*," but not "*Buenas noches*" up here, especially in the middle of the afternoon. He ambles out of his office to the counter. I'm his only foot traffic.

"Excuse me?" I say to his Spanish greeting.

"Where are you from?" he asks in English.

"California," I tell him, showing my passport. He just glances at it and waves me into fortress America with a congenial, "Okay!"

It was, until the 2020 pandemic, not much more difficult for a Canadian to come south into the United States and travel around the 50 states. Canadians were – prior to the Covid-19 theoretically temporary travel restrictions – allowed to enter with no paperwork other than proof of Canadian citizenship. They could travel the country with no geographic limitations and stay as long as six months with no need for a visa. Mexicans, by stark contrast, are not allowed to travel beyond 25 miles of the U.S.-Mexican border (75 miles for those who enter at ports of entry on the Arizona-Mexican border south of Tucson) and can only stay for 72 hours, unless they carry visas allowing for a longer stay with further travel. Mexicans wishing to take advantage of even the restricted border visits must produce documents authorizing those trips.

In late 2003, several south Texas congress members signed a letter to Homeland Security Department Secretary Tom Ridge drawing attention to these inconsistencies and the hardships they cause to both Mexicans and Texas business.

"Hundreds of Mexican nationals cross our southern border each day for business, education or entertainment, and our local merchants and towns rely on their business to stimulate the economy," wrote the representatives, including former Congressional Border Caucus co-chair, Solomon Ortiz.

We should not discriminate against Mexican citizens who legally enter the United States. Fairness demands we treat our neighboring countries equally and remove the restriction imposed on Mexican nationals crossing into the United States legally with a laser visa. Fairness further demands we extend the seventy-two hour stay to parity with the six-month visits allowed for Canadians.

Despite the pleas the rules have not been changed.

Mr. Rogers Checks In

"Down with the Changers!" was King Friday's battle cry in one of the first episodes of "Mister Rogers' Neighborhood." The children's television parable against exclusion aired in 1968. King Friday was defending the new wall around his castle, his wall against change, "cuz we're on top!"

Just before he died in 2018, border state Arizona Senator John McCain made clear his point of view regarding walls. "We weaken our greatness when we confuse our patriotism with tribal rivalries that have sown resentment and hatred and violence in all the corners of the globe," he wrote. "We weaken it when we hide behind walls, rather than tear them down, when we doubt the power of our ideals, rather than trust them to be the great force for change they have always been."

The next year Pope Francis, speaking to a crowd of believers in Panama City, talked walls and blamed the devil. "We know that the father of lies, the devil, prefers a community divided and bickering," he preached. "Those builders of walls sow fear and look to divide people."[9]

Yet President Trump continued to whip up his rally crowds throughout the United States with stories about his wall, stories triggering the "Build the Wall" chants. Illegal crossings continued from Mexico into the United States, and a theme park in Mexico continued to offer a three-hour nighttime hike that replicates conditions experienced by border crossers—tough terrain, blanks shot by actors dressed as Border Patrol officers and staged assaults by marauding thieves. Is the night walk across a pseudo border a lesson for Mexicans not to go north illegally? Or is it a boot camp that teaches survival techniques to migrants?

LAND MEXICO LOST IN 1848

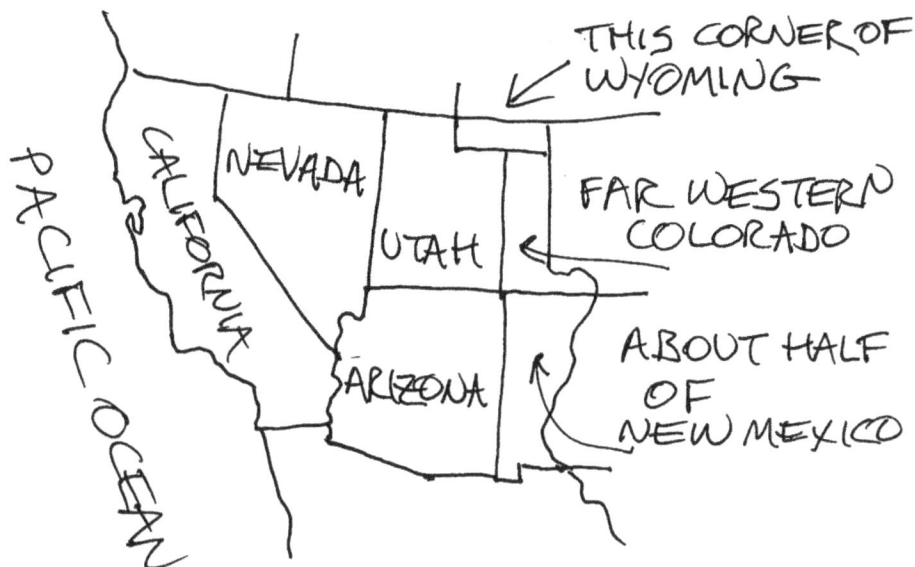

THIS CORNER OF
WYOMING

CALIFORNIA

NEVADA

UTAH

FAR WESTERN
COLORADO

PACIFIC OCEAN

ARIZONA

ABOUT HALF
OF
NEW MEXICO

AND THE 1854 GLADSDEN PURCHASE

Chapter 9

U.S. ANNEXATION OF HALF OF MEXICO

"**G**eorge Bush is a thief," Samir told me. We were driving through the labyrinth of Cairo streets, sweltering in the jammed traffic. Samir is an Egyptian journalist and there was no question in his mind that Bush invaded Iraq for oil. That same week, the *Economist* agreed with my colleague Samir in a special report analyzing America and its empire. "America, it is said, is the world's latest imperial power," headlined the *Economist*, "Don't believe it."[1] The article argues that the nineteenth-century policy called Manifest Destiny was simply the beginning of empire building that continues today.

Back in the 1950s, when I was in grammar school, we were taught Manifest Destiny as heroics. I remember studying maps and dreaming of how swell it would be were that fat mass of Canada part of the good old U.S. of A. Such indoctrination dates from another journalist, John O'Sullivan, editor of the *Democratic Review*, a political journal he co-founded in 1837. O'Sullivan came up with the term and used it in an empire-building 1845 *Review* editorial. "The American claim is by the right of our manifest destiny to overspread and possess the whole continent which Providence has given to us. It is in the Future far more than in our past that our True Title is to be found."[2]

More Manifest Destiny propaganda was splashed across a Sullivan-founded newspaper, the New York *Morning News*, in an editorial rationalizing the annexation of Texas. "It is surely not necessary to insist that acquisitions of territory in America, even if accomplished by force of arms, are not to be viewed in the same light as the invasions and conquests of the States of the old world," argued the paper as it attempted to explain away the double standards of American policy. "Our way lies, not over trampled nations, but through desert wastes, to be brought by our industry and energy within the domain of art and civilization. We are contiguous to a vast portion of the globe, untrodden save by the savage and the beast, and we are conscious of our power to render it tributary to man." The paper made clear just who this "we" was. "The solitudes of America are the property of the immigrant children of Europe and their offspring," it claimed without the vision to forecast that those immigrant children of Europe (read white, of course) would be a minority in California by the beginning of the twenty-first century (and soon across "that whole continent which Providence has given to us"). After asserting that Manifest Destiny would stop the expansion of the United States only at the natural border at the Pacific, the editorial concluded, "With the valleys of the Rocky Mountains converted into pastures and sheep-folds, we may with propriety turn to the world and ask, whom have we injured?"[3]

Those calls to conquer echoed the 1845 inaugural address of another president who lost the popular vote, James K. Polk. Polk campaigned

Figure 9.1 The wall of one of the "slave castles" on the Ghana coast. Through holes in the walls like this one captive Africans were loaded on ships bound for slavery in the Americas.

promising to make Texas a state, despite Mexico's continuing claim to the breakaway republic. The Mexican state of Texas in the 1820s was filling with foreign immigrants, mostly Anglos from the United States, along with northern and central Europeans. The Anglos, for the most part, were not assimilating into the Mexican culture. Many violated Mexican law by bringing slaves across the border into Texas (Figure 9.1).

Artificial Borders

Since they were established, both the Mexican and the U.S. governments have struggled to secure their national borders. Many of the longtime original residents of North America who lived on the changing line between the two countries were nomadic. Arbitrary borders meant nothing to them. Long before the United States worried about illegal immigration from Mexico, Mexico labored to stop illegal immigration from the north into its state of Texas. By 1824, Mexico decided to combat the border crossers by creating a system to legitimize and control the incoming migrants. The government offered foreigners Texas land if they would agree to farm or raise animals. Spanish was mandated as the official language for business, and immigrants were required to be Catholic.

Soon Texas was swarming with newcomers, most of them from the States. As they settled in, building a permanent Texan life for themselves, they started thinking about Texas as their own, or part of the United States. An 1827 rebellion against Mexican rule by a handful of these Anglo settlers was quickly suppressed. But the so-called Fredonia uprising stirred the expansionists in Washington. The U.S. government expressed official interest in buying Texas, an idea Mexico rejected. Charged with studying the growing territorial crisis in Texas, Mexican general Manuel de Mier y Terán came up with a dire conclusion for his country. "Texas is contiguous to the most avid nation in the world. The North Americans have conquered whatever territory adjoins them. In less than half a century, they have become masters of extensive colonies from which they have disappeared the former owners, Indian tribes. Either the [Mexican] government occupies Texas now or it is lost forever."[4]

Mexican troops moved north and—just as the frustrated gringos did about a century later—in 1830 Mexico canceled its liberal immigration law and ordered the Texas border with the United States sealed. And just as it is for the Americans today, it was an unenforceable policy. The Anglos kept coming south, illegally crossing into Texas and settling. There they joined forces with Hispanics in Texas who were discontent with the Mexican government and in 1836 declared their independence and established the sovereign Republic of Texas. Almost ten years later, Polk looked to Texas as he stated his presidential aspirations:

> Since the Union was formed the number of states has increased from thirteen to twenty-eight. Our population has increased from three to twenty million. Multitudes from the Old World are flocking to our shores. Foreign powers do not seem to appreciate the true character of our Government. To enlarge its limits is to extend the dominions of peace over additional territories and increasing millions.[5]

The speech was part of Polk's strategy to grab Texas and more from Mexico. When his administration officially offered statehood to Texas, Mexico severed diplomatic relations with Washington in protest, and the Texans joined the Union on July 4, 1845. Polk increased tensions between the two countries by offering to buy New Mexico and California, dismissing Mexico's heritage in those states as unimportant compared with the mandates of Manifest Destiny. Meanwhile U.S. troops were on the move. Under the command of future president General Zachary Taylor, the U.S. army advanced to the disputed western Texas border. For Mexico, that border was the Nueces River. President Polk declared it further west, agreeing with his new Texan constituents that the Rio Grande (called the Río Bravo by Mexicans) was the frontier, embracing a borderline created by an act of the Texas Congress in 1836.[6] Polk's interpretation of where the borderline ought to be drawn was not fixed by the U.S. Congress when it resolved to annex the new state. That resolution acknowledged with precise language that the specific frontiers were in dispute, describing the Texas borders "subject to the adjustment by this government of all questions of boundary that may arise with other governments."[7] Polk decided that if Mexico refused to accept the Rio Grande as the border, the U.S. Army would enforce an "adjustment." Washington ordered 4,000 soldiers to duty, assigned to defend a Texas defined as stretching to the Rio Grande. To put this number in perspective, the U.S. Army totaled just over twice that many troops at the time. Polk was looking at the contested border as an excuse for a war of conquest with Mexico.

Contemporary critics tried to rally public opinion against Polk's empire building. "Occupation," the opposition newspaper *National Intelligencer* said about U.S. troop movements into the territory between the Nueces and the Rio Grande,

is nothing short (as everybody knows) of an invasion of Mexico. It is offensive war, and not the necessary defense of Texas. And should it prove, as we think it will, that the President has gone this additional length, then the President will be MAKING WAR, in the full sense of the word, on his own authority and beyond all the plea of need, and even without any thought of asking legislative leave.[8]

An anonymous critic of the war wrote a dramatic and colorful rant to the *Cambridge Chronicle* newspaper making it completely clear why he intended to reject recruitment efforts of the Massachusetts Volunteer Regiment. Solicitations posted after the shooting began included promises of pay up to ten dollars a month and a mustering out bounty of more cash and land. "Neither have I the least idea of 'joining' you, or in any way assisting the unjust war against Mexico," he wrote.

I have no wish to participate in such "glorious" butcheries of women and children as were displayed in the capture of Monterey. No sir-ee! As long as I can work, beg, or go to the poorhouse, I won't go to Mexico, to be lodged on the damp ground, half starved, half roasted, bitten by mosquitoes and centipedes, stung by scorpions and tarantulas—marched, drilled and flogged, and then stuck up to be shot at, for eight dollars a month and putrid rations [...].

The refusenik addressed the recruiting officer,

As for yourself, you are employed at an intensely mean trade. Human butchery has had its day. The time is rapidly approaching when the professional soldier will be placed on the same level as a bandit, the Bedouin, and the thug. You had better quit the business: and in return for your offer and information, if you wish to engage in the woolen manufacture (which is my trade), I will give you all the information and assistance in my power. I am satisfied with my condition. I think a man is more nobly employed, drawing a spinning jack, assisting to clothe his fellow "humans," than even leading an army to slaughter them.[9]

Mexican general Maríano Paredes marched to Mexico City and forced President José Joaquín de Herrera from office. Herrera had been unsuccessful seeking a peaceful negotiated solution to Polk's expansionism, a policy unpopular in Mexico. Paredes installed himself as president and announced reclaiming Texas as his priority. Polk reacted by ordering U.S. troops past the Nueces River and on to the Rio Grande. "Hostilities have been begun by the United States of America," responded President Paredes. His commander on the scene, Pedro de Ampudia, demanded in a letter to General Taylor that the U.S. troops depart. "Your government has not only insulted but exasperated the Mexican nation, bearing its conquering banner to the left bank of the Rio Bravo. I require you to break up your camp and retire to the other bank of the Nueces River." Ampudia gave Taylor 24 hours. Instead Taylor ordered a blockade of the mouth of the Rio Grande. Paredes ordered his army to "attack the army that is attacking us."[10] They did just that. First shots were fired at U.S. scouts on April 25, 1846, killing 14 American soldiers.

The attack served well the long-term goals of President Polk and his desire to obtain not just Texas, but New Mexico and California for the Union. Notes to his diary, May 9, 1846, the day he received news of the attack, make clear his choice for war.

Before I had finished reading the despatch, the Secretary of War called. I immediately summoned the Cabinet to meet at half past seven o'clock this evening. The Cabinet accordingly assembled at that hour; all the members present. The subject of the despatch received this evening from General Taylor, as well as the state of our relations with Mexico, were fully considered. The Cabinet were unanimously of opinion, and it was so agreed, that a message should be sent to Congress on Monday laying out all the information in my possession before them and recommending vigorous and prompt measures to enable the executive to prosecute the war.[11]

Polk made his war cry public a few days later, announcing,

After repeated menaces, Mexico has passed the boundary of the United States, and shed American blood upon the American soil. As war exists, notwithstanding all our efforts to avoid it, and exists by act of Mexico herself, we are called upon by every consideration of duty and patriotism to vindicate the honor, the rights, and the interest of our country.[12]

The expansionist Polk found his excuse to start a popular war with the attack on U.S. troops, but it was the United States that sent its soldiers into what, at best, could be called disputed territory occupied by Mexico. Polk had already made clear his intention to take territory from Mexico by force if it would not sell territory desired by the United States. Mexico did little to work toward a negotiated settlement of the dispute, perhaps understandably: the Polk Administration offered nothing but demands and war if those demands were rejected.

Once General Taylor crossed the Nueces River, Mexican president Paredes understandably concluded that the nations were at war. He announced that "hostilities therefore have been begun by the United States of America, who have undertaken new conquests in the territory lying within the line of the Departments of Tamaulipas and Nueva León while troops of the United States are threatening Monterey in Upper California."[13]

Days after Polk's speech asking Congress to declare war on Mexico, and after only brief debate, it did. In addition to the fight along the Texas border, Polk dispatched troops to seize Mexico's northwest—the land from New Mexico out to California. It was policy that editor O'Sullivan had long predicted in one of his Manifest Destiny editorials with the cry, "Texas, we repeat, is secure; and now, as the Razor Strop Man says, 'Who's the next customer?' Shall it be California or Canada?"[14]

There was no question in Polk's mind what should be next. In his diary he records a meeting with advisers shortly after the start of the war.

I brought distinctly to the consideration of the Cabinet the question of ordering an expedition of mounted men to California. I stated that if the war should be protected for any considerable time, it would in my judgment be very important that the United States should hold military possession of California at the time peace was made, and I declared my purpose to be to acquire for the United States, California, New Mexico, and perhaps some others of the Northern Provinces of Mexico whenever a peace was made.

Polk flirted with the All Mexico movement, a drive to annex all of Mexico, promoted by expansionist newspapers. Typical was the language used by the *New York Sun* editor, Moses Beach, in an editorial reminding his readers that

> [The Mexican] race is perfectly accustomed to being conquered, and the only new lesson we shall teach is that our victories will give liberty, safety, and prosperity to the vanquished, if they know enough to profit by the appearance of our stars. To liberate and ennoble—not to enslave and debase—is our mission. Well may the Mexican nation, whose great masses have never yet tasted liberty, prattle over their lost phantom of nationality. If they have not—in the profound darkness of their vassal existence—the intelligence and manhood to accept the ranks and rights of freeman at our hands, we must bear with their ignorance.[15]

Meanwhile, in the Mexican territory of California, Anglo immigrants followed a path much like their fellow settlers in Texas. In revolt against Mexican authority a handful declared California independent. The U.S. Navy landed in Monterey as the troops marching west overland arrived at the Pacific. When Polk announced California as Union territory, the California independence movement evaporated. Polk rationalized to his diary: "Although we had not gone to war for conquest, yet it was clear that in making peace we would if practicable obtain California and such other portion of the Mexican territory as would be sufficient to indemnify our claimants on Mexico, and to defray the expenses of war."[16]

President Polk's California dream was accomplished at Monterey under the command of Admiral John Drake Sloat, who claimed the land from north of Santa Barbara to the Oregon border. He told Mexican Californians that the United States was not their "enemy,"[17] and that they were free to stay in an American California or return to Mexico compensated with dollars for their trouble. By the end of the summer

American forces seized southern California, while Colonel Stephen Kearny marched his troops west to claim New Mexico with virtually no opposition. Kearny joined his fellow empire builders insisting that they were not conquerors, as this excerpt from his speech to the towns-folk in Las Vegas, New Mexico, makes plain. "People of New Mexico," he announced. "I have come amongst you to take possession of your country, and extend over it the laws of the United States. We come amongst you as friends, not enemies, as protectors, not conquerors. Henceforth I absolve you of all allegiance to the Mexican government."[18] Colonel Kearny continued on to California, leaving rebellious New Mexicans who fought against the occupying Americans until a massacre of rebels at Taos ended their struggle. Many of those defenders of their own country not killed in battle suffered in court, where they were tried (and hanged) for treason against the invading U.S. government.

Californios, Hispanics born in California, revolted against their occu-piers with greater initial success. They took back Los Angeles and held it for several months before the Americans returned in adequate force to control southern California. Unlike the fate of their New Mexican countrymen, the surviving Californios were left free after the battle, welcomed to remain as full citizens.

It was a war "unnecessarily and unconstitutionally begun by the President of the United States" according to a House resolution passed 85 to 81 just before the Treaty of Guadalupe Hidalgo was signed in 1848, ceding half of Mexico to the United States.

Mexicans agreed to the bad deal and remember it well.

Mexican Independence

In the Veracruz *zocalo*, the town square, Mexican national pride is on prominent display as September 16—Mexican independence day— approaches. The facade of one of the colonial-style buildings is covered with Christmas tree–type lights, strung up in the image of the Mexican flag. The words "¡Viva México!" are spelled out in lights. The stand of palm trees in the square is patriotically lit too: sparkling with the Mexican tricolor.

The steamy port is up early. From my balcony at the Hotel Emporio I watch the roll-on, roll-off transport ship *Blue Hawk* fill up with brand-new cars, fresh from a Mexican factory. Across the harbor are the remains of the colonial Spanish fortifications. Tour boats, the *Niño* and the *Isla de Sacrificios* and the *Pirata* bob against their lines along the *malecón*, their crews swabbing them clean. Early lovers stroll and hug. Vendors raise the shutters on their shops peddling T-shirts and straw hats, coffee and post cards.

This is the harbor bombarded by Americans during the U.S. war of conquest of 1846–48, a battle chronicled by one of the invaders in a most amoral war description. "It is a beautiful siege, not a man here that is not in high hopes," wrote Lieutenant Colonel Francis Belton, who was commanding mortar batteries, and studied his handiwork at close range. "The lines and trenches are very safe," he said about his own positions, reporting that all of the firing the day before had done no damage, "but to their own beautiful gem of a church in the cemetery," it was a different story. "I was in it yesterday afternoon. A beautiful chaste altar stands in the center under the dome—which was shelled thro' and thro'. The splendid crucifix on the altar seems a high work of art. I could see it imperfectly by the mortar and lime falling down, the crown of thorns was displaced and fell below. The candles in the sticks were broken, four shot holes thro' the doors and other ruin around. Every wall has traces of shot and also the magnificent entrance." Belton continues with this paean to the wreckage he wrought, adding, "We are in high spirits."[19]

On the other side of Belton's lines, an unidentified correspondent cried out in a report first published in Xalapa and reprinted in U.S. newspapers. "How horrible is the scene we are attempting briefly to describe! What sympathizing heart can behold it without his eyes filling with the bitterest tears of grief?" The reporter assailed the United States for its "barbarous manner of assassinating the unoffending and defenceless citizens." The number of civilian casualties was enormous, "women and children, followed by whole families perishing from the effects of the explosion, or under the ruins of their dwellings."[20]

Veracruz offers an English-language guide for tourists. "The city of Veracruz," the brochure explains, "borned [*sic*] on April 22, 1519, founded by the spaniors [*sic*] and headed by Hernan Cortes, which arrived on the Chalchihuecan beaches where is located the City and the porto of Veracruz actually." The brochure identifies Veracruz as the oldest Spanish city in Mexico and site of the first stage of the country's colonization.

A plaque is mounted on the lemon-yellow wall outside the tourist office. It was placed as a reminder in December 1998, honoring those who defended Mexico against another *la invasión norteamericana* in April 1914. The U.S. meddling in the Mexican Revolution and its after-math included an invasion of Veracruz that year. Four thousand troops landed on April 22 with the murky mission of confiscating weapons at the customshouse. In addition to costing the lives of 17 U.S. soldiers and more than a hundred Mexicans, the landing united Mexicans against a common enemy they remember well as the thief of the northern half of their country. With romantic bombast, Emiliano Zapata announced, "If the Americans send a million soldiers, we will fight them, one man against a hundred. We may have no army or no ammunition but we have men who will face their bullets."[21]

The next year, the U.S. military crossed the border again, chasing Pancho Villa after he raided the New Mexico crossroads town Columbus (the town's infamous name probably did not influence Villa's choice). The Villa raid may have been just a rogue manifestation of Villa's frustra-tion or it may have been a strategy intended to incite a U.S. invasion and a Mexican government counterstrike, creating a confused atmosphere during which Villa could rise as Mexico's savior. The U.S. troops crossed the border and stayed in Chihuahua until 1917, periodically engaging Villa (who ultimately was unable to prevail against various adversaries as his revolution devolved into civil war). By February 1917, U.S. soldiers were back on their own side of the border, Washington now preoccu-pied with the war in Europe.

Two blocks around the corner in Veracruz from the plaque com-memorating the 1914 invasion, where Avenida 16 de Septiembre meets a traffic circle, is another monument. It pays homage to Sebastián Holtzinger, Manuel Busio Cruz, Ignacio Platas, Félix Valdéz, Ambrosio Alcalde, Antonio García and José María Villasanta, identified as heroes who gave their lives in the defense of the fatherland during *la invasión norteamericana de 1847*. Another side of the traffic circle monument lists those heroes, known and unknown, who died during the 1914 attack. This monument is another relatively recent addition to Veracruz. It's dated September 1998.

Citing these memorials is not intended to suggest that Mexico today is revanchistic regarding its territorial losses to the United States. But these attacks and defeats at the hands of its neighbor to the north are a continuing memory in the common consciousness of the Mexican nation. At the same time, few gringos think of their lands from Texas to California as conquered territory. Such selective memory allowed President Clinton to declare in his Memorial Day speech in 2000, "Americans never fought for empire, for territory, for dominance."[22] In fact, that's exactly what Americans fought for when they invaded Mexico in 1846. In his book, The *Annexation of Mexico*, the American journalist John Ross, who reported from Mexico for over a generation, suggests Walt Whitman's commentary in the *Brooklyn Eagle* summed up American public opinion at the time: "Miserable, inefficient Mexico. What has she to do with the great mission of peopling the New World with a noble race? Be it ours to achieve this mission!"

The Treaty of Guadalupe Hidalgo, forced on Mexico in 1848, recognized the artificiality of the border. Article VIII states: "Mexicans now in territories previously belonging to Mexico [...] shall be free to continue where they now reside, or to remove at any time to the Mexican Republic." Those Mexicans living north of today's border were given a year to decide if they wished to retain their Mexican citizenship or become gringos.

Singing the News

Corridos are a form of Mexican folk news reporting; they are ballads sung about specific events. Writer Elijah Wald calls them a newspaper of the people. In his book *Narcocorrido*, Wald cites several *corridos* that lament in detail the plight of Mexican migrants and their relationship with *El Norte*. The Mexican *norteño* band—also extremely popular in the United States—Los Tigres del Norte recorded many *corridos* that tell the stories of bordercrossers. One of them, "La Tumba del Mojado," The Wetback's Grave, was written by *corridista* Paulino Vargas, who says the song reflects reality on the border. "I don't like to invent things, it has to be true. The public knows the difference, it can tell what isn't real and what is."[23] The narrator in the song calls himself a *mojado*, a wetback.

> I didn't have a green card when I worked in Louisiana,
> I lived in a basement because I was a wetback.
> I had to bow my head to collect my week's wages.[24]

The *mojado* identifies the border as the "tortilla curtain" and then cries,

> Mexicali Rose and the blood in the Rio Grande
>> Are two different things, but in color they are brothers,
>> And the dividing line is the grave of the wetback.

Corridos dealing with the border are not a recent phenomenon. The song "El Deportado" was recorded by the band Los Hermanos Bañuelos in Los Angeles, probably, according to author Wald, in 1929. The lyrics sound contemporary.

> The white skinned men are very wicked, they take advantage of the occasion,
>> and all of the Mexicans are treated without compassion.
>> There comes a large cloud of dust,
>> With no consideration.
>> Women, children and old ones are being driven to the border.
>> We are being kicked out of this country.

Good-bye, beloved countrymen, we are being deported,
But we are not bandits, we came to work.[25]

Other *corridos de mojados* deal with the social issues of immigration, such as the intergenerational problems of undocumented workers
who establish families in the United States and raise children who are
U.S. citizens by birth and speak English. "El Otro México" is a Los
Tigres del Norte *corrido* in the voice of a *mojado* who sings about his
experiences and new home in the United States, calling it that "other
Mexico which we have constructed on this soil that was once national
territory."

John Ross liked to tell a story to illustrate how important *corridos* are
to cross-border culture.[26] "An old friend of mine in San Antonio, Texas,
Salomé Gutiérrez, has written ten thousand *corridos*," Ross told me one
evening in Mexico City at his favorite haunt, the bright fluorescent-lit
Café La Blanca.

> Salomé was in the studio recording a *corrido* band. I think it was '72,
> maybe '74, and a famous border narco, Fred Carrasco, breaks out of
> jail downtown. There's a gunfight, three people are killed, Carrasco
> was killed, and one of Salomé's neighbor's sees this, comes running
> out to the studio. Salomé's got the band. He sits down and he writes
> a *corrido*. They cut the *corrido*. In San Antonio, there are three radio
> stations that play *corridos* from dawn to dusk. They ran it over to one
> of these stations, and for most of the people in west San Antonio,
> Salomé's *corrido* brought them the news of Fred Carrasco's escape
> from prison.

Another example of a *corrido* reporting news is the late-1970s border
analysis by Vicente Fernández, "Los Mandados." "I call it the Illegal
Alien Anthem," wrote columnist Agustin Gurza in the *Los Angeles
Times*. "In the *norteño* tune, Fernández brags about hopping back and
forth across the border despite repeated deportation. In one attempt, he

even dyes his hair blond to disguise himself as a *gabacho*, slang for white American. But the ruse fails because he can't speak English." Gurza calls the song "a defiant challenge to the U.S. Border Patrol," that tells the story of "an immigrant who takes revenge on Americans for abuse suffered at the hands of La Migra."

La Migra caught me three hundred times, let's say,

But it never tamed me.
    The beatings they gave me,
        I took out on their countrymen.[27]

Typical of a lack of Mexican and borderlands cultural literacy on the gringo side of the line is the fact that the Republican Party invited Vicente Fernández to sing at the convention in Philadelphia where they nominated George W. Bush as their presidential candidate—not knowing, according to columnist Gurza—that he is "Mexico's working-class hero."

That the border today is porous, that Mexicans and their culture range far north, should surprise no one. Gringos arrived after Mexicans, and Mexicans never left.

Are Mexicans Reclaiming Their Lost Northern Territory?

Some Mexicans may dream of reconquering their lost north. Others simply enjoy watching demographic changes reverse the gringo domination of the Southwestern United States. Not only is Spanish a de facto second language in much of the United States, tortillas subsume white sliced sandwich bread as the most popular vehicle for American sandwich wrappings.[28] Since the early 1990s more salsa has been sold in American grocery stores than ketchup.[29] Bordertown McAllen, Texas, is 85 percent Latino, and home to a growing number of wealthy Mexicans. "You get the ease of a manageable American city where almost everyone speaks Spanish," is how businessman Rubén de León explained his decision to relocate from Monterrey to

McAllen. "Essentially you're in Mexico and the United States at the same time."[30]

If there is any irredentist undercurrent among Mexicans and Mexican-Americans living and working in the United States, it is not motivated by any desire to be reunited with the Mexican national government. Rather it is to empower the Latino population within the United States to take political and social advantage of the demographic change in the early twenty-first century that made Latinos the largest minority in *El Norte*.

One prominent Latino activist group is the Movimiento Estudiantil de Chicano de Aztlán, known by its acronym MEChA. Aztlán is a mythical land of the Aztecs, their place of origin. Some Latinos use the name Aztlán to identify the territory lost to the United States. MEChA was founded in 1969 at the University of California in Santa Barbara, organized in part around a document titled El Plan Espiritual de Aztlán. Its preamble is written in prose typical of 1960s political activism.

> In the spirit of a new people that is conscious not only of its proud historical heritage but also of the brutal "gringo" invasion of our territories, we, the Chicano inhabitants and civilizers of the northern land of Aztlán from whence came our forefathers, reclaiming the land of their birth and consecrating the determination of our people of the sun, declare that the call of our blood is our power, our responsibility, and our inevitable destiny.

Some whites fearful of the growing Latino population in the United States point to El Plan Espiritual de Aztlán preamble as proof that the organization is trying to return the Southwest to Mexican rule. Preamble lines such as "Aztlán belongs to those who plant the seeds, water the fields, and gather the crops and not to the foreign Europeans" particularly upset the critics, as does the logical "We do not recognize capricious frontiers on the bronze continent."

MEChA alumni and activists, or *mechistas* as they are commonly known, more or less patiently point out that the language is not a call for territorial independence or reunification with Mexico, but for liberation. Mexicans and Mexican Americans in the United States are intent on sharing an American Dream: a better job, a nicer house, fluency in English, sending the kids to college so the next generation flourishes—just like the waves of immigrants before them since Jamestown and the *Mayflower*.

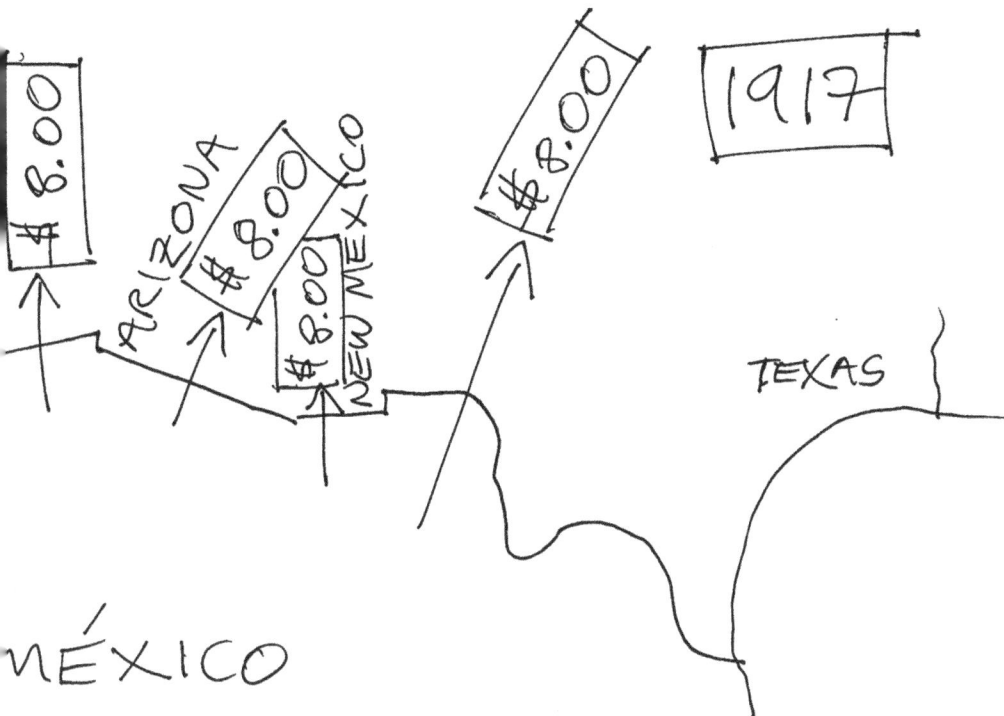

Chapter 10

EARLY BORDER CONTROL

A ttempts to control traffic north across the Mexico border can be traced to the mid-1800s. Once the United States secured the northern territory of Mexico for its own, laborers were encouraged to come to underpopulated California from China. These Chinese migrants worked for low wages, most of them initially employed as manual laborers building the transcontinental railroads. As the number of Chinese in California increased, the migration drew racist opposition along with fears of cheap Chinese labor competing with those European immigrants and their descendants who were traveling west for work. Anti-Chinese riots in San Francisco were followed by efforts to prohibit further immigration from China. Congress finally responded and in 1882 passed the Chinese Exclusion Act. It and further similar laws banned Chinese labor from entering the U.S. labor market. In 1924, a general immigration law extended the ban to migrants from across Asia, a prohibition that stood as U.S. law until 1943 when a quota system based on national origin was first established and very limited immigration from Asia was again permitted.[1]

Not long after the Chinese Exclusion Act went into effect, Chinese who wanted to enter the United States found the southern border a convenient and unregulated portal. Europeans who were denied access at Ellis Island and other East Coast ports of entry had already discovered the Mexico route to the American dream. By 1914, the U.S. government reacted by hiring a unit of border guards and assigning them horses, automobiles and boats to patrol the southern border. These guards supplemented a minimal corps that had been watching the border ineffectively since just after 1900.

Regular army troops patrolled the border during World War I and managed to curtail illegal immigration. After the war, in an effort to combat an increasing number of unauthorized border crossings, the commissioner general of the Bureau of Immigration began attempts to close the border between official ports of entry. It was an impossible effort then, just as it is today.

The first time Mexicans (and Canadians) were subjected to control at U.S. borders came with the 1917 passage of the Immigration Act. Mexicans were charged eight dollars to cross the border, and were required to pass a literacy test. The result: a marked increase in illegal crossings, according to authorities at the time. The institution of the national quota system for visas to the United States in 1924 added to the lure of illegal crossings. The quota system was a failed attempt to design and control immigration along racial and ethnic lines. Congress responded to the press of migrants crossing into the United States from Mexico without papers by creating the Border Patrol. Today Customs and Border Protection boasts some 60,000 employees and, in addition to the horses, boats and cars their predecessors used, today's Border Patrol chases migrants with airplanes and helicopters, bicycles and canoes.[2]

Immigration quotas based on national origin were linked to census figures from the early 1900s when the majority of the American population traced its roots to northern Europe. The quota system kept the number of immigrants from southern Europe, Asia and Latin America at a minimum. Mexicans were exempt from the quota system; there was no limit on the number of native Mexicans who could enter the United States. These racist and ethnically discriminatory rules were tossed out during the reformations of the civil rights era, in 1965. President Lyndon Johnson signed new rules into law calling the old quota system "un-American." Under the reformed immigration laws, a certain number of immigrants were allowed into the United States each year from all over the world. Mexico lost the numerical exemption it enjoyed under the quota system and, like the rest of the world, became subject to a limited number for legal migration into the United States.

But before the establishment of the numerical limits, immigration into the United States from Mexico was consequential, fueled by both jobs and escape from the violence and turmoil of the Mexican Revolution. When the U.S. economy collapsed in the Great Depression, the flow reversed. Mexicans, and Mexican-American citizens of the United States, went south in huge numbers, many against their will. During the 1930s, in numbers estimated by some experts as high as two million, Mexicans and others caught in raids and roundups were shipped south.[3] The motivations for the removal are familiar to the twenty-first century: those deported were charged with illegally taking jobs and abusing social services. The exodus south was labeled "repatriation." But contemporary news reports and later studies make clear that legal, permanent residents of the United States, temporary workers with legal status and U.S. citizens who appeared to be Mexican were forced out of the United States along with undocumented residents. The methods used to rid the United States of these workers during the extreme unemployment of the Depression included "deportation, persuasion, coaxing, incentive, and unauthorized coercion."[4]

Even before the depression, anti-Mexican fervor was again building in official America. Texas Congressman Eugene Black told the House

Committee on Immigration and Naturalization in 1928 that Mexicans were not desirable in the United States because they are "germ-carriers, inassimilable, a people who are with us but not of us, and not for us."[5]

One of the leaders of the offensive against Mexicans during the Depression was Secretary of Labor William Doak. Doak estimated that in 1931 about 400,000 undocumented immigrants were living in the United States. But, just as it is the case today, Secretary Doak acknowledged that he really couldn't cite an accurate figure. "It is obviously impossible," he wrote Congress, "to arrive at any concrete figures as to the number of aliens unlawfully in the United States." He deftly added national security fears to his mission, telling lawmakers in his pitch for direct power to orchestrate the assaults on the immigrant population, "There is a need for strengthening the law relative to the deportation of those aliens who are affiliated with organizations which advocate the overthrow of the Government of the United States."[6]

President Herbert Hoover backed Doak's maneuvers. The secretary ridiculed objections from the American Civil Liberties Union, saying, "The civil liberties crowd always objects, and the worse the aliens are the louder the crowd shouts." In the midst of his crusade to rid the United States of anyone unable to prove legal status, Doak was confronted with a reminder that the United States was founded as a refuge for immigrants. "Yes," he agreed, "and we've been reaping the harvest ever since."[7]

Doak's deportation raids were carried out with heavy-handed police tactics. They were designed not only to round up Mexicans and Mexican-Americans and send them south but also to scare Mexicans who heard about them, in the hopes that they would leave on their own. It worked. By the close of the 1930s the number of Mexicans in the United States dropped over 40 percent, according to official Census Bureau numbers.[8] And that's only figuring those who were counted by the census takers.

Other ethnic groups were caught in the dragnets. The deportations caused stress on the Mexican economy as it tried to accommodate the resettlers and new settlers.

Braceros—Guest Workers or Indentured Servants?

The mood up north changed radically as the war economy took hold in the early 1940s. Labor was again needed, desperately. Congress enacted a series of laws to bring workers across the border, all created in partnership with the Mexican government: the so-called Bracero program. Bracero comes from the Spanish word for arm, and means laborer and fieldworker, referring to the manual labor done with their arms. The Bracero program was supposed to provide needed labor for the United States and a fair deal for Mexican workers. But it was abused from the beginning and the repercussions continued into the current era. Workers were often denied adequate housing and working conditions; wages paid were often below guaranteed standards. The result was that many Braceros left the temporary employment that granted them legal status and disappeared into the underground economy where they sold their labor competitively and illegally.

Songwriter Phil Ochs memorialized the conditions in his protest ballad "Bracero" with the lines, "When the weary night embraces, sleep in shacks that could be cages. They will take it from your wages, Bracero."

Adios, Braceros

After several years of watching its citizens suffer while working in the United States, the Mexican government quit the Bracero agreement, and stopped shipping workers north. Ranchers and farmers panicked at the loss of needed labor and lobbied Washington for help. The U.S. Immigration Service—its roles now performed within the Department of Homeland Security—responded along the Texas border by throwing open the gates to the United States and encouraging thousands of Mexicans to enter the country illegally. Once they were across the line they were arrested and taken into custody by the Texas Employment Commission, which offered them to ranches and farms.[9] Wages slumped as a massive number of workers came north, unaware of the scheme. The two governments renegotiated the Bracero program. Authorized migrations resumed. But, of course, workers without papers stayed.

Official reaction to the illegal migration came in 1954. Robert May Swing, the commissioner of the Immigration and Naturalization Service (INS), created Operation Wetback. Mexicans were seized in the United States and pushed back south. Railroads and ships were used to send the deportees far into Mexico, in a false hope it would discourage them from trying their luck again in *El Norte*. The INS claimed over a million Mexicans crossed the border south during Operation Wetback. That number is much higher than official INS records for deportations, a discrepancy rationalized by the INS because the agency says many more Mexicans were scared south than were officially deported.

It was Operation Wetback that popularized the use of "wetback" as a pejorative for Mexicans. The late University of Texas folklorist John West called the word "a gently derogatory term."[10] The Mexican band Los Norteños de Ojinaga were singing about it as the twenty-first century opened. "We will always be the same, even if you become a citizen," they sang.[11] "In the gringo's eyes, we will always be wetbacks." The slurs were thrown back and forth. Mexicans called deportees returning to Mexico after lengthy stays in the United States "Gringos" (or *agringados*—meaning Yankeefied) for the attitudes and customs they picked up in the north.

The origin of the term "wetback" is obvious. Mexicans who swam across the Rio Grande or jumped off boats along the Pacific coast, came ashore wet. The origin of the word "Gringo" is in dispute. An often-told story is that U.S. soldiers invading Mexico in the Mexican-American War during 1846–48 marched south singing, "Green Grow the Rushes, Oh!" Mexicans condensed what they heard to just "green grow," which came out as the word "gringo." Another theory is that the Spanish word "*gringo*," which means "gibberish," became slang to describe those who could not speak Spanish, and most of those who fit that description in Mexico were from the United States.[12] In one of the Spanish-language dictionaries I use, published in Spain, "gringo" is listed as an offensive term. But from personal experience in California and Mexico, I'd suggest that it could better be characterized as gently derogatory, at worst, unless hurled intentionally as a slur.

Over the 22 years it was up and running, through 1964, the Bracero program shipped about five million Mexicans north. At the border they were stripped and checked for diseases, washed and deloused.[13] Ten percent of many Bracero laborers' wages were withheld as part of the labor contract they signed, money supposedly set aside for life insurance and pensions. The money was transferred into a state-owned Mexican bank and Braceros didn't see a peso of it until a lawsuit was settled in 2008 ordering a one-time payment to some former Braceros.[14] By that time, over half a century after they worked in the United States, too many Mexicans who were owed the funds were dead or could not locate the required proof of employment: original contracts or paystubs.

"It was humiliating," remembered Bracero Manuel Herrera at the age of 75. "They rented us, got our work, then sent us back when they had no more use for us."[15]

Hollywood Wetbacks

Attention to the smuggling of Mexicans across the now fortified border was paid in the noir fifties film "Wetbacks" starring Lloyd Bridges and Nancy Gates. The picture opens with automobile headlights shining out into the night across water. A smuggler is standing by his car, waving at a handful of Mexicans who are struggling toward the shore, sopping wet.

"Come on!" he yells, "Come on!"

In the background we see a fishing boat, and one after another more passengers jump off into the water, swim and stumble toward the beach.

"Why the devil did you bring him out here?" the smuggler asks his partner, who has come off the boat, wading to shore with a gun trained on the captain.

"My friend," says the smuggler from boat about the captain, "was getting ideas." The captain looks stunned. Seems he voiced second thoughts about the mission. "How many you got out there?" asks the smuggler with the car.

"Thirty," says the wet smuggler, as sombrero-wearing Mexicans run past the two of them. "And let's get them out of here."

A truck is waiting to haul the Mexicans north, but suddenly a siren sounds and from a loudspeaker comes an order.

"Stay where you are! This is the United States Coast Guard. You are under arrest. You are under arrest. Do not board the fishing boat! Hold your position. Do not board the fishing boat! Stay where you are."

The Mexicans panic and run back into the water toward the boat. The captain runs along the shore and the wet smuggler fires at him. He falls. The smuggler jumps into the waiting truck and it speeds off. He fires again and the hit boat captain falls face first into the water.

The theme music surges and resolves. The harsh title explodes on the screen, "WETBACKS."

The plot quickly is made obvious. Good guy cops battle ruthless smugglers preying on poor Mexicans. Our hero is another hapless, down-on-his-luck fishing boat captain who struggles with his conscience and smugglers, helped to a happy ending by a Mexican village full of sympathetic supporting heroes.

The next scene is a meeting in the offices of the U.S. Immigration Bureau.

"That was nasty on the beach last night," says the Immigration Bureau chief. He learns from the Coast Guard and the Highway Patrol that all the Mexicans were arrested and that the fishing boat captain died. But he's told the smugglers and their truck were lost in the chase, that it was probably a "souped-up, high-powered job."

"I wouldn't doubt it," says the intense chief with staccato authority. "Running wetbacks across the border is a big business these days."

"Big business?" asks a Coast Guardsman. "How much can those poor Mexicans pay, a couple of dollars a head?"

"Sometimes, yes," acknowledges the chief, and then he lectures the group. "Sometimes a family's life savings. There's plenty of work on the big ranches up here picking cotton and lettuce."

"But how much can these smugglers take in?" he's asked. "Four, five thousand a week," he reports. The Coast Guard officer lets out a low whistle.

"They've really made it a big business," the chief continues. "They hire the Mexicans out to the ranches as farm labor. Truck 'em from one farm to another."

"Yeah," protests one in his audience, "but how much can they net after they pay off the Mexicans?"

The disgusted chief jumps out of his chair and barks, "They don't pay off! They keep the money and run out on 'em." He points to a map of the border. "Gentlemen, they can bring the wetbacks across the border from Texas clear out there to ten miles in the Pacific, and they can cross by land, by air, and by water. Maybe even underground for all we know." He says he needs a couple of thousand more men to secure the border. "This is a war, a war against the most viscous kind of human scavengers."

Hollywood well over fifty years ago.[16]

Those were the days when Tijuana-born Alfredo Santos was busy smuggling Mexicans into the United States. He used trucks and boats to bring workers north, and was paid $200 for every delivery to Los Angeles and $400 for those he escorted to San Francisco. He was caught and served time in U.S. prison. Later in life, after a career as an artist and gallery owner, Santos looked back at his smuggling days without regret. "To me, I didn't see anything immoral. I was sort of a Robin Hood, I thought."[17]

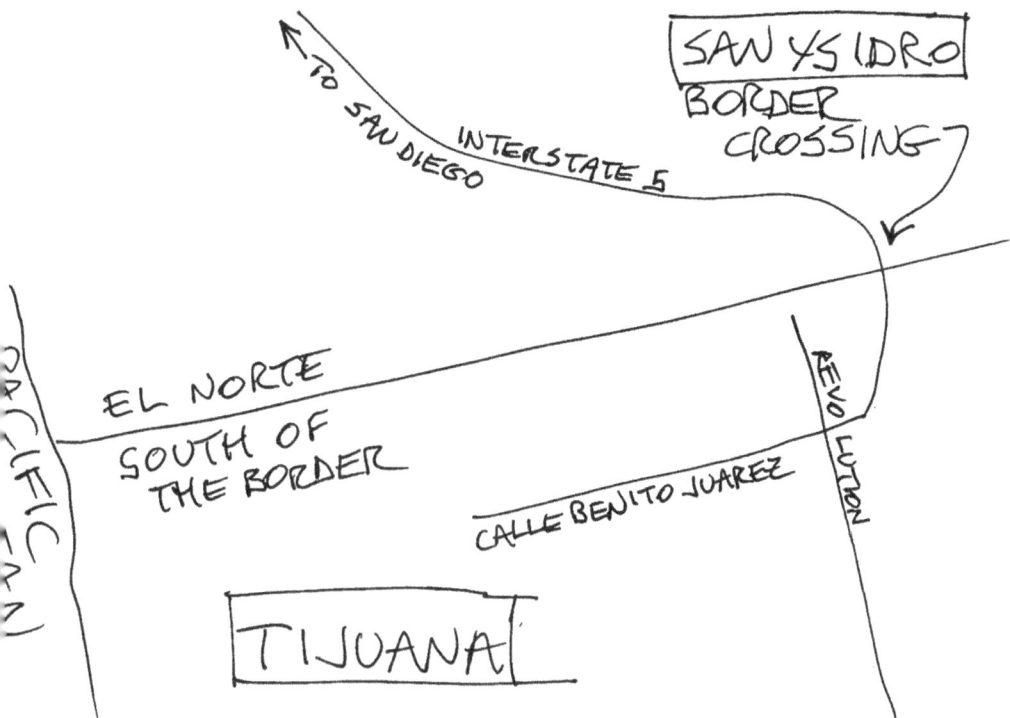

Chapter 11

THE HISTORICAL FAILURE OF BORDER CONTROL

The Mexican border choke point came in the 1980s, and it changed the border completely.

The influx of Mexicans across the border at major urban crossings such as Tijuana and Juárez and Nuevo Laredo increased dramatically while Washington policymakers watched. Failed attempts by the overwhelmed Border Patrol to curtail unauthorized migration at that time set the stage for the disastrous failures the Patrol found itself facing along the rural border two decades later. Those days, in the

1980s, when throngs of Mexicans advanced nightly from Tijuana into San Diego, are a critical moment in the history of the border wars, and a precursor of the ongoing crisis. That unending surge of desperate Mexicans north through shocked U.S. cities precipitated the building of walls designed to keep them out, makeshift walls that were inspiration for President Trump's politically astute and repeatedly stated obsession with an impenetrable frontier wall.

In the 1980s, I went to see for myself how the immigrant flow had begun to swell. First I crossed into Tijuana and stopped for a few minutes to listen to a *mariachi* band playing along the Avenida Revolución. Then I joined Chief Border Patrol Officer Alan Eliason in his squad car for a tour of the scrubby desert no-man's-land separating Tijuana and San Diego. Operation Gatekeeper and the severe wall built between the two were not yet reality. Eventually the wall would send migrants looking east for more susceptible access points along the border. As dusk arrived, we looked down on hundreds of people massing in an open field.

"They are about three-quarters of a mile into the United States at this point," Eliason told me as we looked at the crowd swelling north.

"What's going to happen?" I asked this veteran of the border wars.

"Right now, they're just going to run on back to the south." Eliason saw the same ebb and flow every evening. His arrival merely moves the crowd a few strides away from him until his squad car passes. "If we have a unit behind us, we can maybe cut them off, otherwise we'll probably be running into this same bunch a little further north after dark."

As Eliason and I talked along the border, Congress wrangled with the bill that ultimately became the 1986 immigration law, the compromise that tried to appease citizens fearful of immigrants, documented and undocumented, and at the same time tried to acknowledge the infusion of needed energy immigrants traditionally bring to societies, especially America. While debate continued in Washington, we bounce along the rutted dirt trail toward a man already illegally in U.S. territory.

"We're seeing groups of from fifteen to about forty," Officer Eliason uses his trained eye to access what for him is a routine scene, "marching northward. Usually there is a guide accompanying those people, and the guide knows exactly where he is going to take his group."

We watch a slow and steady flow of people from the Mexican side, people carrying knapsacks, chatting with each other—people on the march.

The border created a clear delineation. A relatively neat row of Tijuana houses, in line on an east-west axis, ended and the scrub began, desert scarred with the trails used by the immigrants and crisscrossed by the tracks and ruts made by the Border Patrol's four-wheel-drive jeeps. The equation is easy to figure out from our vantage point: there simply were more people moving north than Eliason and his men physically could apprehend.

"That's the border," he said, gesturing south to a spot where the masses were congregating, "and these people are on their trek northward right now."

The odds of successfully infiltrating the spotty control were so in favor of the surge north that the sight of our lone squad car did virtually nothing to impede the progress of the evening's movement. Most did not run south. We could reach out and touch Officer Eliason's adversaries. They looked at the Border Patrol-marked car and glanced at us fleetingly to check us out, then looked away. Eliason called out to a few men:

"¡Hola, señores! No quiero molestar. Este señor," he pointed to me and my tape recorder, "quiere no más que hablar con ustedes." I don't want to bother you. This man just wants to talk with you.

Unless Eliason stopped his car and got out, most of the people heading north illegally didn't even bother getting off the dirt road, they simply walked around him. The desert wind blew hot and hard, and one fearless fellow responded to our call and stopped to talk, explaining that he tried first to get into the United States legally and was rejected.

"They didn't want to give me permission." He looked to be in his twenties, dressed in international casual clothes: running shoes, jeans and a T-shirt—ideal for sprinting across the desert and escaping authorities, natural camouflage for disappearing into suburban Southern California.

"Why do you think the authorities refused you permission?"

"Because you have to have some money in the bank in order to get in," was his reply. And of course he had no money in the bank. His primary reason for coming north was to earn money.

"What do you want to do in Los Angeles?"

"Work," he said. His answer is immediate, without hesitation, obviously honest.

"What kind of work do you want?" My question comes from the luxury of a First World perspective—wondering about preference, but he answers politely.

"I am a mechanic," he says, "but I'll do whatever work I can find."

An Arresting Scene

Later that evening Eliason and his colleagues moved against the crush of immigrants pushing north and edging toward the American dream, those hundreds of Mexican nationals waiting for an opportune moment to move past the border. I watched as suddenly an agent jumped out of his four-wheel-drive and ran along the Tijuana River where it separates the two countries. The river runs from Mexico into the United States, dry during the summer but an open sewer when it flows, and it created a break in the fencing between the two countries. The agent chased off a forward group of the Mexicans who had inched into U.S. territory. Another patrol truck raced down the dry river bed, siren screaming, while a helicopter joined the charge, its twin spotlights playing off the surreal ballet below: a mass of immigrants waiting for what they believed will be an ideal time to race north, trying to evade the patrol and disappear into the brush and eventually the urban sprawl of greater San Diego. In the face of the agents' offensive, the swarm of humanity surged back to the sanctuary of Mexican territory. Newcomers to this nightly life-and-death border dance ran south to safety; the regulars ambled. Vendors with ice chests milled around in the throng, selling burritos and beer. The atmosphere was almost festive.

Like herd dogs trying to keep errant sheep in place, the agents scurried around the fringes of the mass of people, looking for stragglers to arrest, hoping to keep the crowd in check. The guards kept in touch over radio.

"There's one right in the middle of Tijuana Road." the officer coming over the squawk box spoke with a thick Mexican accent.

"Is that me you're looking at?" asked his compatriot, "let me give you a light."

"Ah, ten-four."

"Yeah, okay, you saw me going up the side of the levee."

The guards were equipped with the latest 1980s technology. The night was pitch black now and I had moved to about a mile east of the frenzied chases under spotlights in the Tijuana riverbed, to the north side of the 10-foot-high metal fence the United States erected between Tijuana and San Diego, a wall jumped over, ripped apart and tunneled under by motivated migrants. I was at a solitary Border Patrol truck perched high on a bluff overlooking the canyon known as Smugglers Gulch. A starlight camera was mounted on a tower above the truck and inside an agent—one hand on his walkie-talkie—studied a video monitor. On the monitor the brush of Smugglers Gulch is clearly visible, as are the roads and the trails. The agent stared at the screen, saw a group of about half a dozen figures scrambling along a path and picked up his radio.

"I've got a group coming up toward the s-curve," he told agents down in the Gulch.

We watched a Border Patrol truck roar into sight on the screen and lock its brakes to a stop. The band of immigrants scattered, but they didn't stand much of a chance. The screen was equipped with a compass and the agent on the hill was back on the radio.

"Go south fifty yards," he told his colleagues, "they're in the brush."

Moments later the immigrants were surrounded and arrested.

Border Routine

"I'm not frustrated," said veteran Border Patrol agent John Krupa as an immigrating crowd scattered just south of us. "The system works, but the system is overloaded." He looked south and shook his head as he tried to come to terms with his role in these skirmishes. "We get people who come down here and tour the border and they're shocked," his voice included a hint of a drawl, and with his moustache, easy smile and militaristic uniform, Krupa came across like an actor playing sheriff in a television Western.

Later that same evening, he proudly showed off the latest in Border Patrol surveillance equipment, shared some prejudicial Border Patrol humor (Question: Why isn't the border fence electrified? Answer: Because the Mexicans would tap into it to run their refrigerators). At the San Ysidro Border Patrol station where Krupa was headquartered, the driveway was marked with a huge model of a cartoon-looking chicken. Mexicans who cross the frontier illegally are known by *coyotes* and the Border Patrol alike as *pollos*, chickens.

Already then, soon after the installation of the new wall, there were breaks torn into the surplus military landing mats used for the barrier. It was ripped apart in some places and tunneled under in others. Designed to run 14 miles from the Pacific east into the desert along one of the most heavily traveled international borders in the world, the new barrier was not yet finished and already routinely violated. A decade later the rigorous Operation Gatekeeper wall ended the daily dance I watched at Tijuana that night.

Worried Neighbors

"We've got to keep that border closed," insisted Barbara McCarthy to me in the 1980s. She was one of those shocked citizens who toured the border at the invitation of the Border Patrol. An elegant-looking woman with time on her hands ("The kids are gone, and what am I going to do? Play bridge?"), she sat in her opulent San Diego living room, chain smoking Parliaments and glancing occasionally out of her picture windows at the sweeping California-perfect view of Mission Bay. McCarthy was an organizer at the Stamp Out Crime Council, one of several ad hoc organizations that sprung up along the border to lobby for a tougher response to illegal immigration.

"If we were honest with ourselves," she readily admitted, "and we were in the position of those Mexicans, we'd do the same thing." But in the next breath she dismissed the people she wants stopped as "Mexico's problems. When people say we should open the borders I ask, 'How many are you going to take home with you?'" McCarthy smiled, leaned back in her overstuffed chair and took another drag on her cigarette. She saw the immigrants heading in her direction as responsible for much of the crime in San Diego County as well as a drain on local social services such as the public schools. She wanted to rescind the law that guarantees citizenship for everyone born in the United States. She wanted a law against providing a ride in a car to anyone illegally living in the United States. She could have written speeches for Donald Trump were he running for president in 1986.

Stamp Out Crime published a newsletter and organized field trips to the border to rally support for its cause. Despite McCarthy's strident attitude toward illegal immigration, she tried to distance her group from the incidences of violent vigilante activity that sporadically occur at the border. "You do have to look out for the cuckoo birds," she said, "and they're out there. They give others a bad name." McCarthy was adamant that groups like Stamp Out Crime do not encourage freelance attacks on border crossers.

Observers at the American Friends Service Committee office in San Diego agreed that vigilante border violence was a relatively minor problem especially compared with the attacks perpetrated by bandits and the mistreatment undocumented immigrants at times received at the hands of Border Patrol agents. "They're not violent," Roberto Martinez, then the director of a Friends project studying border violence, said about Barbara McCarthy and her ilk, "but they incite violence." He said he was dumbfounded by the xenophobia he encountered in groups like Stamp Out Crime. "They want me to go back to Mexico," he shook his head, "and I'm fifth generation!" His downtown San Diego office was littered with reports and photographs documenting attacks by the Border Patrol on foreign nationals. Martinez and the Friends wanted the Border Patrol to be subject to a civilian review board. "More humane treatment is needed by the Border Patrol," he said. "They have a total disregard for human life."

The human rights organization Americas Watch agreed that the Border Patrol was more of a threat than vigilantes. In a report it charged agents with killing and abusing immigrants. "They're naïve," said Barbara McCarthy about the Americas Watch investigators, "because they believe Roberto Martinez." Stamp Out Crime considered Martinez "a lying paid agitator seeking personal power."

Border Patrol agents don't deny that Mexicans were injured and killed during the free-for-all encounters that occurred along the border. But from the Patrol's point of view, the violence was a result of the illegal incursions into U.S. territory. Nobody would be hurt, they maintained, if no one was breaking the law. And agents felt slighted that they were so rarely acknowledged for the good that they perceive the Patrol accomplished, from regular drug busts to sometimes rescuing immigrants from the bandits that preyed on them in the no-man's-land.

Pert and bubbly Muriel Watson was another high-profile Border Patrol booster. Her late husband was a career agent and she honored his memory with her group, Light Up the Border. Her agenda was direct action. She organized protests by lining up cars and shining headlights south, into the dark fields used as cover by those crossing into the United States illegally. "These were no vigilantes," she said of her compatriots. "You could go from car to car and they were grandmothers, whole families. They'd be sitting with their take-out food and turning on the lights. They understood that something must be done."

Watson saw a direct connection between her protests and the new anti-crime lights along the border, the new access roads for patrolling agents, and especially for the new border fence. Her answer to the problem of illegal immigration was simple: "The only safe passage is for them to come through the port of entry and get on the trolley. They should do it legally." Of course, most of those who might follow her advice and try to cross legally would not gain legal entrance into the United States.

Later that night, while one bunch of immigrants was identified by the starlight scope, and another bunch was being chased off the Tijuana River levee, hundreds more were making their way past the Border

Patrol, past any marauding vigilantes, safely into the United States. "We have to stimulate the Mexican economy," said agent John Krupa. "We've got to get business down there to provide a job base." On this point Roberto Martinez and Krupa agreed. "In the final analysis," said Martinez, "it has to be understood that 99 percent of the people crossing are just poor working-class people."

On a typically bright and sunny day on the border I crossed into Mexico unimpeded. In the 1980s Mexican officials just waved travelers in; it was the taxi drivers who asked the questions:

"You need a cab? You want a girl? Hey, hey, joint *de* marijuana?"

On the other side of the crossing station U.S. customs guards studied the never-ending train of cars coming into California. Some drivers were diverted to a secondary inspection lane where more searches were conducted. A stream of pedestrians came north through the border station, too. A Border Patrol truck was parked on a knoll east of the official crossing. But there could never be enough trucks and agents.

There, in the broad daylight within sight of dozens of the guards, I watched as first one head and then another appeared at the top of the new fence. Experienced eyes took a quick look at the road and saw no visible hindrance to their passage north. There was a yelp of "Come on!" The bodies connected to those heads appeared and two young men quickly let themselves down into the United States. In seconds they were followed by a half-dozen more men flying over the fence, all dressed in that usual uniform of border crossers, attire that defies the stereotypes of poor Mexicans: jeans, a T-shirt and running shoes.

"Nothing is going to stop them," agent Krupa said. "These people are going to keep coming as long as the jobs are here."

The group ran north, across Interstate 5, and disappeared into the brush under the Camino de la Plaza overpass from where they could easily vanish into the teeming neighborhoods of San Ysidro, the southernmost suburb of San Diego.

Border Strategy Architect

The Southwest Border Strategy moved those dramatic encounters I witnessed in the 1980s out of the sight of urban San Diego into the empty deserts of the Southwest. In his Washington office, former Congressman Silvestre Reyes—who takes and gets credit for coming up with that idea—talked about the border he tried to enforce during his long career with the Border Patrol. "I was born, raised, worked on the border all my life." He knew the two extremes in the border debate: some Americans want to eliminate all border restrictions while others want to seal the border with the U.S. military. He rejected either as an agenda "that doesn't take into account those of us who know, understand and love the border." The border, said Reyes, is a necessity. He pointed to national security, the economy, public health and crime as reasons to restrict access to the United States.

There was a replica of the Statue of Liberty in Congressman Reyes' crowded Capitol Hill office, along with military mementos of his workload on the Armed Services Committee. His grandparents emigrated from Mexico, he's a product of the American Dream, a fact he considered part of his routine while working his Border Patrol beat, chasing Mexicans. "You recognize that there but for fate, you might be going. You have a full understanding of the implications of what you're doing." Reyes is a stout man, gray showing in his neatly combed and clean parted hair. His military posture reflects his years wearing a badge. Smiles came easily as he talked about the issue he knows intimately and from a unique perspective. No other member of Congress had served on the borderline, patrolling the U.S. frontier. "One of the things that always frustrates those of us who wear the Border Patrol uniform is the fact that depending on the political climate and the economic climate, we're expected to have what we describe as 'spigot enforcement.' You either turn it on or shut it off. We cannot work under those circumstances with any degree of success."

Advocates of sealing the border do not understand the "cultural mixing, the economic diversity and vitality that the border region represents to the two countries," said Reyes. He patiently explained that his years of experience taught him that controlling traffic on a border such as the one separating the United States and Mexico is a matter of compromise, and that controlling about 85 percent of cross-border traffic is about the best the United States should expect. "If we learned anything from the Berlin Wall, it's that you can't build a wall to keep people in or out. We need to recognize that." But he was convinced the government must make a 100 percent effort to achieve that 85 percent control.

Reyes talked passionately about human costs he's seen on the job. He lost border patrolmen under his command to attacks from smugglers, saw close-up the violence of border bandits who cross into the United States and rob, witnessed the heartlessness of *coyotes* who abandon their clients when a crossing goes wrong. "I investigated a case where a train caught eighteen undocumented people in the middle of a trestle. They had to jump off—it was a calamity of major proportions. Some of them died and some of them were mangled. Those kinds of things really tear at your gut."

Yet Reyes did not think opening up the border was a viable solution to the heartbreak he'd experienced in the field. Instead, he said, the resources must be allocated to control it and from his perspective that was not happening. "Now that I'm in this position," he said about his role in Congress,

> I'm frustrated because I can't influence policy fast enough to make a difference for those [who die] in the boxcars and the eighteen wheelers. Not only has that happened way too many times in my lifetime, but unless we get serious about managing the border the way it ought to be managed, and with the cooperation of Mexico, then people are going to continue to be doomed to die in those kinds of circumstances.

Managing the border, he said, includes freedom of movement for those with proper documentation who want to cross back and forth to shop and visit friends and relatives—but it does not include opening the border for all of the Mexicans who want to come north to work or join their families. "We cannot afford a willy-nilly, chaotic border as long as the economies are so disparate, as long as we have a First World economy butting right up against a Third World economy."

If and when Mexico develops an economy and a society equivalent to the United States, Silvestre Reyes speculated the southern border could evolve to be as free a passage as the U.S.-Canadian frontier.

> There isn't a trick to it, it's just the economy of the country. Mexico is a very rich country. They've got oil. They've got natural resources. The only thing they don't have is the ability to manage it in a way that benefits the Mexican people. I think it's unfair to put the burden on this country for the well-being of Mexicans.

So Congressman Silvestre Reyes kept working the halls of Congress, soliciting votes from his colleagues to bolster the Border Patrol.

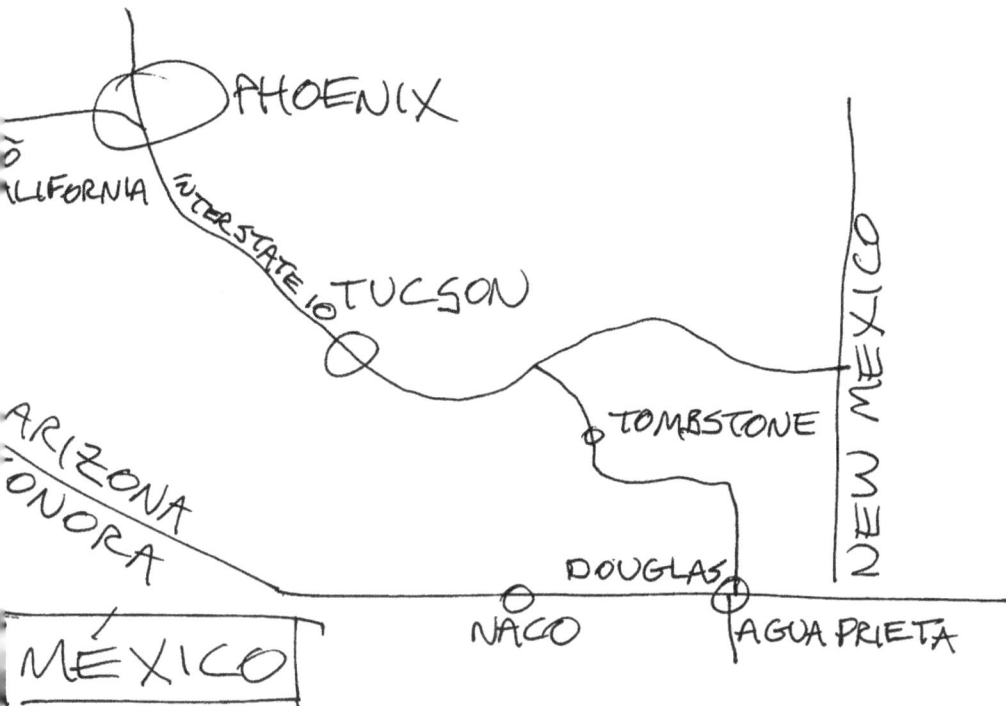

Chapter 12

THE VIGILANTE
MOVEMENT

With increasing regularity in post-Berlin Wall Germany, neo-Nazis attack foreigners. In Dolgenbrodt—a city in what was East Germany—for one particularly nasty example, prominent citizens hired an arsonist to firebomb a hostel for immigrants. Mayor Karl Pfannenschwarz rationalized the attack saying, "Look, we are a small village of 300 inhabitants that lives off tourists visiting our lake. How are we supposed to react when the state tells us to find rooms for eighty-six Gypsies or Africans?"[1] (Figure 12.1).

Figure 12.1 Along even the most fraught borderlines in the world—such as Checkpoint Charlie at the Berlin Wall—barriers eventually become routine stops for tourists' smiles at the camera.

In the ongoing attempt to wall us off from one another, there are scores more barriers lining national boundaries than there were when the Berlin Wall finally was breached in 1989. The push of cheap undocumented labor from the poor Global South into the rich Global North is creating new battlegrounds worldwide.

At the southwestern border of the United States, Mexicans at times surge and at other times trickle north illegally to fill jobs in states as distant as Washington and Maine, Americans in border states such as Arizona bear pain from this illegal migration. They fear drugs, disease and violence from across the frontier—fear fueled by President Trump's xenophobic speechifying. The mood of many Americans on the Mexican border often seems similar to that of their anti-foreigner European cousins. But despite rising waves of desperation and frustration in the United States, anti-foreigner behavior does not approach the widespread lawless terror of Germany's neo-Nazis.

Yet a long list of grassroots organizations has lobbied, propagandized and agitated to seal the U.S. border with Mexico. They echo Trump's

"Build the Wall!" chant with their rhetoric and their actions. Glenn Spencer and his American Border Patrol operated a flashy website that offered detailed advice on how to turn in neighbors. "These are the numbers to call to report employers you suspect are employing illegal immigrants," it instructed. "You may also report immigrants themselves if you believe they are in the country illegally, whether they are working or not. You should have the address of each suspected violator at a minimum, and as much additional information as you can obtain."[2] When his operatives spotted what they considered suspects, they say they called the Border Patrol. The continuing worry is that these types of freelance border guards add to the danger on the border.

Ranch Rescue advertised "operations," inviting volunteers to come join them in Arizona for Operation Thunderbird, in Colorado for Operation Foxbat and in New Mexico for Operation Jaguar. They said their volunteers stopped trespassers, most of whom they suspect of being illegal aliens.

All trespassers were given food and water, examined for injuries by a certified EMT, and evicted off the property by our volunteers. These trespassers were told not to return, and to spread the word among the rest of their criminal element not to come onto our property. Return to the property by these individuals will result in Citizen's Arrest for Criminal Trespass.

The Ranch Rescue now-defunct website was illustrated with dramatic photographs of volunteers in military-looking fatigues on patrol with their automatic rifles. Their faces were covered with camouflage paint, their hats festooned with shrubbery.

The names sound at least quasi-official: Civil Homeland Defense Corps, Ranch Rescue, American Border Patrol. But they were not part of any government agency. Instead, the independent groups were composed of angry and frustrated Arizonans who said, since the federal government failed to secure the U.S. border with Mexico, they were going to do what they could to keep immigrants without valid papers out of Arizona.

Migrants are killed along the trails from Mexico into Arizona. Reports of unsolved shootings along the border are commonplace. Border Patrol agents are targets; migrants are targets. Who is doing the shooting? *Coyotes*? Bandits? Drug traffickers? Vigilantes?

A Visit to Tombstone

Tombstone, Arizona, is a typical Western tourist mecca. In the late nineteenth century the mining boomtown's saloons really were full of outlaw gunslingers. Today busloads of tourists come to Tombstone looking for the warm Southwest sun and to cheer the actors who recreate the famous gunfight between Wyatt Earp and the Clanton Gang at the O.K. Corral.

But underneath the veneer of simple, friendly locals catering to out-of-town visitors, the Tombstone I visited was a simmering cauldron of conflict. The Mexican border is just a few miles south. Tombstone lies directly in the path of undocumented migrants heading to Tucson, Phoenix and points farther north.

Several months before my first trip to Tombstone, an out-of-work California kindergarten teacher drifted into town and took a job washing dishes in the O.K. Café. Before long, Chris Simcox hung up his dishtowel and went to work as assistant editor at the weekly newspaper, the *Tombstone Tumbleweed*.

"The owner had basically given up on this paper." Simcox told me. Soon after he went to work for the paper, he bought it. Local gossip says the capital came from his new girlfriend, the owner of the O.K. Café. "The paper was failing horribly. We were barely selling—maybe four hundred copies a week. It wasn't making it. You know, no advertising." The previous owner put the paper up for sale shortly after Simcox joined the staff of three.

His post-9/11 takeover of the *Tombstone Tumbleweed* is a story Chris Simcox told often. Reporters worldwide wanted to hear him complain about illegal immigration into Cochise County, and about how he founded the vigilante group he called the Civil Homeland Defense Corps. After he bought the paper, Simcox turned the weekly into a propaganda sheet for his group's border activities. "It's been nonstop," he told me. "I mean I've done hundreds and hundreds of interviews. It's working."

What's working? I asked him. What are you accomplishing?

Getting everyone across this country to understand what's going on down here in this border. That it's ridiculous. We've been at war since 9/11, basically. We were attacked by people who came in, and then you watch what goes on at this border and you think, my God, it's a free for all. There is no real national security when you have an open border like this one here. Our government will not protect our borders. That's my number one concern.

This concern filled the 16-page paper each week. The January 30, 2003 issue was typical. The editorial complained that a couple of tourists from Oregon were unable to get the county sheriff or the Border Patrol to respond when they called after they "spotted a group of eight suspected illegals walking just off the road." Frustrated, reported Simcox, the couple came to the newspaper's office because they had heard about the Civil Homeland Defense Corps. "There are so many illegals every-where we go," he quoted them as telling him. "We can't even take a hike anymore without running into a group. We think this will be the last time we winter here in the south near the border. Our government had better do something!"

Simcox ended his editorial with his call to action. "Sounds like it is up to us, friends, the citizens. If you don't like it or it scares you? You can hide, or run, or you can join us as the eyes and ears of the citizens who can make a difference. Civil Homeland Defense is the only imme-diate solution." In a following editorial he charged that five thousand "illegals" came through Cochise County while Border Patrol officers watched the Super Bowl. "*Hasta la vista*," he wrote, "welcome to the United States. Hope you enjoyed the game."

Forty-two years old when we talked in 2003, Chris Simcox looked much younger. His office was cluttered, dominated by his computer and his electronic drum set. He wore the Tombstone uniform: work shirt, blue jeans, cowboy boots.

"I want America to know that they're not getting the real story," he said about his newspaper's perpetual lead article. "I've created a group of volunteers. And we go down to the border and we actually help do the job. That's the Civil Homeland Defense Corps. We are aiding and assisting the Border Patrol and plugging the holes on the border."

Simcox was wide-eyed and excited.

> I mean, granted it's, you know, the little boy with his thumb in the dike basically. But we go down to the border when we can and with however many numbers we can put together and we help patrol that border. Using the same tactics and the same procedures and the same humane interaction that the Border Patrol uses. We work shoulder to shoulder with Border Patrol. We're on Border Road, which you'll see when you go out with us. We're in our vehicles. We drive back and forth. We create a presence that says, "There's activity here, don't come across."
>
> They're human beings. I mean, there's a reason why they're coming across, and that's because Mexico's not taking care of their needs, their own government. I've seen people out there in bad shape. But I've also been shot at by, you know, drug dealers. There's been so many drug busts, it's incredible. Something's not right.

It's impossible to determine if Simcox slowed migration from Mexico, but he certainly managed to disrupt life in Tombstone. As I hired a room at Curley Bill's Bed & Breakfast ("The Best and the BADDEST in Tombstone! Wyatt Earp Slept Here—You Can Too!!!"), a few blocks across town from the *Tombstone Tumbleweed* offices, Larry "Curley Bill" Alves expressed disgust with Simcox's talk about guns and shooting. "His military training was in the Boy Scouts," he said. "I'm a conservative Republican, but I'm an ex-senior non-com in Vietnam. He's a little kid who never got to play soldier as a kid." Alves saw a direct relationship between his bed and breakfast business and Simcox's ability to draw national news coverage. "This militia stuff hurts tourism. People in this town don't like this at all."

At breakfast the next morning Alves's wife, Sally, continued the verbal assault on the new guy in town and his antics. "Local people are sick of listening to all that crap," she said about Simcox's tirades in his newspaper. "If you could still run people out of town on a rail, he'd be run out of town on a rail. I've had a couple of people cancel reservations, afraid Simcox and his group were walking around with assault rifles and camouflage. It's too bad when a guy doing something bad owns the town's newspaper."

But Simcox insisted Sally and Larry Alves are wrong.

"We do nothing but identify where they're coming across," Simcox explained his tactics. Yet a few days before we talked, he and one of his troopers were arrested by a National Park ranger for straying onto federal land at the border. The specific charges were carrying a loaded weapon inside a National Park and interfering with law enforcement. Rangers confiscated Simcox's patrolling gear: a pistol, two-way radios, a police radio scanner, a mobile telephone and a camera.

"Why were you armed?" I asked him.

"It's my Second Amendment right. The U.S. Constitution and the Arizona State Constitution give us rights to keep and bear arms. I have a concealed weapons permit. I refuse to be a victim. I've had eight death threats since I've started this. So, you know, I'm not going to be a victim."

"We're neighborhood watch volunteers," was how he defined his role. The Border Patrol was less enthusiastic. "As long as they don't impede our duties in the field, we don't really deal with them," was the official response from the Border Patrol's Tucson sector spokesman Frank Amarillas.[3]

As he quickly skipped through his biography, Simcox highlighted an event that may well explain his fixation about Mexicans coming across the border.

"I've been a victim of crime by a guy who didn't speak English in New York City. I was mugged."

I pointed out the fact that just because the guy didn't speak English doesn't mean he wasn't born in Manhattan.

"True. True. It's just a crime. Crime is out of control. Drugs are out of control." Simcox quickly changed his target and blamed the federal government for failing to secure the borders, "so it's just my basic patriotic duty to do what's necessary."

Not that Simcox and his ilk believed they alone could secure the border with Mexico, not even just the Cochise County border with Mexico. They hoped their efforts would force Washington to militarize the border. Trump's election, still years distant, would be their dream come true.

"Troops on our border," was the solution Simcox sought. Troops would create "a true sense of national security. When you talk to the folks out there that's the only thing that will deter illegals from coming across. We've talked to them. I talk to them all the time. They're not afraid of us. They're not afraid of the Border Patrol. They're not afraid of anything. They're going to come in to America because we leave it wide open and it's so easy. Troops on the border would force Mexico to deal with their own people, to start spending some of its money to support the citizens of that country. Build infrastructure. Improve their cities, improve their schools, improve their education. That's why they come here, because they admire our system. Well if they admire it why the hell aren't they doing it themselves?"

"Chris Simcox's principal malady is that he is an incurable racist," responded Miroslava Flores on the website La Voz de Aztlan. Another La Voz de Aztlan writer identified Simcox as a "vigilante thug calling for anti-Mexican armed militia."

Not so, Simcox protested. "Since when do your nationalistic views and your patriotism and your wanting to provide security for your neighbors and fighting crime make you a racist?" And he insists he was not a vigilante. "A vigilante is someone who is judge, jury and executioner basically. Someone who certainly takes the law into his own hands. We don't. We report illegal activity, that's it. That's all we do. And we create a deterrent to anyone who would break the laws of coming across that border."

Despite his protestations, when I first called his office to arrange a meeting, his assistant said he couldn't come to the phone because he was keeping Mexicans he suspected of being in the United States illegally in place under a Tombstone tree while a colleague tried to summon the Border Patrol.

"We do not apprehend." It's obviously a matter of definition. "We locate. We don't hold 'em. We just follow 'em. We give the Border Patrol the coordinates of where these people are, whoever they may be. It's not about racism, this is about national security."

Chris Simcox told me he knows what to look for when he patrols the border. "People who've entered this country illegally, it's quite obvious most of the time." Of course, even trained Border Patrol officers make identification mistakes. The mayor of a Los Angeles suburb—Latino, but a native U.S. citizen—was famously picked up in an INS raid, and Cheech Marin starred in a tragicomedy film about such a false arrest, *Born in East L.A.*

It's was a Friday. Chris Simcox invited me to hang around with him and his group all weekend. The plan, he said, was to meet at the newspaper office at 5:30 Saturday morning and drive south to patrol the border. Dawn is a prime time for illegal crossings, he said. The weekend days are scheduled to be filled with classes for his posse provided by an ex-Delta Force Special Ops trainer. Another border patrol outing was planned for Saturday at dusk.

The Pragmatic Local Mayor

A half-an-hour south of Tombstone is the dusty border town of Douglas. The two-lane blacktop from Tombstone to Douglas is tumbleweed and sagebrush studded, punctuated with billboards addressed to President George W. Bush. They sport the international "no" sign, a red slash through the word "invasion."

"Mr. President," reads one, "Mexican Federales and Soldiers Are Shooting At Our Border Patrol. Order Your Friends to Stop!" Another is a reference to 9/11. "Mr. President: Homeland Security Starts Here, Cochise County, AR, USA," and adds a sardonic, "Maps Available." The map offer is used on another sign that says, "If This Were Crawford, TX, The Marines Would Be Here." Crawford was the locale of Bush's Texas White House. Still another: "Mr. President. Don't Forsake Our Sovereignty For Votes. Send the Army—Ours!" And: "If This Were Scottsdale The National Guard Would Be Here."

Cross-border traffic became a crisis for Arizona when the U.S. government reinforced patrols at San Diego, El Paso and other urban border crossings. When the wilds of the Arizona desert became a favored crossing point for migrants without proper papers, it wasn't only the migrants who suffered. Arizona became overrun with desperate trespassers. The Border Patrol increased its manpower on the Arizona line exponentially in an effort to try to combat the sudden flow of huge numbers of migrants moving north across the desert.

"I was born and raised here." In the modern Douglas ("The premier Southwestern border community") city hall, a block from its fading Main Street, I'm talking with then-Mayor Ray Borane. "I've seen illegal immigration all my life. I remember when I was a kid there wasn't any fence." Mayor Borane is disgusted with the likes of newcomer Chris Simcox. "I am part Hispanic. My mother is half Mexican. I was raised in this town and I was raised with her side of the family, the Mexican side of the family. All through my life I have been very sympathetic, very compassionate towards the plight of Mexican people."

When the harsh Arizona desert corridor turned into a highway of death for many of the migrants, Mayor Borane says he felt compelled to respond. He complained to his congressional representatives, the president, the attorney general. He wrote an op-ed for the *New York Times* addressed to "those who live in the nation's more wealthy places." Borane lectured *Times* readers. "Do you have any idea what havoc you cause in our area and in other border towns, all because you hire illegal immigrants to make your beds, mow your lawns and cook your food?"[4]

The mayor paraded statistics. He cited the more than two hundred thousand Mexicans and other migrants deported by the Border Patrol in just the six months prior to his screed. He told the story of 28 migrants suffering from heat exhaustion rescued in the desert the week before he wrote to the *Times*, all evacuated by helicopter to local hospitals where one died. He recounted a shootout between *coyotes* and their clients, a highway wreck that injured 33 people jammed into an old van.

Don't blame the migrants, Borane insisted. "Can you even begin to fathom the arduous, debasing journey people endure to serve you comfortably in the luxury you are so accustomed to?" He noted the armed vigilante groups that responded to the crisis, calling their actions wrong and added, "But it is what your demand for cheap and unregulated services has driven them to."

As we sit and chat in the company of the American flag in the mayor's office, Borane is agitated, calling the technology and manpower assembled on the U.S. side of the border a charade.

> The only thing it lacked was a fucking idiot like that guy Simcox up the road. Excuse me, but it gets me really frustrated when I talk about this. Simcox writes that idiotic call to arms and they make him a media idol. Not because he's saying things that are going to be effective, but because it's so outlandish and it's reminiscent of the Old West. He's a fraud.

Mayor Borane is disgusted that the Border Patrol puts up with the meddling of Simcox and the other vigilante groups. "He's insincere. He has no depth. There's no fiber to what he's doing. He has no *cojones*, you know? He just threw that bomb out there and he never knew he was going get all that attention. And he liked it."

One of the reasons Ray Borane expresses such disgust with Simcox and the other vigilantes is because their patrols add to the problems faced by the migrants without preventing illegal cross-border traffic.

> People think I'm a bleeding heart for the illegals. I am in a way. They're being used and they're being abused by their own people. They're robbing them on that side. They're being abused over here. And they're on their way to work. They're going to work. They're going to jobs that are given to them by Americans. Jobs that Americans don't want. And they're risking their lives to do it, to support their families. You know

why Simcox is a problem? Because while those people are lying there in Mexico having to wait for him patiently to play his little game—his childish game—they won't go across the border because they don't know what to expect from him. They're suffering in the weather. They have no money. They're enduring at night the cold, and during the summer the heat, because assholes like him are out there playing a game. They're just sitting there waiting him out.

Families Ripped Apart

In Mayor Borane's *New York Times* op-ed he cites what was then a little-known group of victims found along the border. "Children are often separated from their parents in Border Patrol roundups and end up in shelters," he wrote, years before Trump-era ICE and Border Patrol agents made headlines tearing thousands of children from the arms of their parents—figuratively and actually—and locking up those children in appalling, filthy cages. I walked across the border from Douglas to Agua Prieta to learn more. Borane had sketchy information for me: the children were taken to a shelter called Casa Pepito, he told me, run by a woman named Sylvia—he could not remember her last name.

I found Sylvia Villalobos with little trouble. Along one of sprawling Agua Prieta's main streets is the storefront office of a local legislator. I asked the two men at the desk for directions to Casa Pepito. "You want a ride?" one of them offered me a lift in his truck with a hospitable, "We are friends, *señor.*" I had planned to walk, assuming quite incorrectly that Agua Prieta is a sleepy crossroads like its across-the-border neighbor, Douglas. On the contrary, Agua Prieta is bustling, and stretches miles south into the Sonoran desert, with a population approaching ten times the fifteen thousand living on the United States side. As is the case for so many Mexican northern border cities, Agua Prieta is booming as a jumping off place for Mexicans heading north and a center for border trade and industry.

The U.S. Border Patrol, in addition to the brutal Trump policy of forcibly removing children from their parents' custody, sometimes picks up children who accidentally get separated along the border from their parents during a family crossing. Other children are entrusted to *coyotes* by parents already living in the United States who wish to reunite their families. If these smugglers are caught, U.S. authorities send the children back to Mexico. The Border Patrol also finds children wandering the border area alone. Some decided to attempt the crossing alone, others were abandoned by *coyotes* who feared capture.

"Sometimes the children cross separately," Sylvia Villalobos is explaining to me how children end up at Casa Pepito. If they're found by the Border Patrol, they're turned over to the Mexican consular officials in Douglas who send them over the line to Casa Pepito. "We look for the mother or any relatives." During the search "they stay in Casa Pepito. We give them medical services, we feed them. We try to help them with psychological help too so they don't feel so bad. It's like a home. They live as a family."

On Villalobos's desk is a fat binder, filled with forms and pictures. For each child processed there is a before-and-after photograph: when they first arrive at the shelter and when they are reunited with their family. "When we talk to them we ask, 'Where is your mother? Do you have a phone? Where do you live?'" Local social services in the hometown are then engaged to help. The success rate for finding those families is an extraordinary 100 percent. "Sometimes we have hard times. We have had two children who spent six months here. Sometimes the families cannot come and pick them up and we have to travel all the way to Mexico City or Guadalajara to return them to their families. But usually they stay one day or two."

Of course not all the children can offer their phone number and other critical information. On one page of the binder I spot the photograph of case number 114, who arrived at Casa Pepito December 1, 2002, from Chihuahua, age 17 days. Others are 5 months, 1- or 2-years old. Such little children are either traced by their birth certificates or are reunited with their families when the parents send word to the Mexican authorities that they lost track of them. "Sometimes the parents cross through the desert while the children cross by the water." The parents go without the children, worried that "the crying of the baby is an alert for the immigration people," and turn their children over to *coyotes* who take the children across—for a fee, of course. "Sometimes they are so intent to go across the border, I think they don't care who does the work, as long as they get their children across." She shows me the picture of a teenage boy, turns the page of the binder, and there he is again, with his father.

These must be highly emotional reunions, I say, looking at the before-and-after faces in the binder.

"Oh, yes. We feel very proud of doing this. This is a great job." She sighs.

Sylvia Villalobos is a sophisticated woman, part of the Agua Prieta elite. Her sister is the mayor. As she looks at the photographs of the scores of children she's helped, she tries to understand the choices their parents make. "Sometimes we know the parents are going to try again to go to the United States, even though they have suffered so much. But they are on the line. They won't go back to their towns. They'll try and try and try until they make it." She flips the pages, child after child, many just months old. "They travel two days on a bus. They get here and we say, 'Where are you going?' And they say, 'We're going to New York.' You never know how much they suffer in their own towns so they do all this just to get across. And sometimes they don't need to go, but they want to, and they do."

I walk back over to the U.S. side. The immigration officer asks me what I was doing in Mexico and I tell him about my visit to Casa Pepito. He nods. "It's a continual problem." His face turns soft, in stark contrast to his starched uniform and shiny badge. "It breaks my heart to see kids suffer. See these gray hairs? I'm only forty."

With the Vigilantes

"That asshole!" says the bartender with disgust. I'm in St. Elmo, a rowdy saloon in Bisbee, the old copper mining town between Douglas and Tombstone that's now filled with gentrifying urban refugees. Buzz Pearson is tending bar, talking about Chris Simcox. "The guy has no idea what's going on." Buzz sports a shaved head and graying goatee, a big silver earring in one lobe. Powerful arms tattooed, arms that won him the power lifting championship of Arizona. His band plays at St. Elmo: Buzz and the Soul Senders. "I've 86'ed him from St. Elmo," says Buzz about Simcox. "I'm not down with his thing."

"It's too complicated," Buzz says about the border, "to have a bunch of yahoos patrolling on their own. I'm sure it'll cause problems. Somebody will get shot. A lot of them are looking for excitement," he says about Simcox and the other vigilantes. "I think it's going to blow up in his face. Something bad is going to happen or people are going to realize he's in it for his ego."

"Chris Simcox is an idiot!" Susan Nunn spits out the words. She knows Tombstone from a vantage point few enjoy. She was the night manager at the Tombstone Best Western motel, the Lookout Lodge. "Quiet and peaceful," offers the Lookout Lodge's advertisements, "Rooms with views. Walk to town." Views, yes. Quiet, not very. Walk to town, walk from Mexico.

The Border Patrol was hustling in the late 1990s to find additional agents to assign to the border around Tombstone. "They brought a bunch of guys down from Washington state," Nunn remembers, and these out-of-state agents needed temporary housing. They took rooms at hotels along the Arizona border. "I had a bunch of them at the Best Western. In the evening they'd go out and they'd be all over the hills all night long. When they were gone was when all the illegal immigrant traffic was coming by the hotel with their problems."

At 10 o'clock each night Susan Nunn locked the Best Western's front door. A telephone just outside the door was available for late arrivals to call the motel office; it also rang in Nunn's bedroom.

"The immigrants would pick up this telephone because they needed help, they needed a room," Nunn tells me.

All night long they would be on the phone—"We're in trouble. Our people are wet, our people are cold. Please come help us." I'd ask them if they were illegal, and if they said yes I'd figure they were honest enough that I could help them. If they'd lie to me, I'd say, "Walk on downtown, it's another mile."

If the migrants admitted to Nunn that they were in the United States illegally, she'd check the register for vacancies.

> If I had a room, I'd put them in it. I didn't care how many people. They're wet. They're cold. They're crying. They're old. They're young. They're babies. I mean, my God! They were coming at us in all directions.
>
> My theory at that hotel was, I am not the law. I have no right to discriminate. If someone comes up here and they have the money and they have an ID, I do not have the right to say you are not allowed to have a room.

The travelers paid. "They put their money in a plastic bag so it wouldn't get ruined if they got wet."

The Best Western rooms typically contained two beds, "and they would put maybe fifteen people in that room." Nunn says she would make it clear that she didn't mind the crowds and that she had no intention of calling the authorities by holding her index finger up to her lips to indicate their secret was safe with her. She brought food to the rooms and never needed to warn her guests from south of the border that Border Patrol agents were their neighbors. After resting, the migrants were back on the road. "In the middle of the night they'd be gone. As soon as they got dry and warm they would move on."

Rained out Vigilantes

The morning after I met Chris Simcox I crawled out of bed at Curley Bill's into a frigid sunrise, warmed up the car and headed across Tombstone to the newspaper's office. Simcox said his posse would convene at 5:30. Southern Arizona heat is murderous in the summer, but winter cold and rain and snow also abuse the migrants. Tombstone is 4,500 feet above sea level. I sat in the car with the heater on listening to radio stations from Dallas and Salt Lake. I waited. I read the *New York Times* I bought the day before in Douglas at the Gadsden Hotel, the architectural star of Douglas's fading main street. The Gadsden features twin marble staircases leading up to a huge Tiffany stained glass mural of the desert. I waited. It got light. I waited. Chris Simcox was a no show.

I drove the few blocks over to the O.K. Café and nursed a cup of tea. While I was deciding what to do next, I started to overhear bursts of conversation from the table next to me. "Twit […] ego-driven […] underqualified." A man was talking to a woman. "It was terrible, I was pulling my hair out." And I started paying close attention when he said, "Chris can't shoot for shit." This was the day Chris Simcox told me his troops would be trained by an ex-military expert marksman. The fellow at the next table looked the part, with his trimmed moustache and Airborne baseball cap. "He's so enamored of all the attention." I got up and introduced myself to James Garrett, who was only too happy to talk about his client, Chris Simcox.

"This is such a complex issue that is being so grossly oversimplified," he begins. "Normally I run under just a code name down here, for obvious reasons, because this is going to get ugly at some point," Garrett tells me. But he says he decided to identify himself to me and speak on the record because of his concerns. "At the highest level it is a political problem," he says of the border, "because it's about sovereignty. I think sometimes we all slip into clichés because they fit, not because we're intellectually suffering from a deficit but because they simply are able to capture in a pithy way a conceptual issue." It's six in the morning, but he's fired with emotion and energy.

A nation without borders is not a nation. And we have lost control of our borders. At the more immediate level, we have an abrogation by state, certainly federal—and I would also suggest local—law enforcement of the responsibilities for protecting the citizens that live along this border. When citizens cannot leave their home without a radio and a gun, when they escort their children to the bus stop under arms …

He pauses with disgust.

As a Vietnam combat special ops veteran, I did not fight for this. For me it's a very personal issue. I have to be somewhat careful at times not to let that personal focus cloud my strategic judgment.

Veteran Garrett tells me he is "tactical officer" for the Civil Homeland Defense Corps. It is a "very uneasy" relationship, he says. His job this day is to provide concealed weapons permit training to the group. But he's rethinking his role after working closely with Simcox. "He mentioned to me the other day that he wants to start doing night ops, and he has no clue. At night the rules change big time. During the day I think it's a great idea to have citizens taking an active part. And if that deters, good."

But Simcox, worries Garrett, is not the man to lead such a movement. "He's made an absolute fool of himself. He lacks the intellectual basis for the issue. At some point it's going to turn into a tactical issue," Garrett says about the border. "I think it's going to turn into a shooting issue. But right now it's a political issue and it has to be handled with a serious degree of sophistication. It has to be packaged very carefully."

Then why would Garrett want to get involved with Simcox?

Because I think the model we're working up has the potential to be the most effective and the least offensive—as opposed to Ranch Rescue, which is running around in camouflage. That's just a wreck waiting to happen. Or like the American Border Patrol which takes photographs, and okay, so what? Simcox is the only game there is because he has that newspaper. It's a voice. Without that, you have no voice.

An accurate example of the power of the press, at its most local level, influencing the global agenda.

We head back over to the newspaper office to collect the students where a sheepish Simcox apologizes for standing me up. "I forgot to tell you. If it's raining we don't go out."

Borderline

Our motorcade heads south out of Tombstone. We get off the blacktop and speed along dirt roads, past a scattering of homes, finally turning into Ray Bouton's driveway. Two nooses hang from trees. Three flags fly from his big red Ford pickup: Old Glory, the Marines flag and the

Revolutionary War's Don't-Tread-On-Me banner. Bouton offered his land for the concealed weapons training class. We're less than a mile from the border.

Ray Bouton wears blue jeans and boots, a work shirt with snaps and a black cowboy hat. A loaded automatic pistol is shoved into his belt, and he offers to show me his personal war zone.

"These trees out front here," we're walking past the nooses,

which are probably sixty, seventy feet from my house, I've come out and found—the politically correct phrase for it is illegal aliens[5]—but I call 'em wetbacks. They actually camped in front of my house in those trees. My daughter's bedroom is over here.

He makes clear the proximity between the ad hoc campground and his girl's room. "They come through from the border. They walk through here, cut my fences. I find 'em out here, trash all over the place." And as we walk he shows me the trash, piles of it. Liter-size plastic water bottles with Spanish-language labels, soiled diapers and baby wipes, bottles of electrolyte supplements. And pair after pair of women's underwear. Ray Bouton's theory is that the discarded underclothing suggests rape victims.

Bouton regularly encounters the trespassing migrants.

Sometimes they ask for water. None of them are violent or aggressive. I don't consider them a real threat. But they don't come with signs stating that their intentions are good. I happen to think that their intentions are to look for work. But when I find bottles of tequila, empty cans of Tecate beer, pornographic magazines and pornographic comic books, I do have a concern for my daughter and the children around the area.

What I usually do is grab a pistol, if there's only several in a group. If there's a large group—thirteen, fifteen, twenty, I usually grab a rifle, and go out with a rifle. I've got a rifle that holds thirty rounds in a clip. I walk out with that because these people are desperate. I don't know what a desperate person's going to do. Our only line of defense right here is me. We don't rely on the Border Patrol or police at all.

Bouton's place is remote. A call to the authorities, even if they were to respond, would mean a long wait for a patrol car. "They couldn't get here to do anything to protect you in time." Not that he would expect the cops to care.

Most of the Border Patrol and the police have become so apathetic with the numbers of illegals that come through this area, that they don't bother. It's just another day in the office for them. They can put their eight-hour day in and they can go home. They don't have to think about it. I have to live here, with the fear of it, twenty-four hours a day. I live by the weapon here.

Once he has the trespassers under control, Bouton just wants to get rid of them if he senses no threat.

They're usually trying to get north. I just direct them, tell 'em, "*Vamos! Andale!*" and point. Then I go in and call the Border Patrol and keep an eye out. I don't go out and hold a gun. I don't hold 'em on the ground or threaten in any way. But I do want them to see that I do have a firearm, a defensive firearm with me.

Bouton says he just wants them off his property. "They have more rights in this country than you or I. I can't hold 'em. If I hold 'em at gunpoint, I'm detaining these poor or pathetic migrants that are just coming up here," he trails off, resigned. I find it hard to believe he'd face any difficulty from the authorities if he detained a trespasser on his own property. But he tells me I'm wrong.

Even if they do come through and cut the fence—and they've cut my fences—it's not worth what would happen to me. These wetbacks that have come through from another country—criminal trespassers as far as I'm concerned—have filed lawsuits against ranchers and other people in the area, just because they have come out and detained them. I have seen, with my own eyes, down on the border, Mexican civil rights groups handing them water, food, and pamphlets telling them where to go in the United States for help, how to get north. Maps and phone numbers of civil rights organizations. If they're in any way detained by any of us legal American citizens, then we're the ones at fault. We're the ones in the wrong.

How often does this happen? Does this happen once in a while, does it happen every day? Is it something that you're thinking about all the time? Is it just a part of your routine?

"Pete," he addresses me with the informality that comes fast in the rural West, "this is something I think about all the time. How many Americans do you know who live with a gun. I sit with my family at night and watch TV with a pistol by my side. When I go to bed at night there's a pistol by my bed, there's a rifle in the corner loaded, ready to defend my home."

"So you're living scared on your own ranch," I suggest.

"I'm not scared," he rejects the characterization. "But I'm apprehensive. I'm on edge all the time."

I ask him again how frequently he encounters trespassers.

"It's every night of the week."

"Every night of the week?"

"It's every night."

Bouton says migrants use his hoses to secure water, sleep in his hay or the beds of his pickup trucks. Sometimes the bolder or most desperate of the intruders ask for provisions.

I will give them water. There's no person in this world that I could refuse a drink of water unless it was a child molester or a rapist or murderer. They could die of thirst as far as I'm concerned.

I happened to be sitting right on this porch here one day this summer, and of all things I was doing, I happened to be cleaning a rifle. And this wetback walks around the corner. It was in the summer, it was in the high nineties, and this guy was just completely done. I could see the signs of heat stroke, heat exhaustion. I work in the Grand Canyon, I'm familiar with the signs. I ran a hose over him. Then I went in the house and got a tortilla and loaded it up with grape jelly and sugar to revive him. Then I called the Border Patrol. I eventually got out of him that he was going to Wilcox. He had a brother in Wilcox and he was going there to look for work. But he was lost. He didn't know where Wilcox was or how to get there. When the border patrol came he got up and, and went toward the border patrol vehicle looking to get in it because of the air conditioning.

"It's a human tragedy," I say. "Aside from whatever problems you have with your fence and your own concerns for your safety, it's a human tragedy."

"Oh, it is," Bouton agrees.

I have no hatred for these people. I know the Mexican people. I've lived here with the Mexican people for I don't know how long. I have friends that are Mexicans who don't like what's going on here. I don't blame these people at all for wanting to better themselves. I do blame the Mexican government for not doing more for their people. I think the Mexican government condones what's going on here.

"What's the solution?" I ask him.

I would like to ask politicians why we're so afraid of Mexico. Why we are afraid of putting the military on this border. I would like to see the military put on this border. I could actually probably heave a little bit more of a sigh of relief knowing that the military was on this border. The other thing is, I've been in Mexico, three hundred miles south of the border to the beaches, back into the interior, in the mountains. It's a beautiful country. That country supposedly has as much resources as the United

States has. Plenty of oil. Look at the Marshall Plan. Look at Japan. Every country that we've ever had a war with, we go back in and build them up to become one of the most prosperous countries in the world. These people are our neighbors, next door, but we don't seem to want to do anything for them. I think the Mexican government is just set up as a cash system for the superrich. To me Vicente Fox is the biggest pimp in the world. He prostitutes his people to the United States so he can live in a lap of luxury. As long as they can come up here and bring billions of dollars every year into the Mexican economy, he doesn't have to do anything.

Ray Bouton's analysis is a little rough around the edges but packed with eyewitness reality. I ask him why he doesn't just sell the ranch and find a safe place, say in Montana, hundreds of miles from these daily crises.

Pete, I'll tell you what. I lived at one time six hundred yards from the border and I was in a major shootout down there. I stood out in the front of my house and my at that time four-year-old daughter was lying in her bed with her little pink teddy bear pulled up over her head while there were bullets flying around outside because there were four criminals from another country that came into our country that were robbing people. They called them the border bandits. We've got enough criminals in this country, we don't need more.

"So why not get out of here?" I ask again.

Six hundred yards from the Mexican border or six hundred miles, I'm still an American citizen, and I shouldn't have to run in fear because of criminals from another country. I've got too much pride to turn around and run. Americans are known for standing and fighting. We as Americans don't turn our back and run because Mexicans are going to come up here and run us out of this country. You hear Hispanic pride, Mexican pride, we're proud to be Mexicans. Well if you're proud to be

Mexicans, stay in your country and effect some type of change in your country. We did it in our country. Do it in your country.

Strange words from a settler whose ranchland was in Mexico before President Polk's war of conquest.

In an out building on Ray Bouton's border land, the motley bunch of about a dozen self-appointed border patrol volunteers gathered by Chris Simcox assemble for class. Generic country music plays. A sign on the wall proclaims, "Hunters, fishermen and other liars gather here." The decor includes guns and knives, cell phones and walkie-talkies. Stacks of *American Rifleman* magazine are scattered about the room.

"My name is Storm," James Garrett introduces himself only with his nom de guerre. He makes no mention of being "tactical officer" for Simcox and his Civil Homeland Defense bunch. Instead he specifically announces that he is not formally connected with them and is on the scene only to teach what the state of Arizona requires a citizen to know in order to obtain a concealed weapons permit.

I spent ten years in Special Ops, United States Army Special Forces. I spent combat tours in Vietnam, and Central and South America. I was an instructor at the commando school for U.S. Army Special Forces at the Special Warfare Center. I did almost ten years in law enforcement beginning with the LAPD, and my last tour of duty was as a Border Strike Force Ranger in New Mexico on the drug deals over there, one of the dreaded "Men in Black." I've been teaching weapons and tactics for about thirty-seven years. I don't know it all. But I've had to learn a few things because I'm alive and some other people aren't. Last year I retired as a professor of criminology and forensics. I could just no longer teach in the current higher education environment of political correctness. You will find out from me from some of the remarks I make in here that I am anything but politically correct.

"That's okay," interrupts one of the eager students. "Neither are we." The group laughs.

Storm tells his students to introduce themselves and explain why they want to be licensed to carry a gun. One more thing: if they were to be reincarnated as a wild animal, Storm assigns the group to announce which animal would they choose to be.

"My name is Chris," says Simcox. "I want to learn how to avoid park rangers." His bunch laughs. He gets serious and says he wants to learn more about the law "and come back as a bear."

Ray Bouton introduces himself and says he's pleased to be the host of the event. He's already taken the course, he tells Storm, so he'll skip the class. But first he wants to explain why he chose not to apply for a permit after he took the course. "I thought that communist-slash-socialist Gore was going to be president. I figured getting the permit would be just an open door for him to come down with the storm troopers and bust through the door. That's what I think of the government."

"Right on!" says someone.

Ray says he'd like to come back as a poodle with free run of Hugh Hefner's mansion.

Around the room the responses are more predictable.

"I want to come back as a lion."

"Alligator."

"Eagle."

"A fly on the wall."

"I want to carry a gun to protect myself, my wife and family from nuts."

Another eagle.

A coyote (!).

"I want more confidence handling confrontation situations."

Still another eagle.

"What I want you to notice," says Storm "is all the predators. Being a predator is better than being prey."

Storm refers repeatedly to his work toward a PhD as he warms up the class for the two days ahead of them. "I can teach a chimpanzee to shoot. I can't teach a chimpanzee judgment." His automatic pistol is strapped to

Figure 12.2 The Virgin of Guadalupe provides comfort—faded, peeling and sharing a sun-bleached wall with graffiti tags in El Centro, California.

his belt. "I've done my share of killing and I do not take any pleasure or pride in it. If you do, leave." About controlling suspects, he teaches, "If you don't intend to shoot him that instant, keep your finger off that trigger."

"We need the revolution in this country," Storm tells me after the class, frustrated about "my government that precludes me from fighting these Mexicans" (Figure 12.2).

Another Porous Borderline

One of the places where those Mexicans that Storm wants to fight come across the border is at Naco on the Arizona Sonora border. I'm in the Gay 90's Bar. You can't get any closer to Mexico: the parking lot is right on the border. Pool balls are smashing as I chat with the owner of the bar and dance hall. Lionel Urcadez was born and raised in Naco, on the U.S. side.

The wall of corrugated metal on the far side of the Gay 90's parking lot is not dressed up to hide its utilitarian purpose. It's a nasty-looking slab of a barrier, lined with lights and cameras. It is impossible not to compare it with the harshness of the Berlin Wall. Except, of course, that the U.S. wall is designed to keep them out, not keep East Germans in. Just as was the case in Berlin, though, it doesn't work. Lionel Urcadez sees the failure every night from his bar's southside doors.

"The border wall hasn't stopped anything," Urcadez tells me. "It doesn't do any good at all. They just jump the wall." The migrants put steps on the Mexican side to climb up the wall, then use ropes to lower themselves into the United States. "It's a complete waste of money, the Border Patrol. I've never heard someone from Mexico say, 'It's too rough. I can't get across.' They get across. I've seen people who get caught ten times. But still they keep trying, keep trying until they get across."

Directly across the street from the Urcadez saloon is the official port of entry for the United States. But the proximity of the government office does little to deter migration.

Right there where the border station is where most of the people come through. Every night. There is not one night when we are closing up that they're not jumping the fence and coming through. You can watch them. Sometimes the Border Patrol is right there in the middle of the street and they're just running past them. They chase them. But they get away. Every night. Every single night.

Urcadez appreciates the frustrations of ranchers and other property owners along the border. "I get mad when they come through here. They come in my bar. Then the Border Patrol comes in and disrupts my business. That happens almost every day. It's harassment." With all their cameras and manpower, Urcadez figures the Border Patrol should be able to do their job without busting into his bar.

More work visas for Mexicans is the obvious solution, says Urcadez. "I can't get anybody to work," he reports about finding legal local labor. "People don't want to work. These people come to work. They'll work twelve hours a day and work seven days a week. They want to make

money so they can go back home. It's hard to get good help to work."
The migrants he sees are passive, scared and no threat. To Urcadez these
are tragic, desperate people being taken advantage of on both sides of
the border.

A statue of the revolutionary priest Miguel Hidalgo y Costilla
dominates the main drag in Naco, Mexico—Hidalgo breaking a chain,
one broken link in his outstretched right clenched fist, in his lowered
left hand the rest of the chain far from the broken link. I watched a stray
dog forage for scraps in the gutter, unconcerned about the passing cars
just missing him.

I crossed back through the elegant adobe-style U.S. border station
where the bored solo customs agent on duty looked up from his super-
market tabloid to ask, "You an American citizen?"

"Yup."

"Okay."

This marked the first time I ever crossed a U.S. frontier without
showing identification. I looked at his newspaper.

"Studying for the lieutenant's exam?" I asked, pointing to the tabloid.
He laughed.

A look later at the Police Beat column in the *Bisbee Observer* was a
reminder of how easy it was to get across the border, and that migrants
without documents can't let their guard down until they are far north
of the line.

February 6—Bisbee police reported undocumented aliens on Mill Road
and turned them over to the Border Patrol. February 8—Bisbee police
reported four undocumented aliens on Warren Cutoff Road and turned
them over to the Border Patrol. Bisbee police reported 20 undocumented aliens near the Bisbee overlook and turned them over to the
Border Patrol. Their vehicle was impounded. February 9—Bisbee police
reported three undocumented aliens in front of the Anniversary Home
and turned them over to the Border Patrol. February 10—Bisbee police
reported two undocumented aliens on Mill Road and turned them over
to the Border Patrol.[6]

Real Justice versus a Vigilante

Despite the missteps of Chris Simcox and other vigilantes on the border, the official response suggests little worry. "I've seen a lot more concern expressed about what these groups could do or might do as opposed to anything that they actually have done." Russell Ahr told me when he was the special assistant to the Immigration and Naturalization Service Arizona and Nevada district director. He all but endorsed the vigilantes. "My understanding is that these groups engage in patrol activity. They drive around and attempt to spot groups entering. They try to communicate with the Border Patrol to alert them about groups that they might otherwise not be aware of." Nothing illegal about that, says Ahr. He suggests Simcox and others study regulations carefully when they patrol public lands while armed because of the varying rules regarding firearms and that they know they must get permission to patrol on private property. But he understands the concern for self-defense, telling me his officers are finding more and more people smugglers resorting to the practice common among drug smugglers of protecting their illicit businesses with potent firearms.

"If I'm understanding you correctly," I say to Ahr, "you guys don't mind and maybe you're even glad these private patrols are there."

"I didn't say that," he protested. "We don't support anyone undertaking any activity that is illegal. But by the same token we don't oppose anyone engaging in any activity that is legal."

"Are you glad that they're there?"

"Personally?" he asks.

Yeah. I'll be frank with you. I'm afraid they may encounter some circumstances they're not prepared to deal with. I'm a little concerned if they end up encountering an armed group either of narcotics traffickers or alien-smugglers. The Border Patrol will tell you there have been occasions when they run into groups that may have an advantage firepower-wise over the agents themselves. That's got a real potential for tragedy. These groups haven't shown much reluctance to fire at federal agents so I'd really be amazed if they'd show reluctance to firing at people who are not in uniform.

One vigilante who won't be back on the border anytime soon is Chris Simcox. In 2016 he was sentenced to nineteen and a half years in Arizona State Prison.[7] The mother of the little girl he was convicted of molesting told reporters after the guilty verdict, "This conviction is for all of the children he hurt," adding, "I hope he meets karma in prison."[8]

Law and Order

If the lawlessness along our southern border is breeding the beginnings of a homegrown American-style fascism among some border dwellers, at least for now it's a less ugly than the murderous border wars roiling Old Europe. But Washington ignores its responsibilities to maintain order on the border at great peril. Valid arguments can be made for militarizing the border and tightly controlling all movement across it. Valid arguments also can be made for legalizing the cross-border trips of Mexicans who want to come north and take the jobs American employers urgently need filled. But there is no good argument for maintaining the status quo: a lawless and dangerous frontier attracting desperate migrants, lined with frustrated residents tempted to take the law into their own hands.

Further fodder for the debate comes from the words of comic Rene Sandoval who feigned confusion regarding those fighting to deny education and health care to migrants during the campaign for Proposition 187, the California referendum struck down by the courts as unconstitutional. "They love our food, our music and our culture," Sandoval said. "They love everything about us—except us!"[9]

UNITED STATES OF
AMERICA

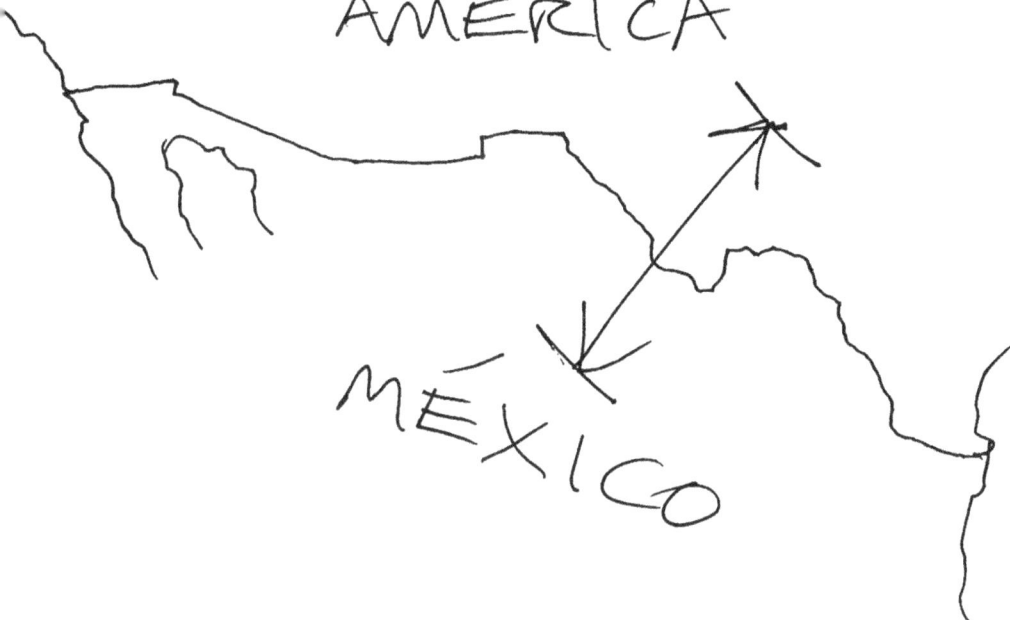

MEXICO

Chapter 13

AMERICANS PARTY SOUTH, MEXICANS STRUGGLE NORTH

O n the volatile border with Mexico, the heavy traffic goes both directions. Mexicans struggle north for jobs, desperately searching for survival work—usually underpaid and often taken advantage of, they labor for food and shelter and a few extra dollars to send home to extended families. At the same time, wealthy—or at least wealthy by comparison—Americans hurl themselves south, seeking recreation, renewal and fulfillment—a spiritual and leisure regeneration too often elusive for them during their driven routines back home. And usually it's a sanitized vacation, segregated in touristic enclaves from the realities of daily Mexico routines.

At the same time the cruise ships dock at Ensenada and planes land at Cancun, Manuel is making his third trip north—illegally—across the Mexican border and into the United States.

Manuel is in his late thirties when we first meet. He is a round-looking man, still boyish with an open, ready grin under a mustache that looks stereotypically Mexican. We sit and talk in the kitchen of one of his employers as he eats a burrito lunch. He works as a day laborer, traveling between his adopted work home of Marin County, California, and his family home in Sinaloa, Mexico.

This day he's cleaning out a backyard, loading old fence poles into a truck, preparing a garden. His yellow T-shirt is dirty from the work, so are his running shoes and his jeans. Back home in Mexico, Manuel earned his money performing stoop labor on local farms. The most he could manage to make was about five dollars a day. The simple economics of the job market drives him north.

On this last trip north—well before the Trump era and his wall, before post-9/11 border hardening—he picked Nogales as a crossing point "because there are so many Latinos living on the Arizona side." He's proud of the fact that this time, for the first time, he didn't need to pay a *coyote* to help him cross the frontier. He's an old hand now himself; he knows the ropes. "I must be watching all the time," he says in Spanish between bites of tortilla, "so I'm not grabbed by the *migra*." He's serious as he talks about the Nogales crossing. "It was cold and raining. I just walked across in the middle of town. No one stopped me." Manuel hitched a ride up to Phoenix where he hopped on an airplane to San Francisco and with a contented smile figures that the total elapsed illegal travel time from Mexico back to Marin County was about five hours.

His two earlier trips were not so easy. For the first Manuel paid a *coyote* $55 to hide him in a van that passed through the Tijuana checkpoint, its dozen or so undocumented passengers undetected by overworked and overwhelmed U.S. border guards. The passengers all jumped out near San Clemente, where the Border Patrol maintains a secondary checkpoint. "We ran into the brush and put a dark blanket over ourselves. When we felt it was safe we started walking north." A car stopped and a woman offered Manuel a ride up into Los Angeles for $30 dollars—there's plenty of ad hoc money to be earned throughout the borderlands. He grabbed the chance, spent the night at her house, and started working the next day.

"We were making fiberglass molds for ceiling tiles," he says. A friend from Sinoloa found him the job. It was piecework. He made five dollars for each mold he finished. But he could crank out as many as a dozen a day. From there he made his way to better working conditions at a factory producing fiberglass pipe. Eventually he quit that work and headed up to the San Francisco Bay Area where friends and relatives already lived. He found work painting apartments for eight dollars an hour.

After several months he saved almost $2,000 and sent most of it home to Sinaloa so his six brothers and sisters could join him in California. At Christmas time, Manuel went home for a visit, stayed a week and paid another *coyote* $300 to help him back across the border. "Again we were placed in a packed van." They crossed at Tijuana. "When the border agents are changing shift, they are not paying as much attention."

Why did he rush back to California after only a week? "There was no work at home." And home it continues to be for Manuel, even though he's spent most of the last three years in California. "I am a Mexican, but I am in the north. I don't feel like a *pocho* [...]"—a Gringo-tainted Mexican who has lost his sense of being a Mexican.

Manuel hoped to study at a university in his earlier years. He finished secondary school and two years of college preparatory work but then lacked enough money to continue. "I feel I lost a chance at a better-paying profession," he now says. During his last trip south, his father died. "It's all my responsibility now," he says of his mother and the house his father left behind.

The Sinoloa house still suffers from a dirt floor kitchen, is equipped with just an outhouse and needs plenty of other work. So Manuel labors in California and sends money south, money known in Mexico by the

Spanglish word *migradollars*. The brothers and sisters are back home, the undocumented life in California not to their liking.

Some half dozen years after that lunchtime interview with Manuel my phone rings. It's Christmastime 2003, and an excited Manuel is on the line. He's celebrating in California with his wife and their two children. "It is the best Christmas present!" he tells me. The three of them managed to get visas to the United States, and joined him the night before Christmas Eve. A few days later we all met at a local Starbucks. Manuel is rounder—he pats his belly and laughs—but retains his baby-faced look. His smile is permanent as he introduces his 8-year-old daughter and 9-year-old son, both of them shy and equipped with barely a word of English. They sit quietly while we talk, eating sweets and looking angelic.

While his wife and the children are in the United States legally, Manuel is still without papers. He all but shouts, "¡Soy el Ilegal Fuerte!" I am the Strong Illegal! We agree to meet again in a few days to talk about the changes in his life. This time it will be at the local Chevys, the Americanized Mexican restaurant chain developed by PepsiCo.

Mexican music is blaring when we get together after the New Year at Chevys, and we find a booth over in a far corner of the dining room, searching for a place where we can hear each other talk. The place is filled with both Latino and Anglo families, the waiters and waitresses easily slipping back and forth between English and Spanish, as needed. We're hundreds of miles north of the border. Manuel has been back and forth three or four times in the last several years. "It was terrible," he says. "I was caught by the *migra*, two or three times. They caught me and I was in jail until the next day when they kicked me out. The first time was in Agua Prieta, the second time was in Nogales." His travel route was dictated by the Southwest Border Strategy, when the border controls were buttressed in California and Texas, choking much of the illegal trafficking of Mexicans up to the Arizona-Sonora desert frontier. There the self-appointed vigilantes patrolled on the north side to combine with harsh weather and the Border Patrol as a barrier to entry into the United States.

"We crossed during the afternoon," Manuel says about the Agua Prieta escapade. "Later, when the sun was going down, we walked the whole night, until dawn, about five or six in the morning—more than twenty miles."

"You climbed over the fence?"

"That's right, we climbed over the fence and then walked through the *Cañón del Diablo*. In the morning, at the rising of the sun, is when we were caught by the *migra*. We were really tired." He says they were bruised raw by the chaffing of their clothes against their legs; their feet were blistered. When the Border Patrol showed up, Manuel says he and the group of about a dozen fellow travelers from his hometown weren't afraid. They were so tired that they were relieved. "There were a lot of poisonous animals. Snakes. It was really cold. During the night it was really cold. We had to walk in order to keep our bodies warm. We were really tired. The *migra* told us, 'You guys sit down!' And we said, '*Gracias*. Thank you very much!'"

The Border Patrol officers took Manuel and his compatriots back to the border where, he told me, they were forced to agree to accept so-called voluntary deportation. Manuel signed the required paperwork. He was photographed and fingerprinted. And then he jumped the border once again. "Of course," he says—a necessary part of doing business. He was caught and deported a second time before successfully running the gauntlet and returning to his work in northern California.

"Finally, the third time I got here. That time it was harder," he says. He and his colleagues headed north without a guide, confident that their own experience would serve them as well as a *coyote*. "We had to walk the whole night, and then the next day the whole day we walked through the rivers and streams. The whole night, the whole day. We arrived really tired in the evening and we slept." Where they arrived was still out in the middle of nowhere: the Arizona desert. But it was far enough north that they felt it safe to rest. "We were so tired we simply collapsed without eating. We woke up because the sun was so hot. We were hungry, thirsty." Help came from the original Arizonans, local Native Americans, who gave them water and offered them a ride out of the desert. "They drove us to the Phoenix airport. Just to be driven from Papago territory up to Phoenix we had to pay $400 or $500 each."

Tribal Divides

Papago was the name the Spanish gave to the Tohono O'odham, whose lands extend throughout the Sonora Desert across the arbitrary borderline that separates the Mexican state Sonora from its neighbor, the American state Arizona. The Tohono O'odham nation opposes the Trump wall across their territory. Tribe leaders say construction jeopardizes burial and other cultural sites that date back some ten thousand years while it bifurcates tribal communities.[1]

Across the Southwest the border barrier impedes the movement not just of people but of migratory animals. The native ranges of threatened and endangered species, such as jaguars, ocelots, Gila monsters and the Sonoran pronghorn antelope, are blocked by a wall that stops wildlife but is breached by migrants.[2] Another unintended consequence of the wall builders: in some locales the pragmatic route of the barrier is determined by topography, bizarrely leaving U.S. territory on the south side of the border wall—ranches, wildlife preserves and private homes.

Landowners with property in the path of the proposed Trump wall who do not want to sell their holdings fought eminent domain demands from the government, legal proceedings that added to delays plaguing the project.

No More Commuting

Manuel was making his arduous commute in order to visit his wife and children in Sinaloa, and he's had enough. "Now I don't want to go back." The hardened border turned Manuel into a permanent U.S. resident. When his family arrived two days before Christmas, they had been separated for the two years following the 9/11 attacks. His wife and two children arrived in the United States on six-month tourist visas, arranged for by one of Manuel's employers. Manuel smiles. "But I don't think they're going back there. The kids are in school."

Manuel's immigration status, of course, was still undocumented. But he acts fearless.

No, I don't have papers. But if the INS kicks me out, I can always find my way back here. Not my family. That's different. I don't want my wife and my kids to do that because it is very, very dangerous. There are rapes. There are a lot of bad people all around. There are people who take the wives from the husbands at the time they are crossing, just to rape them. That's the reason they separate the wives from the husbands when they are crossing the border. It's terrible. They take your money. But I can do it myself. I don't have a passport. But I am here. What do I need a passport for? I am the one who has to work. And I work here.

He sounds like the character in *The Treasure of the Sierra Madre* who famously jeers at Humphrey Bogart, "Badges? We ain't got no badges. We don't need no badges. I don't have to show you any stinking badges." It's a crazy situation, a crazy life he's been leading, I suggest.

"Give us a work permit," is Manuel's answer to the border wars. He says the powerful drug and immigrant traffickers do not want such a solution because an end to the chaos on the border would be bad for their business. "We found forty pounds of marijuana packed along our path. One of my friends got it and hid it. He marked where he hid it. He and his father went back to get his stash and moved it over to Phoenix to do the business." That forty pounds of marijuana was worth much more than the price of the two-hour ride in the Tohono O'odham Good Samaritan/entrepreneur's car. "On the border you really get a lot of corruption. And things are getting worse. That's why I don't want to go back. I want to stay at least five years here without going back home."

But Manuel's mother is still in Sinaloa, and he expects he'll make more clandestine trips south, insisting he's *el Ilegal Fuerte*, and unafraid. "If they kick me out, I'll get back here. I know how. I have to do it. I have to work." By this time his hourly rate was up to $25, and he's complaining about new immigrants from Mexico and Central America working for far less money, endangering his flush pay scale.

The cheery bilingual waiters and waitresses at Chevys are singing a Spanglish version of Happy Birthday to a customer a few tables from us, while Manuel paints a picture of the misery and desperation he's seen along the frontier.

So what are you now, I ask him, a Mexican or Gringo?

"Both. Because I have to spend part of my life down there and part of my life up here. I like it here and I like it down there. I have friends here and I have friends down there. Part of my family is down there and I have family up here." He gestures to his daughter and son, happily drawing with crayons in Chevy's coloring books.

I want them to study here now, so they realize what life is all about. I want them to know what it means to be here, so they are not being told what the United States is like. I want them to know what life is here and also down there. Then they will have an opportunity to figure out for themselves where they want to live. They can take more advantage of what's available here than I can, because I am older.

We're speaking Spanish; Manuel speaks minimal English. "They're going to speak both languages, so they can figure out both sides."

So Manuel has one foot in Mexico and the other in *El Norte.* "That's right," he readily agrees,

with the border right between my legs, right. But that's not going to change. Who is going to change it? These presidents, Fox and Bush? When Fox comes here he comes to just wander around and have a good time. When Fox took office he said that he was going to fix the problem. How many years have already passed! He cannot even fix the problems in Mexico. How can he fix the problems up here?

We move over to the table with his family, order quesadillas and burritos, wine and tequila. A waitress brings ice cream for the children and Manuel's little boy tells me in school this day he's learned how to say "yellow" and "blue" in English.

Chapter 14

THE POROUS, SHIFTING BORDER

"*Joven! Joven!*" the Mexico City cop called out to me, motioning me to pull over where he had already stopped another car. I would have kept going, but the light was red for me and traffic blocked my path.

"You didn't signal left," he announced. I told him I knew I had, in fact, signaled. He ignored me, pulled out his ticket book and gave me a quick lesson in bribery.

"You want to take care of this right now?" he asked, after writing "1500 pesos" on the back of a ticket blank (while holding my driver's license and passport for the ransom). The alternative was to follow him to the station house.

"I don't have that much," I told him, and I didn't—in Mexican cash. "How much do you have?"

I asked Sheila to look for some money knowing she kept her pesos in a separate purse and that she was carrying only a few hundred. She pulled out two hundred and I passed it to the cop.

"More," he said. Sheila fished deeper in her purse and came up with another fifty. "That's all we have," I told him as he relieved me of the money.

"Put your seat belt on," he ordered as he handed back my papers and waved us off, pocketing our money.

Workers throughout Mexico rely on such bribes for survival. Corruption pervades the government, corruption used to obtain and maintain power. Toughs and their gangs extort protection payments from businesses. Drug traffickers exacerbate the ongoing crisis with their easy access to phenomenal amounts of cash. The dysfunctional Mexican economy is the prime force that pushes migrants north working in ballet-like precision with the pull of *El Norte* economy's lust for cheap labor.

Bribery 101

Cruising south on Interstate 5 in San Diego in the silver Chevy Malibu I rented from Avis at the airport, my immediate destination was Tijuana, across the busiest frontier in the world. Tijuana brags about itself as "The World's Most Visited City."

At the U.S.-Mexico border the First World meets the Third World face to face across an artificial boundary. It's because this man-made delineation remains so porous that, even after the events of 9/11, most clever and determined Mexicans (or other non-U.S. citizens) could make their way illegally over the line and into the United States. The result of this continuing migration is a border that manifests itself in a variety of forms far north of the actual international boundary.

The car-renting experience is one example. Few U.S. companies allow their cars south of the border. Avis allowed such travel, for an extra 24 dollars a day in insurance charges. The insurance comes with a booklet titled, *How to Handle an Accident in Mexico*.[1] Except this brochure fails to report some critical news. "If there are injuries in any vehicle involved [in an accident]," it instructs, "you and the adjuster may be asked to accompany the police to the precinct house."

As a matter of fact, if there are injuries, all drivers involved in the accident might well be arrested and kept locked in jail until the cause of the accident is determined.

The booklet continues, "The adjuster will handle all details with the police." Well, he or she may well do that. But note that the booklet does not suggest how long it may take to handle those details. Meanwhile, the drivers can languish in jail.

Avis also provides renters with a handy bilingual booklet called *Tourist Guide Tijuana*, published by the Tijuana Tourism Board.[2] On a page headlined, "Recommendations for Visitors," it advises, "No police officer is authorized to receive money." Of course not. That could be considered a bribe and would be against the law. But most motorists experienced traveling in Mexico would probably agree that it is naïve to consider—even since the reforms of the Fox Administration—that a deftly placed peso note no longer works to alleviate problems with the law.

A better source than Avis is Carl Franz's classic, *The People's Guide to Mexico*. Franz offers this advice: "Even though Mexicans claim that the *mordida* (the bite) no longer exists or that it is unnecessary, we have found it alive and working quite well in all parts of the country. I have given 'considerations' to everyone from post office workers who couldn't seem to remember my name to border officials who didn't like my looks."[3]

Franz offers a practical guide to the *mordida*.

You don't bribe someone by stuffing a wad of bills in his pocket and saying, "Here ya go baby, a little something for the wife and kids!" There are more subtle and respectable techniques used to feel out the other person on their attitude and price. The easiest of these for the inexperienced person to adopt is the, "Gee whiz, I sure wish you'd tell me what to do" angle. Other effective openers to the pay-off are: "Is there any way this can be worked out?," "Will there be an extra charge?," and the national favorite, "Is there any other way of arranging the matter?"

News you can use, despite the posters that papered Mexico City featuring an apple and the legend: *Por un México íntegro, ya no más mordidas*. For a Mexico with integrity, now no more bribes.

I pull off Interstate 5 and park the rented Chevy on the U.S. side. I want to experience the walk into Tijuana again. At the time there was no overt immigration control for those of us heading south by foot at the world's busiest international border crossing, just the incessant click-click, clatter-clatter of the one-way turnstile rattling against the mechanical device that makes walking through it northbound impossible. The foot traffic continues past the Mexican customs office and the sign indicating a required stop for those traveling with taxable goods.

Ha!

A lone customs officer sits out front sipping a soda, watching without expression the constant flow of people past customs. No one is stopping to declare "taxable goods" and he's inspecting no one. Just before the business district, a couple of border guards with machine guns strapped over their shoulders chat with each other. The sun is setting through the golden smog. (When I took the same walk a few years later, in 2017, the passage into Mexico required a quick stop for a tourist visa.)

The first sign I see is huge: "CIPRO," it yells, offering for cut-rate prices what the drug store claims is a generic version of the anti-anthrax drug.

I walk on toward Avenida Revolución, Tijuana's main street, past Club Fetish.

"Hey, *amigo*," calls out the barker. "Hey, professor!" It must be my beard. "Check it out. Nice looking girls. Naked."

I've only been in Tijuana a few minutes and I've already received some basic news about drugs and sex: both easily available. It reminds me of the popular Manu Chao song lyrics: "Welcome to Tijuana: tequila, *sexo*, marijuana." It's a catchy tune that ends with a blast of machine gun fire and the sound of an eerie empty wind.

I walk on, up on the pedestrian bridge over the Tijuana River—a concrete culvert as wide and as flat as the I-5 freeway, with a foamy brown trickle down the middle. A little girl sits with a plastic cup in front of her, squeezing random chords out of a toy accordion and singing out with great gusto an atonal, "Ahhhahhh! Oooh!" She manages to collect a few coins.

Football stadium–type lights shine from the U.S. side on the Berlin Wall–like barrier that's been forcing illegal crossings eastward into the deadly heat of the desert. The lights are a visible landmark at dusk from Avenida Revolución, the strip already throbbing before dark with blaring techno music.

Try as some might in Tijuana, the border town can't lose its reputation as a sin city.

"I've got the camera ready, señor!" says the photographer working with Pepe, the Zebra-stripe-painted donkey. Nearby is a sign in English: "Welcome to Tijuana. You can be arrested for immoral conduct. For more information visit or call us." It's signed, Baja California Secretary of Tourism.

Sometimes it's the Tijuana police who are arrested for immoral conduct, perpetrated against naïve or unlucky gringos.

"I feel lucky to be alive," Ron Terwilliger told *San Diego Union* reporter Sandra Dibble after he made a shopping trip across the border. He said he was handcuffed by police, threatened with a gun and forced to withdraw money from his bank at a Tijuana ATM before finally being released from custody. Tijuana officials acknowledge that corruption continues among some police, and they insist they will prosecute officers who take advantage of Americans if the U.S. citizens will cross back to Mexico and testify against them.[4]

Dianna Murray came forward and announced herself as a victim of the Tijuana police after reading that she was not the only American to suffer at their hands. She says she was raped by two Tijuana policemen after a minor traffic accident, raped "right on the street," within sight of the U.S. border, and left on the curb bleeding. "They laughed a lot," she said of her assailants. Another woman reported to California police that after she and her boyfriend complained about a restaurant bill, a waiter called police. She says she was taken to a hotel, handcuffed to a bed and raped by four officers. Still another woman was stopped after using a script from the United States to buy a prescription drug at a Tijuana pharmacy. She says she was raped by four policemen, one of them a supervisor in a division of Tijuana's police department that specializes in providing help for tourists. He was arrested, jailed and charged with the rape.[5]

Journalists in the Crosshairs

Just as border-created problems are not confined to the borderlands but reach throughout the 50 States, so do they stretch south throughout Mexico. Crooked cops and institutionalized bribery remain endemic, despite the promises of reforms. The corruption is especially problematic regarding the news media in a Mexican society in transition, a society trying to redefine itself as at least an emerging democracy. As long as the news media are targets of intimidation, abuse and bribery, the economic crises that drive migrants north will likely persist. Mexico remains one of the most dangerous places in the world to practice journalism. Scores of reporters have been killed in recent years, the murderers silencing their victims and enjoying impunity. Threats to journalists understandably lead to self-censorship. The result too often is a void of news about the perpetrators of heinous crimes.[6]

My first Tijuana appointment this trip is scheduled with the cofounder and codirector of the crusading weekly *Zeta* (slogan: "Free like the wind."), J. Jesús Blancornelas. In 1997, Blancornelas was the victim of a vicious assassination attempt that left him permanently injured, and killed his bodyguard. As he tells the story, his car was cut off in the

Tijuana traffic by gunmen who pumped over one hundred rounds into it. Seeking cover as soon as the shooting started, Blancornelas managed to avoid all but four of the shots, one of which just missed his spine. He spent a month hospitalized, more time recovering at his home, and finally returned to work.

But the attack on Jesús Blancornelas was not the first attempt to silence *Zeta*. His partner, the paper's cofounder Héctor Félix Miranda, was murdered in 1988. Neither shooting slowed down the crusading reporting *Zeta* was famous for, on the contrary. Instead the paper and Blancornelas became examples of a new type of Mexican journalism: investigative and courageous. He won international reporting awards until his death from stomach cancer in 2006; *Zeta* continues its crusading work.

Zeta's offices are south of the Tijuana tourist strip, in a residential neighborhood. A tiny sign identifies it, but the building is easy to spot: a long Mexican military Chevrolet SUV, with smoked windows and a telltale communications antenna on the roof, is parked out front. Across the street sit two old Ford sedans, plainclothes guards waiting and watching inside.

In the compact courtyard of the house that's been converted into *Zeta*'s headquarters, two plainclothes "greeters" confront me with a casual, *"Buenos días."* One of them makes a practiced parting of his jacket front to clearly display the automatic pistol stuffed into the waistband of his trousers.

"You here to see Blancornelas?" one asks. They seem to know of my appointment, and let me pass.

In the small waiting room I sat by a photograph labeled "Luis L. Valero E. 1959–1997," the bodyguard murdered. I'm told Blancornelas is delayed.

Zeta was founded in 1980 and quickly gained a reputation for disclosing Mexican government corruption and reporting on the activities of drug traffickers. These investigative stories were a surprise for Tijuana readers accustomed to government corruption and drug trafficking being glossed over in most papers. Cash payoffs to publishers and their reporters—in the form of government advertising (de facto subsidies with implied editorial influence) or outright bribes—long kept most Mexican papers filled with celebrity gossip, violent street crime news and bland political coverage that was little more than the official ruling-party line.

The sprawl of Tijuana—from the tourist traps downtown to the *maquiladoras* luring factory workers up from the interior, to the squalor of its slums, to a burgeoning art scene, to the never-ending border stories—is a mix resulting in a vibrant news town. *Zeta* made its pages come alive with the details inside that sprawl, providing a tribune for politicians and covering the illegal drug scene infesting the borderlands.

After a long wait, I'm told my meeting with Blancornelas must be postponed. He's still behind closed doors and won't be available as scheduled. I find out why a few days later when the next issue of *Zeta* hits the streets. Blancornelas's byline is trumpeted throughout the paper over articles about the presumed shooting death of one of Tijuana's most feared drug smugglers, Ramón Arellano Félix. Blancornelas had been working the story in meetings with Mexican and U.S. authorities and other sources while I was waiting for our delayed interview. The photographs in the paper of a cadaver reputed to be Ramón are gory, reminiscent of the New York tabloids in the thirties and forties, a drool of blood flowing from his open mouth. This is big news along the border, where prominently placed wanted posters on both sides offer a $2-million reward from the U.S. government for each of the notorious Arellano brothers. At about the same time Ramón was killed, the other brother, Benjamín, finally was arrested. Blancornelas believes it was the Arellano brothers who hired the gunmen who attacked him in 1997.

A few weeks later I return to Tijuana and am warmly received at *Zeta* by Jesús Blancornelas. Dressed in a black leather jacket, white slacks and a sports shirt, he is relaxed and pleased to take some time to philosophize about his career, Mexican journalism and the border. His closely trimmed gray beard and gray hair, and his black frame glasses, add a professorial touch to his appearance.

Blancornelas says his paper's troubles with the Arellanos began when *Zeta* published a letter from the mother of a trafficker allegedly killed by Ramón Arellano. In the letter, the mother called Ramón Arellano a coward. "We published the whole letter, publicly telling him he was a coward. He got mad and came against us."

Zeta now is an armed camp. He says his notoriety works to his paper's benefit because it attracts important sources. "The protection came after the attack. The fact that I am in this office without the freedom to go out in the field results in more people coming to me with information. The only thing that the Mexican media needs in order to gain credibility is to tell the truth. Nothing else."

Credibility, maybe. Security, no. For that, the impunity long enjoyed by those who intimidate, assault and assassinate Mexican journalists must end. In early summer 2004, another *Zeta* editor and investigative reporter was gunned down in a Tijuana street. Francisco Ortiz Franco was murdered as he sat in his car with his two children. A blatant example of the result of such attacks and the resulting impunity for the killers was the screaming last headline in 2017 of the Ciudad Juárez newspaper *Norte*. "*Adios*" was its one-word message, followed by a final editorial signed by A. Cantú Murguía:

> Today, dear reader, I am speaking to you to inform you that I have decided to close this daily because the guarantee for the safety for us to continue journalism does not exist. Everything in life has a beginning and an end, a price to pay. If this is what life is like, I am not ready for one more of my collaborators to pay for it and I am not either.

Six journalists were killed that year in Mexico and 14 went missing.

Jesús Blancornelas says that in addition to its aggressive reporting, *Zeta* rejects *gacetillas*, those press releases disguised as news stories that are so common in Mexican papers, press releases not identified as the paid-for-advertisements they are, often placed by government agencies. The income from *gacetillas* historically forces newspapers into a compromised position of dependency on the government, since the government can yank these pricey ads from any paper that fails to fill its news pages with content acceptable to government media manipulators. This policy of rejecting *gacetillas*, says Blancornelas, costs *Zeta* a great deal of lost revenue.

As we were saying our good-byes, I ask J. Jesús Blancornelas if he is a role model. "No, no, no, no," he insists. "There are no role models except the truth. The truth is the role model."

Fluid Border

Carlos Fuentes deals with the fluidity of the border and the exchange of information across it in his novel, *The Crystal Frontier*. A character named José Francisco is stopped at the border on his motorcycle.

> José Francisco brought Chicano manuscripts to Mexico and Mexican manuscripts to Texas. The bike was the means to carry the written word rapidly from one side to the other, that was José Francisco's contraband, literature from both sides so that everyone would get to know one another better, he said, so that everyone would love one another a little more, so there would be a "we" on both sides of the border.
> "What are you carrying in your saddlebags?"
> "Writing."
> "Political stuff?"
> "All writing is political."
> "So it's subversive."
> "All writing is subversive."
> "What are you talking about?" "About the fact that lack of communication is a bitch. That anyone who can't communicate feels inferior. That keeping silent will screw you up."[7]

Cash for the Taking

Atzimba Romero rushes over between assignments from her newsroom on the south side of Mexico City to meet me in a glitzy bookstore and coffee shop in the posh southern California-style shopping center Perisur. She's youthful, intense and anxious to tell her story.

It was the seventy-eighth anniversary of the founding of the Mexican railroad union, an important event on the Mexico City news calendar. At the ceremony to mark the occasion were the labor minister, the railroad owners and officials from the union. "Lots of reporters were there," Romero tells me, "Perhaps because they knew it was payoff day."

This is not a memoir of scandal-ridden days of Mexico's long-ago past, but a report from early 2002, when Romero worked as a reporter at TV Azteca. This is not a report from the impoverished and marginalized provinces, but from urbane Mexico City.

After the formal ceremony reporters had an opportunity to obtain comments from union leaders. The reporters then were invited into an anteroom at the union headquarters. "The cameramen and the cameras were ordered out," Romero says, "and the door was closed. Another door opened. I was nervous. What was going on?"

The railroad union was not Romero's beat. The regular union beat reporter was ill that day, and the assignment desk sent her to fill in for the celebration story.

After the second door opened, the reporters lined up.

"I kept asking, 'What the fuck is going on?'"

"A man, a Televisa reporter, said, 'Little girl, stop asking. We're going to get our payoffs. It's embarrassing, but we're going to get our *chayo* [a Mexican fruit and the slang word for bribe commonly used in journalism].'"

"Then it was my turn," Romero continues, "and I came up to a short man who was handing out envelopes. He gave me the stapled envelope and I said, 'What is this?'"

"He was very surprised and upset and insisted I take it and leave. I said, 'Don't mess with me!' I threw it in his face."

"I left really upset and a reporter for *Reforma* came up to me and said, 'We are the only two who did not take the money.'[8] He told me he was going to run a story about the bribing the next day, but he needed to know how much was in the envelopes."

Romero said she found the Televisa reporter who had suggested she just take the money and approached him with a microphone but no camera.

"I asked, 'Señor, how much did you receive in that envelope?'"

"The only reason he did not beat the crap out of me is because there were so many people there."

"He asked me, 'Why didn't you take it? You could have given it to your crew.'"

"I asked, 'Did you take it?'"

"He said with a shrug to suggest the answer was obvious, '¡Sí!'"

"I said, 'You make me sad. I'm embarrassed for you.' And I left."

Reporter Romero got into her company car with her crew and they left the union building. About twenty minutes later, she says, while they were still on their way back to TV Azteca's studios, the dispatcher called on the mobile phone and told her that the reporter who usually covered the railroad union beat wanted to talk with her cameraman. The dispatcher told her to put the cameraman on the line and that she would patch through the call from the beat reporter. The cameraman talked for over twenty minutes, she tells me.

"When we arrived back at the station, the cameraman asked, 'What are you going to do?' He told me it wasn't really the beat reporter who was on the phone, but someone who told him, 'You don't know me, but I am the person in charge so that everything goes smoothly at the union.'"

Atzimba Romero told me she thinks the cameraman does know whom he was talking with at the union and that he was threatened or pressured. The cameraman warned her. "If you say anything," he told her, "all the reporters who took the money will be against you and say it's not true." He told her it happens every day in Mexico and there is nothing she can do about it.

"The cameraman was so insistent that I realized he was scared."

She kept asking him where the money came from. Did it come from the labor minister or the union? "He told me, 'Please do it for me because I have a labor related problem and they're helping me at the Labor Department.'"

"I told my cameraman, 'Ahah! This is coming from the Labor Minister!' He said, '¡No sé, no sé, no sé!' I don't know, I don't know, I don't know."

Romero decided to bring the matter up with her bosses. She approached the vice president for news, identified the incident as a direct threat and asked what action the company intended to take. She announced that she wished to do a story on the payoffs.

"He congratulated me and told me the network would back me." But no story was broadcast because she did not actually receive any money.

And she feels the effects of her actions on the job. "When I go to news stories now and run into reporters who took the money, I am shunned."

Atzimba Romero is convinced that poor pay is no excuse for taking bribes. "It's not a matter of having money or not. It's values. It's something you have inside. It was so routine, so natural, so part of the day's work for everyone in that line. It can't be a problem of poor people, you can't justify it as poverty in the DF [Mexico City]."

We leave the exclusive shopping center, walking past the armed guards protecting the upper class in their oasis. I take a taxi back to my hotel, across miles of miserable traffic, air so smoggy it seems you could chew on it, and a cityscape that defies routine maintenance: unfinished, crumbling, paint peeling. I pass the fortress-like American embassy and hawkers working the cars stopped for the red lights, hawkers selling such an odd array of unneeded goods: Spider-Man dolls, inflated plastic rackets equipped with balls tied to them with elastic, steak knives, fly swatters. Who impulsively buys their steak knives from a transient vendor at a red light?

Bags of Bribes

Another day in 2002, en route to a meeting with a colleague, I made my way at dawn to the Observatorio bus station on the north side of Mexico City to grab a bite to eat before my first-class bus ride to Morelia. A cheese sandwich on a fresh roll with onions, avocado and refried beans looked good. And coffee. The clerk handed me the sandwich and a cup of hot water. "*No, no. Café con leche,*" I protested. She said, yeah, yeah, and pointed me to the adjacent table where the jar of Nescafé sat with a spoon. "Make it yourself," she instructed. Four hours and two B Hollywood English-language subtitled movies on the shrieking video monitors in the bus later, we had climbed out of Mexico City's smog, up and over conifer-covered mountains into Michoacán and down into its capital, colonial Morelia.

"Call me from Café El Centro just after eleven," Francisco Castellanos told me when I contacted the journalist from Mexico City. I called. No answer. I bought the magazine he writes for, *Proceso*, ordered a coffee and orange juice, waited and read. I called again. No answer.

I decided I better sit back and relax. I looked at the cathedral. I ordered breakfast. There was nothing else to do yet. Finally the waitress told me I had a phone call. "Sorry I'm late," Castellanos said, "I'll be right there." At a quarter to one, he showed up, all smiles, sat down and said hello to me and then proceeded to chat up the guy at the next table until finally our appointment started, some two hours late.

We hailed a cab and started talking. As the taxi barreled along the mountain roads, Castellanos regaled me with details of the bribes and payoffs enjoyed by Michoacán reporters, editors and publishers. These payments were often in a form called *convenios* in Spanish, an agreement by politicians to pay the newspapers for publishing notices from the government as a device to funnel money to the papers. Control, or at least great influence, is the understood commodity being purchased by the *convenios*, along with the similar paid copy, *gacetillas*.

Francisco Castellanos punctuates his tales of corruption with specific ideas of what can be done to work to change the endemic problem of tainted news reporters. "What we need here is to have a conscience, because most of my mates are *empíricos*—that is they are self-taught. They are not professionals. They did not study at the university. They just got a press card and automatically they were journalists."

These "journalists" make little money at the papers and hence are susceptible to corruption. "Let's make a comparison. A correspondent for a big newspaper in Mexico City who is working in Michoacán, receives about two hundred U.S. dollars a month. But when you add all the money he gets underground, it totals about eight hundred dollars." In addition to payments from the government, he tells me, the reporters could get payments directly from the political party that controls the government. The Fox government says it will end all these *convenios*," says Castellanos "They say there will be no more corruption. So you can understand why all the journalists are really mad now, because it was their source of income."

Not that every reporter in Michoacán was corrupted by the endemic status quo, says Castellanos. "But only three or four of us who are correspondents here did not take the money, out of more than three hundred journalists in Michoacán who did."

Castellanos says he has been offered overt bribes and payoffs. "But I haven't accepted them. I have been offered bags full of money, I do not know how much." The blatant and insidious nature of the corrupted relationship between government, business and media in Mexico is made clear in one of his examples.

On the holiday *El Día de la Libertad de Expresión* [Free Speech Day!], one official of the government approached us with a big brown bag, like a bag for bread, full of packs of five-hundred-peso bills.

"He told me, 'Here. This is a present from the governor.'"

"I said, 'No thank you, I don't want to have anything.'"

"He said, 'You don't want the governor to be angry with you.'"

I told the guy, "I don't care." I said I was sorry he was going to be mad but I couldn't accept money from the government because I was an independent journalist and I had to write whatever I wanted. If I accepted the money, I would be obligated to say and not say certain things. I was with a *compadre* who is a publisher of two newspapers, one in Apatzingán and one in Uruapan, so they broke the advertising agreements [the *convenios*] with him in order to try to pressure me to accept the money. My friend called me later and said, "*Compadre*, if you don't take the money they'll take the *convenios* out of my newspapers."

But Castellanos tells me he nonetheless refused.

The *mordida*, the bite, is a kind of *ballet folklórico*, engrained in Mexican culture. Author Tom Miller, who made a coast-to-coast trip along the frontier for his book *On the Border: Portraits of America's Southwestern Frontier*, saw it repeatedly.

I wasn't sure of the etiquette in a situation like this. If twenty pesos was not enough he might be insulted. If it was too much I wanted change. Every Mexican official I have ever seen take a *mordida* uses a graceful and smooth motion for grasping and pocketing money. I flicked a twenty-peso bill toward the Juárez cop. In one sweeping motion the bill disappeared in his right hand while his left hand returned my driver's license.[9]

Cultural Indigestion

I found examples of the fluid and extended border during a day of study at a Spanish-language traffic school, where the instructor explained how to avoid police profiling. At the traffic school, hundreds of miles up into California from the border, I was the only gringo in attendance. I was stopped for an illegal U turn in downtown Santa Rosa. Since part of my penalty was traffic school, I figured spending the day in a Spanish-language traffic school would at least provide me with a day of language lessons. The instructor overtly announced it as a survival school for Latinos facing an often-offensive dominant culture. He made it clear he was going to provide important news during the day. "Gringolandia is like baseball," he explained, "If you don't understand the system, you're out."

He was specific, calling Republicans hypocrites for advocating state's rights but trying to use state and local governments to enforce immigration laws. He explained how corruption in the United States takes a different form than the Mexican *mordida*, using special-interest big-dollar donations to the Bush campaign as an example.

"Corrupción republicana," he called it.

"Who makes the laws?" he asked, answering, "Special interests who get the ear of politicians with soft money."

This was scarcely the type of traffic school the courts expected.

"Whoever has the money gets to sit on the *burro*," he taught us. The lessons came one after another.

"If you don't have medical insurance they will treat you like a dog in this country. ¡*Hasta la vista, chica!*"

But there is a law requiring emergency medical attention be provided, protested one student.

"Ha," he responded. "They won't give it to you. Try it out!"

More advice: "Watch out in Oakland and L.A. where the cops will go after young men and pretty women for little things."

He explained how the police obtain DMV records when they swipe the computer strip on a driver's license, "So don't lie."

The students, all in the class for the opportunity to remove a violation from their records, paid rapt attention. "Watch out," insisted the lecturer about the propensity of the police to stop Latinos, "they're after you."

This sort of nontraditional news reporting directed at Mexicans far north of the nation's political boundary is an example of the subculture taking care of itself. The traffic school instructor was not out of touch with reality. His classroom was in Novato, California, in Marin County, just north of San Francisco. There, at about the same time, Novato High School senior Andrew Smith was busy on the final draft of an editorial for the school newspaper, an anti-immigrant rant targeting Mexicans.

"The American culture is being disintegrated through this multicultural atmosphere that everyone's trying to push," was Smith's point of view.[10]

If you don't have a country that's strongly based on one type of culture, then there's no glue that will hold it together in a crisis. There are a whole bunch of illegal Mexicans coming over. People come across the border pregnant, have a kid, and now the kid is a burden to the United States because their parents are not able to take care of them. We're just allowing people to take advantage of us. It's going to end up destroying everything that's good here.

Where does Smith learn this rant? He studies at the speakers of his radio, listening to the pantheon of right-wing talk show hosts. One of his favorites is the hate-mongering immigrant basher Michael Savage. "It's a good way to get information," Smith says of the Michael Savage program, "The Savage Nation," a barrage of misinformation, opinion and vitriol. "You don't have to search for it, it's presented to you." Asked if he ever checks on the veracity of what he hears, his response is sad. "I would if I felt the need to. Usually I just listen to what's been said and think it over and discern what I think is true and what I think is false. It helps me form opinions on topics I wouldn't normally have heard about."

In sleepy Rohnert Park, a tract house-filled Sonoma County bedroom community, the president of the local high school's Conservative Club, Tim Bueler, created a long-running crisis with an essay in the club's newspaper assailing undocumented immigrants. The motto of Bueler's club is "Protecting our Borders, Language, and Culture." In his diatribe, Bueler identified migrants without proper paperwork as "unsophisticated, poor and uneducated, who do not in any way hold strong family values." He struck out not only at immigrants, but also at those who disagree with him, saying "liberals welcome every Muhammad, Jamul and Jose who wishes to leave his third world state and come to America—mostly illegally—to rip off our health care system, balkanize our language and destroy our political system."[11]

The assault earned Bueler, who says he also studies at the feet of Michael Savage, a coveted interview with the right-wing former Fox TV star Bill O'Reilly. "I'm going to try to give you some advice," O'Reilly said during the interview, telling Bueler to watch his rhetoric, because it was getting him into trouble and it "clouds the issues you want to talk about." O'Reilly knows. He tried to carefully walk a line between his inflammatory language and the issues he wished to rant and rave about (until his TV career collapsed around charges that he sexually harassed colleagues, colleagues who were paid millions to keep quiet). In an interview with Texas Congressman Silvestre Reyes, O'Reilly promoted militarizing the border, at one point telling Reyes, "We'd save lives because Mexican wetbacks, whatever you want to call them, the *coyotes*—they're not going to do what they're doing now, so people aren't going to die in the desert. So we save lives, all right, and we seal it down and make it one hundred times harder to come across."[12] During the controversy that resulted from O'Reilly's use of the word "wetback," his employer suggested it was just a "gaffe" and O'Reilly dismissed it as "slang." He told the *New York Times*, "I was groping for a term to describe the industry that brings people in here. It was not meant to disparage people in any way."

Congressman Reyes doesn't accept the excuse. He called O'Reilly's use of "wetback" an insult. "Bill O'Reilly is an entertainer," said Reyes. "Off camera he's actually a nice guy. Turn on that damn camera and he becomes an entertainer, and he likes to be outlandish and he tries to be overbearing." People such as O'Reilly, said the former Congressman after the exchange with the TV showman, "are not trying to solve anything. They're actually trying to exploit people who are well intentioned and who are trying to solve some of the most complex issues and problems that our country faces. That's his livelihood, but he's still accountable."

A quick look at the website promoting Michael Savage's book and radio show made it clear where Conservative Club President Bueler got his inspiration. "Save America Now," screamed a headline on the site when it solicited contributions to something Savage founded called The Paul Revere Society, which stands "for the reassertion of our borders, our language, and our culture." That is the same language used by Bueler's high school club to explain their purpose. On his website, Savage explained further,

Some say that the borders are arbitrary, English is only one of many languages in our new "Multicultural America," and that we share

Figure 14.1 Sound walls keep much of the roar of traffic confined to the Autostrada without blocking the view at Arno in Tuscany.

no common history or values. We believe in the Sovereignty of our Nation. That English is our national "glue." And that we all do share in the pillars of the Bible, the U.S. Constitution, and the Bill of Rights. These documents and what they stand for are our common cultural heritage.[13]

The Tim Buelers out in radioland obviously listened carefully (Figure 14.1).

Undocumented immigrants could well be attending California traffic school classes in order to resolve a traffic citation. The state does not require proof of legal residency in the United States as a criterion for obtaining a license to drive on its streets and highways. And in California the driver's license test is administered in several languages, including Spanish. The policy makes perfect sense. Yet a majority of states forbid licenses to those who cannot prove legal residency. By denying undocumented immigrants driver's licenses, we fool ourselves if we think the lack of a license will keep them off the highway. Instead, they likely will drive without insurance and perhaps without knowing the rules and customs of our roads since they are not forced to learn them in order to pass the test that we're not allowing them to take.

The driver's license bill was drafted by former California state senator Gil Cedillo. We met on a cool Sacramento day in his Capitol office. Cedillo expressed worry about the potency of right-wing talk radio to perpetuate fear and hate against migrants. "In those cars," he says about California's commuter culture, "there's some buffoon who is blaming every problem that they have on immigrants. The white working class is frustrated," he understands (long before Donald Trump was elected president). "We're into this generation where the children are not going to do better than the parents."

"They're not just frustrated," I say. "They're scared."

"They're scared," he agrees, "and it's fueled by this phenomenon of AM radio," he says about talk shows that blanket the airwaves. "Shock jocks who pretend to be serious thinkers play a major role."

The hypocrisy frustrates Cedillo. "Thousands of people are dying," he says about immigrants trying to cross the border.

Should they survive, we're happy to have them take care of our kids, take care of our parents, pick over 90 percent of the foods in the Central Valley. If you really don't want immigrants here, stop using them. I guarantee you, whether you're eating Moroccan food or Chinese food or Italian food, in the best restaurants in Beverly Hills or San Francisco or Carmel, there are Mexicans out there making it in the kitchen.

Gil Cedillo calls himself a typical Mexican-American. He didn't learn to speak Spanish until he was an adult. He grew up in Los Angeles, rooting for the Dodgers and studying at UCLA. "My only experience as a kid with going to Mexico was going to Tijuana to visit my grandmother." When I suggest that the Mexicans crossing the border bring positive energy to American culture, he gets enthusiastic, saying he's pleased to find them in his district. "They are vibrant. They're innovative. They're industrious. I just love driving around L.A. and seeing these guys who grow corn in their backyard. They get a cart." He imagines them selling their homegrown corn on the streets of his district. "These guys will probably be owning a chain of markets in one or two generations, starting with a little corn stand." He's laughing now, enjoying the image. "Oh, yeah! That's these crazy Mexicans people complain about."

The arguments against allowing undocumented drivers a license include the fact that they broke a law crossing the border so they should not be afforded the privilege of driving. Of course they drive nonetheless. But the government is inconsistent. Many undocumented workers pay federal and state income tax. The tax authorities don't check to make sure that they are working in this country legally before withholding their money. And the U.S. Supreme Court has ruled that legal residency in the United States cannot be used as a test to prevent students from studying in public schools.

Another argument against issuing driver's licenses to undocumented migrants is that the official government document helps legitimize the residency of people who are in the United States without proper paperwork.

"Yeah, that's valid," Cedillo says about such complaints. "But it's a good thing. It facilitates the process of immigration for the millions here, working. They are imbedded in the foundation of our economy. It would be tough for us to prosper without their labor."

Senator Cedillo (because of term limits he left the legislature in 2012 and was elected to the L.A. city council the next year) and I finish our interview about licensing Mexican drivers, but we keep talking—two sons of immigrants swapping stories about the American dream. Cedillo describes swank restaurants in L.A. once more, and the valet parking scene. "There is a significant number of valets in California who have no license," he's shaking his head at the paradoxes that surround us prior to the license law changing. "We won't let them drive themselves to work, but we'll put the keys of a Porsche and a Hummer and a Jaguar in their hands in a heartbeat."

We chat for a few minutes in Spanish, entertaining each other with stories about the difficulty of learning languages as adults. But as I'm about to leave he gets serious again, talking about the extraordinary

Figure 14.2 The pragmatic use of a Portland, Oregon, wall: advertising.

number of deaths along the border since the immigrant trail was forced into the deserts.

"We made it more dangerous to come. People die. The question I ask is: How many people die before your policy is a policy of genocide? What's the number? When do we say this a policy that's designed with a consequence that people are going to die?"

Cedillo likens the attempts to keep Mexicans out of the United States to Prohibition. "We wanted to regulate the consumption of alcohol. So we did that. It didn't work. We changed the law again to recognize reality." Reconcile the border law with reality, he says, and open the U.S. border to Mexicans who wish to come north. "We have a trade reality. We have a need for human capital. We want security. We want things to be done orderly. These things argue for a different type of border and a different type of understanding of our relationship with Mexico" (Figure 14.2).

SAN DIEGO

CALIFORNIA
MÉXICO

FIVE MILES

TIJUANA

LA MESA PRISON

Chapter 15

ILLEGAL AMERICANS

Mexico fights its own illegal immigration on its southern border. Central and South Americans slip into southern Mexico without proper documents. They're seeking a better life in Mexico, or more likely, hope to use Mexico as a bridge to the United States. The Mexican border guards at the Chiapas-Guatemala frontier struggle to identify foreigners. Physically there is nothing to distinguish a Mexican from a Guatemalan, and the 620-mile southern Mexican border with Guatemala and Belize is mostly wild and unguarded jungle. One device the Mexican border patrol agents have used is to demand the travelers sing the Mexican national anthem, and not only the first verse but also the second and the third. Imagine the scene at San Diego if instead of asking "Are you an American citizen," border guards demanded returning tourists sing the second and third verses of "The Star Spangled Banner." (The final verse includes an arrogant line particularly poignant if sung at the border with formerly Mexican California: "Then conquer we must, when our cause it is just.")

For an American heading south, border formalities remain minimal. A trip overland to a Mexican border city does require a tourist permit—a simple form to complete. Longer stays and business trips demand more complex paperwork. But compared to the northbound trek for most Mexicans, Mexico's border is wide open to gringos.

Mexico operates a national immigration detention prison in Mexico City where those caught entering the country illegally are held while their cases are pending. Deported Americans usually spend only a few days locked up and then are bused from the prison to Brownsville or Laredo. Mexican authorities do not go looking for Americans without papers, they stumble on them when the gringos are stopped by police or seek help.[1]

Americans in Mexico legally can and do end up in Mexican jails and prisons for breaking Mexican laws. Heading south on Interstate 5 from California to Mexico, signs suggest travelers tune into the radio station broadcasting at 1700 AM. It transmits endless repeats of recorded bilingual border information advising travelers regarding Mexico's rules on importing automobiles and its prohibitions on guns and ammunition.

Mexican authorities spot-check incoming cars. Drivers who didn't listen to the radio alerts and passed the big signs reading WARNING ENTRY OF FIREARMS INTO MEXICO PROHIBITED can find themselves in accommodations they did not expect and probably could not imagine. "I made a bad, bad mistake. Ruined my whole damn life, I guess," said Johnny Manuel from prison in Ciudad Juárez. Manuel claims he took a wrong turn and ended up crossing the bridge into Mexico by mistake, with three of his fiancée's guns in his car. Mexico sentenced him to five years behind bars.[2] His is not an uncommon story.

Americans stand out on in the crowds on Avenida Revolución in Tijuana just as conspicuously as the street corner donkeys that are so curiously painted up to look like zebras. The hustlers bark their wares at the gringos; the cabs cruise by slowly, cabbies yelling.

"Taxi?" asks still another driver.

"You want woman?" is the next question. It is especially easy to get into trouble in Tijuana and other Mexican border towns.

South from the tourist strip that hugs the international frontier, the nightclubs and trinket stands give way to upholstery shops, car dealers and a more residential district. There, miles from the tawdry downtown but still within sight of the hills of San Diego County on the north side of the border, La Mesa Penitenciaría is a temporary home for Americans who found trouble in Tijuana and got caught.

"I had a car accident," Keith Prohaska didn't mind his name being noted. He had been locked up in La Mesa for three weeks when I met with him in the 1980s, charged with drunk driving and destruction of private property: the parked cars he hit. But he talked like a prison veteran, "You learn real quick, Spanish is not the language here. Money is."

We were standing around the noisy open yard inside La Mesa. Word spread that I was looking for Americans to interview. Prohaska, the drunk driver, still sounded dazed about his sudden confinement, "I had several drinks at dinner. I don't know how long I've got here." He was already disgusted with his own government. "The American Consul is absolutely useless. All they do is call home collect and give us vitamins."

Alex Hines was a little more than a third of the way through his seven-year sentence for possession of one gram of marijuana and contributing to the delinquency of a minor. "It was just seeds," he complains. "If I had killed somebody I would have been out already." For almost two of his years inside La Mesa, Alex's wife and two small children lived in the prison with him. "Oh yeah, my wife was here. Everyday she'd go out, go to the store, shop, do what she had to do, do laundry, whatever, come back in. We'd walk around the field."

A Marine serving five years for counterfeiting tells me life isn't so bad for him, considering he is in prison. "There are certain benefits you can't get in the States: women and bottles."

Another Marine agrees. "This is a better jail than jail in the States. Let me put it this way: If you've got the money, you can get anything you want."

"Except out," interrupts Phil Trembley who says he has been locked up for a year, and then looks at his watch and adds, "and eleven days." The charge was homicide, but Trembley had not yet been tried, let alone convicted and sentenced.

"I was in a bar," Trembley says. "Somebody slipped me some drugs. They tried to rob me and I killed somebody. Okay?" As is the case with so many people locked up, Trembley feels wronged. "Whether I'm guilty or not, there's a lot of extenuating circumstances. I'm not going to say my hand didn't do it, but I'm going to say I feel, personally, that it was self-defense."

Trembley's story is a typical border tale. He was picked up by the police after the killing, he says, and then abused. Then he languished in prison, wishing and expecting his own government do more to help him out of his predicament.

"I was beat and electrocuted and locked in a little room for the first five days I was in Mexico," he says coolly.

The first three days no one knew where I was at, including myself. I didn't even know what part of Mexico I was in. I was cold. My clothes were completely ripped. They had electrocuted me. They tied wires to my testicles. They put soda up my nose. They beat me. You know, they beat me in the eyes and the kidneys where there were no marks.

Trembley says it was three days before the Shore Patrol and the U.S. Consul showed up with a few blankets.

I got in trouble the last day in January and you can imagine how cold it was. I was in a little cell and there was defecation about five inches deep and I was handcuffed with my hands behind my back for three days solid, day and night. So I slept with handcuffs on, in defecation. In the mornings the Mexicans, when they brought my food, it was two corn tortillas with some beans. They threw it in my cell. I wasn't allowed fresh drinking water. We drank water from the tap. I was terribly sick. I was throwing up.

The U.S. Navy started shipping him bag lunches so he wouldn't be forced to eat jail food. But his stomach was a mess. "I had diarrhea, I was freezing at night, I was cold. I had to fight to get a bed, to get a place to sleep, thankfully I'm large enough that I did win out. I got a place to sleep."

After his arraignment, Phil Trembley was moved to La Mesa to face an open-ended period of incarceration while the authorities put together their case against him.

The high walls of La Mesa didn't keep the outside world away from the convicts, they just kept the inmates away from the outside world. When I visited, guards armed with rifles crouched on top of those walls, looking sinister in their blue jeans, T-shirts and baseball caps. There was something especially threatening about their lack of official uniforms, a reminder that the authority they represented did not necessarily answer to a government that controls them. They looked like freelance toughs, adding to the mood of whimsical justice that pervades the Mexican legal system.

One guard was on duty at the front gate of the prison, a swinging door in the chain link fencing, working alone. The gatekeeper casually cradled a machine gun and watched over a steady stream of visitors coming and going, deciding who could come in and who could not, a decision based as much on deals and bribes as on law and order. Searches of visitors were cursory operations. Inmates could buy just about anything they wanted or needed inside the prison.

The warden was expecting me; I called ahead. He looked smart in his suit and tie. Four shotguns in a case scattered with boxes of shells were behind him. He smiled and offered me free run of his teeming institution.

Behind his office, in an open alleyway leading to the yard, the warden had collected La Mesa's American inmates, all were eager to talk: the alleged murderer, the counterfeiters, the drunk driver, a robber, all in their twenties, and a convicted child molester serving a 30-year sentence.

The stories come fast, tumbling out all at the same time, all rejecting the American government as worthless to their causes. None of them knew when they were getting out of La Mesa; all agree that they were being treated better than most other inmates because they were Americans, Americans with money.

In the yard—which looks like a stage set for a small, poor Mexican village—the inside of the actual prison wall is difficult to see. In most places it is covered by what the Mexican inmates call their *caracas*, private quarters referred to as "houses" by the Americans. They are tiny but adequate private rooms built onto the prison's walls. Furnished with shag rugs and TVs, equipped with padlocks controlled by the inmates, they bring to mind kids' clubhouses more than prison cells.

"I did all of this," one of the counterfeiters proudly shows off his studio apartment, barely larger than his bed. An English-language San Diego television station is coming in loud and clear on the black-and-white set. "I did all of this, even the wiring." Where did he get the wire and the connectors and the electrical outlet? "A hardware store delivered it."

Some of the houses are up on a second floor, complete with balconies, barbecues and a sweeping view of those close San Diego hills.

"At first it was really scary," Alex Hines, the inmate doing seven years for marijuana possession, says. But soon he learned to deal with his new routine.

> I get up, eat, go with a few other Americans who are in here, you know, we just talk. That's about it. Watch TV. Listen to the radio. Walk to different places back and forth in here, to different cells people are living in in here. That's about it. Then go eat, go to sleep, and occasionally, like when I have visits here, like when my wife's here and stuff, we go eat and, you know, everything else you could probably do on the outside.

Alex's house includes two bedrooms, a bathroom and a kitchen. He has room for a couch and apologized for the mess, but the day I visit the Mexican woman prisoner who cleans for him hadn't made it over to his place from the women's side of the prison. With a smile and wink, Alex suggests she performs other services for him too, when his wife isn't visiting or living with him. We run into his maid later over in the women's section of the prison. They hug and hold hands while we talk. The guard escorting us hoots over the handholding, Alex just smiles. Cooking, cleaning and prostitution are the most common chores available to the women inmates for making money in the prison economy.

"It's pretty well set up," Alex says proudly about his house. "You'd be surprised, this is like no prison at all. This is like, they just take me off the street, and they put me in another world, but away from everyone else. And I have to get along with all these people in here." Hines tells stories of stabbings and killings in La Mesa. "I never thought about death until I came here," he says. But on the high-rent side of the prison where his and the other Americans' *caracas* are scattered, life is relatively quiet. The nasty fights and fires usually occurred across the yard in the maximum-security section of the prison, or where the poorest prisoners shared unlocked cells. "Where I live, it's fine. It all depends on how you're set, financially. If you've got a lot of money you can do anything here."

Alex Hines's *caraca* cost him about five hundred American dollars to secure and furnish. For the duration of his sentence, it is his. The prison administration takes time payments for the house. Alex and the other inmates buy what they need from the outside, get it from visiting friends and relatives, buy it through the prison marketplace or do without. Nothing is free. Even the routine beans and rice from the prison kettle require a payment to the guards.

Mordidas these daily expenses are called, that ubiquitous word in Mexico for bribes, the little bites needed to do business in Mexico. Everything in prison carries a price: blankets, cots or the more comfortable beds, showers and, of course, illegal recreation like drugs, alcohol and sex. The guards provide the goods, take a cut for themselves and augment the warden's salary with his percentage. This controlled, market-driven economy keeps prison costs low for the government, and makes the job of guard and warden appealing because there is plenty of extra money to be made for warders who knew how to work the system.

Radios blare pop music throughout the prison yard, competing with the official announcements coming over the loudspeakers. The prison doesn't appear to be a penal institution as much as a walled city.

The Americans order out to Tijuana restaurants or grocery stores for their food, or eat at one of the inmate-owned-and-operated restaurants in the yard. These are actual private eateries. The open-air restaurants are complete with hand-painted signs, just like those seen out on the streets of Tijuana. *Cantina* announces the restaurant's brightly colored sign. Up on the makeshift wall is a listing of the hamburgers, fries, and other menu offerings. The counter, too, is restaurant-issue Formica. Commercial bottles of ketchup are set out with the meals, along with restaurant-style napkin dispensers. Both inmate and guard customers sit on red Naugahyde-covered swivel stools. A juke box pumps tunes out into the yard.

"I'm never going to come back to Mexico again," Alex Hines tells me about his plans after his release from La Mesa. "Never." He goes back to a game of Risk with his friends.

Alfredo Anzaldúa served as the U.S. government's consul for American citizens services in Tijuana. That Americans were packed into La Mesa was no surprise to him. "They come here to do things they would never think of doing in the United States," he said about Americans who cross the border and get into trouble. "They get blind drunk. They buy drugs. Then they try to buy their way out of trouble."[3]

La Mesa seems a macabre variation on Ambrose Bierce's *adios* punch-line: "To be a Gringo in Mexico—ah, that is euthanasia!"

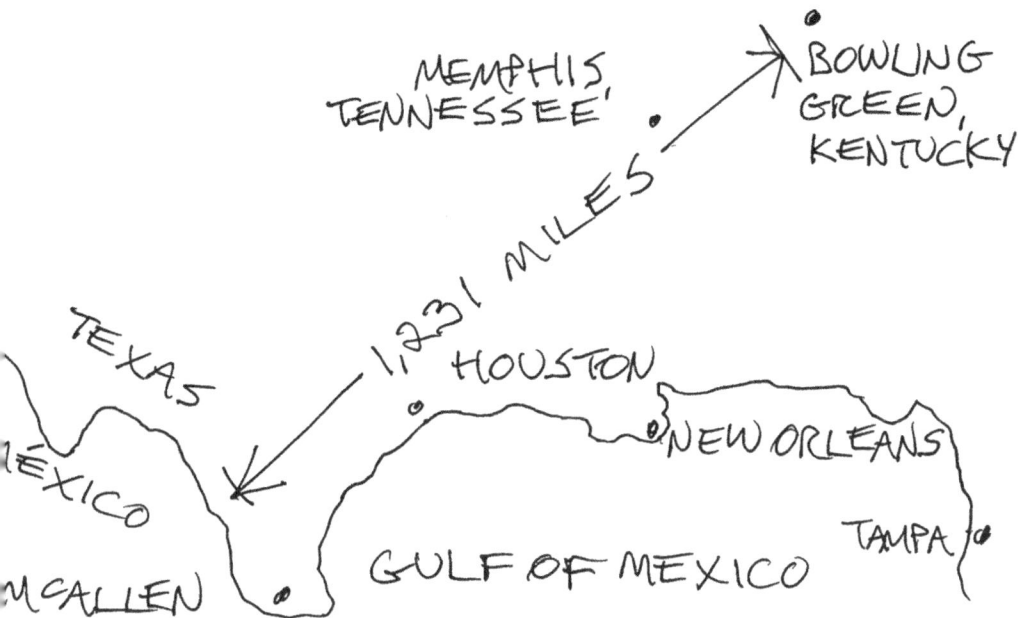

MEMPHIS, TENNESSEE

BOWLING GREEN, KENTUCKY

TEXAS

1,231 MILES

HOUSTON

NEW ORLEANS

MEXICO

TAMPA

MCALLEN

GULF OF MEXICO

Chapter 16

ON THE KENTUCKY-MEXICO BORDER

The late Professor David Coffey lived in a revitalized Victorian home on an all-American-looking tree-lined main street in Bowling Green, Kentucky. Coffey was an agricultural sociologist at Western Kentucky University, and he found plenty to study in his rural home state, where he watched the Latino population grow at an astounding rate. As his state's demographic makeup changed, Coffey became a strong advocate for the minority. "They're working in tobacco, landscaping, horse farming, poultry processing, fruits and vegetables, and forestry," he told anyone he could get to listen. "These are the people who roof our houses, mow our lawns, paint our houses, wash our dirty dishes in restaurants and clean our dirty laundry in hotels." Dr. Coffey estimated that only about 15 percent of the Latinos living in Kentucky enjoy legal immigration status, and he was fascinated by the underground subculture that exists in Bowling Green, invisible to most citizens. His enthusiasm for the social changes infecting Middle America from its neighbor to the south was perpetual.

One evening when we were sharing a meal at a Mexican eatery, Coffey introduces me to the employees, many of them relatively fresh from south of the border. "They work for three or four dollars an hour when they first arrive, working ten- and twelve-hour days," he tells me with his lilting Southern accent. "They get one day a week off and all they can eat." When the busboy is caught up with his work hustling dishes, Coffey motions him over to the table. He is a newcomer, just arrived in the United States a few weeks earlier but proud and happy to show off the few English phrases he'd already learned.

"How are you?" He smiles. "Want more soda?" He smiles again, and then again he offers, "I love you, baby!"

"They're the slaves of the new century," says Coffey. The busboy will likely be working long hours for low pay until he pays off the fees he owes the *coyote* who ferried him across the border. Coffey points out a table where a young Anglo couple are eating, washing down their enchiladas with frosty Mexican beer. They look college student age, but not necessarily beer drinking age. "The help asks them for proof of age," Coffey is explaining another effect of the influx of Latinos. "Then they study the driver's license, give it back, and serve the beer. Of course they can't read," he laughs.

The busboy's boss walked across the border several years before this night. I ask him why he chose to stay in Bowling Green. "Because no problems," he tells me. "Here there are no problems and lots of work. The Americans of Kentucky," he says, "are *muy amables*," kind and friendly. "There are no problems because Mexicans work hard." He believes Coffey estimates high when he guesses about the number of documented border crossers in Kentucky and that only about 5 percent of the Latinos in Bowling Green were authorized to immigrate. But he points out that all of them probably carry papers testifying to their legal status. A set of U.S. identification papers, from a driver's license to a social security card, takes just a few hours to procure on the Bowling Green black market. The going rate rarely exceeds $20 a card.

The restaurant manager goes by at least a couple of different names, not unusual in the Latino migrant community. He asks me to call him Israel. Israel came to Kentucky from Veracruz where he was friends with the Cabrera brothers—Pioquinto and Guillermo—two of the men who were packed into the death trailer at Victoria, Texas. It was Guillermo I met with in Kentucky, the dairy farm laborer who told me how his brother Pioquinto died while they were heading north through Texas, back to work in Kentucky. Israel took Pioquinto's body back to Veracruz.

"I knew him when he was a little boy," Israel says. "I'm older than he was, probably five years. I knew him in Veracruz and when he came to America. He used to work in Oregon, then he moved to Glasgow, Kentucky, to work in the milk." Pioquinto took a leave from the dairy farm for an emergency trip back to Mexico. "His daddy was sick. That was the reason he went to Mexico, to see his daddy. And when he was coming back, he died in Texas. They put him in that trailer." Pioquinto had made the cross-border trip successfully about three times, Israel tells me, and he expected no trouble.

"Let me tell you something," Israel leans forward. "He was talking to me probably five days before he died. He was talking to me and he say, 'Hey, *pues cómo no*, are you okay?' And I say, 'Yeah, where are you?' And he say, 'I'm in Texas.' " Pioquinto was checking to see if Israel could help him make the trip back up to Kentucky. Getting across the border from Mexico is only half the battle for migrants coming north without proper documentation.

Twenty to fifty miles north along the border, the Border Patrol stops traffic on northbound routes: trucks, cars and busses. Typical is the Sarita Checkpoint blocking Highway 77 from McAllen and Brownsville to Kansas City and Chicago, Memphis and Louisville. And Bowling Green. "Inspection station," explains the green highway sign diverting traffic to a stop, a wait that can stretch to hours when inspectors decide to make thorough searches. Usually they spot-search the cargo, look under the chassis with mirrors on poles, just like those the East Germans used to find their citizens escaping through the Iron Curtain to the West. Police dogs sniff for drugs and explosives and people. Drivers and passengers are asked, "Where are going? Where do you live? Are you an American citizen?" If the agents don't like the answers they receive, they say, "Prove it!" They demand identification. If they suspect the identification that's presented to them is stolen or faked, they detain the traveler and begin deportation proceedings. The Border Patrol and ICE officers roam beyond these official checkpoints, and conduct raids and random checks wherever they suspect illegal immigration. Pioquinto was asking Israel for help getting past those secondary checkpoints.

"I said, 'Absolutely, I can do my best.'" Israel tells me. "But he said, 'I'm not asking you only. If I need you I'll call you.' I said, 'Yeah, no problem. Take care of yourself.' He said, 'Take care of yourself too, buddy.' And that's the last time I heard from him. Later his brother called me and said, 'Hey, you know what happened? Pioquinto died.'"

Well established in the United States with a decent job, Israel says he's helping the family, sending some money whenever he can afford it to Pioquinto's wife and daughter who moved back to Veracruz after his death.

They need money to live in Mexico. I don't send a lot of money, but like a couple months ago I sent her three hundred dollars. I don't make very much, you know. He got a little boy and he got two little girls. The middle girl is my godchild. I talk to them sometimes on the phone. I ask his wife if they are okay and how is the little girl.

Israel shakes his head. "It was really sad, and really hard times."

Israel favors temporary work visas as a solution to the border crisis that killed his friend. "Whatever money that you make, you can pay tax to America and you keep the rest for your family in Mexico, so you don't have to pay *coyotes*."

But Israel is another immigrant who came across without papers who does not favor an open border between his old and new countries.

> The problem in the States is too many peoples, you know? If they open the border, everybody will want to come to this country. This country is number one in the world and it's really nice, and I know that this country is nice to everybody, but see what happened September 11th because they give a chance to anybody coming here. I don't say that everybody is mean. Some people we are nice, but some people, we are stupid. We got shit in our mind. So I think it is a great idea if they make a contract, if the Mexican president talks to the American president and says, "You know what? I've got a thousand people. Please let me give a job for these people and I promise to you that in six months they'll come back."

Revolving Door

For migrants picked up by the Border Patrol, stopped as they cross the border, immediate deportation can become just part of their commute routine. The Border Patrol packs them onto busses and escorts them back to the border and they walk back into Mexico. Such "voluntary return" allows the seized migrants to avoid the more serious consequences of a court date and formal deportation.

The "voluntary return" arrangement is a revolving door. Migrants come north, get picked up by the Border Patrol and sent back south. Then the next day, or even the same day, they come north again. Eventually, if they're persistent and stoic, they may make it into the United States. New policies of the federal government are designed to reduce the number of such repeat attempts. "What's happening now," Barbara Hines already saw long before the Trump administration's extreme border control efforts,

> is that the databases are more sophisticated so they can tell that somebody was picked up yesterday. A lot of those people are now prosecuted criminally for criminal re-entry. It's not just a civil violation to come to the United States breaking the immigration laws, it's actually criminal.

So some clients have to serve sixty days or ninety days in jail, and then they go into the deportation system.

Others are freed pending a court date that they may well skip—a practice referred to by Trump's disparaging propaganda as "catch-and-release."

Another tactic the Department of Homeland Security uses to find undocumented migrants is to knock on the doors of local jails. Along the border the ICE police look at the sheriff's rosters and interrogate inmates they suspect are outlaw border crossers who got in trouble in a saloon or were picked up for wife beating or drunk driving. Old-fashioned immigration raids still occur. The raids are another source of suspects for agents who go after Mexicans in shopping center parking lots or restaurant kitchens or factory floors. The sanctuary city movement is designed to prevent such local cooperation with ICE. If residents—documented or not—fear their local police will turn them over to ICE, cooperation with law enforcement regarding routine law and order matters likely will collapse.

Captured Mexicans, along with migrants from Central and South America, and all over the rest of the world, are shipped to a holding pen. The DHS Port Isabel Processing Center in Texas or the CoreCivic facilities in Laredo or Taylor, Texas, are examples. CCA and CoreCivic are both corporate identities of the private company Corrections Corporation of America. It runs detention facilities as a contractor for the federal government. The Taylor lockup operates under the Newspeak-sounding name of the T. Don Hutto Residential Center; Hutto was a CCA founder.

The deportees held in Texas and then sent south out of Texas are not necessarily just those who were picked up along the vast Texas-Mexico border. The Border Patrol is continually inventing new procedures for dealing with the migrants they arrest. One experiment was to fly migrants seized along the Arizona-Mexico border east to Texas and then to deport them through Texas ports of entry. The idea was to make it more difficult for the migrants to repeat the crossing; an anticipated benefit of shipping the border crossers hundreds of miles east was to disconnect them from ties they may have along the Arizona border to *coyotes*, family and other logistical support. The immediate result of the human transshipments was to create a homeless problem in the Mexican border cities of Cuidad Juárez, Nuevo Laredo, Reynosa and Matamoros, metropolises already teeming with poverty and unemployment, slums and overcrowding.

South of the Rio Grande, city governments complained. "We don't like Juárez being used as a point for massive deportations," was the response from Ricardo Chavez, a Ciudad Juárez official. "The city is not prepared to deal with this, and there is already a shortage of jobs here. It's a bad situation. People are sleeping in parks and under bridges." One of those deportees sleeping on the streets of Juárez succinctly analyzed the new problems created for him, "They shouldn't deport us so far away, to places where we don't know anybody." Another complained bitterly about the shackles used to confine the migrants during the plane trips to Texas. "If they have to deport us, they shouldn't treat us like criminals. It's humiliating. We're just working people."[1]

Lawyer Barbara Hines sees his point, especially when migrants are housed in jails and prisons alongside hardened criminals. "A lot of these people have never been in jail before. Even if you're not co-mingled it's a very frightening experience. Because to immigrants it's a labor issue and for the United States it's a criminal issue." The U.S. government calls the long-distance deportations humane because they deter the repeated attempts at crossing the harsh Sonora desert, the wildlands where thousands of migrants have died since the California and Texas borders were fortified.

Bowling Green, Kentucky versus Bowling Green, Mexico

On the other side of the old Louisville and Nashville Railroad tracks from David Coffey's elegant Victorian home and from the city's historic main square is what long was the wrong side of the tracks and, like Poletown in La Porte, what became home to Latino immigrants. There they can shop at the general stores named *La Mexicana* and *La Pearlita*, the *Mercado Hispano* and *Los Camarades*. Prominent banners on the facades of the stores offer the services of express companies that will ship money to Mexico and other points south. They do a big business in prepaid telephone cards that offer cheap rates for calls to Mexico. The marquee on Teresa's Restaurant urges, "Pray for our troops open 6 am." Nearby is the *Luz del Mundo* church. Up the street is Don Chuy's bar and dancehall, its advertising limited to a simple, *"Baile Vie. Sab.,"* Dance Fri. Sat.

In the late 1990s Coffey secured a grant from the U.S. Department of Agriculture to teach a few Spanish words and phrases to Kentucky farmers and basic English to Latino migrant workers so that some of the mutually dependent strangers could begin to get to know each other. Because the classes were subsidized by the federal government, undocumented workers were not allowed to attend. His Latino students all held H2A visas, the visas granted to agricultural workers for specific jobs for specific periods of time during the growing and harvest seasons. "Mr. and Mrs. Farmer came in first, workers second, separated. The first night, it was quite apparent that the Latinos were scared. They were very subservient to the gringos. The first night we did body parts. We had them pronouncing each other's names, shaking hands, and naming body parts." They were instructed to touch each other as they named the arms and legs, heads and shoulders.

> I'm sure most of our growers had never touched a Mexican. And most of the workers had never had an encounter touching a Gringo. As a result, after they touched each other and started pronouncing names, giving a *"¡Mucho gusto!"* and the handshakes, everything just melted, and we started laughing with arms around other and all that, which to me was worth the grant.

They walked into the schoolhouse separately, but they walked out arm in arm.

Coffey loved surprising the two groups by bringing them together to socialize—"We had Thanksgiving meals in Mexican restaurants." Most of the workers in the class came from Nayarit, and after the harvest he organized a trip for some of the growers to tour the Mexicans' villages.

"We flew to Guadalajara. They took us on a tour of Tequila, and we sampled tequila. Which was really interesting for a group of Baptists away from home, so they got mellow. They were treated royally." The Mexicans showed off their homes and were careful to point out their microwave ovens, their televisions, the rooms that they had added on to their houses—all as a result of the money that they had earned working in Kentucky. The Kentucky farmers were amazed at the poverty they witnessed. "They had never thought about how poor some of their workers are and how much they're really helping them out by bringing them to Kentucky and how much they appreciate it."

The process for obtaining an H2A visa is complicated. The grower must show that no U.S. citizen wants the work and then solicit workers in Mexico, usually through an intermediary who acts as a fixer. Once a deal is made, the worker goes to the American consulate and secures the visa. The grower must provide the transport from the border to the jobsite and back, along with food and housing during the period of employment. The worker cannot change jobs and must return home when the crop is harvested. A tiny minority of the millions of Latinos working in the United States do so with H2A visas.

Immigration lawyer Barbara Hines says the H2A visa is unpopular with both employers and workers.

An H2A is for seasonal agricultural work and it has all sorts of restrictions. The problem with an H2A is that it only gives you permission to work for a certain contractor. An H2A means that if you find a better job or you want to move to Chicago you can't. The problem with these temporary visas is they're employer-tied. That raises all sorts of issues about labor conditions.

Another unpopular alternative, says Hines, is the H2B visa.

An H2B is a temporary visa which allows you to work in any industry— but it must be a temporary job. So if someone wants to hire you as a dishwasher in their restaurant, you don't qualify for an H2B because the employer needs a dishwasher all year round. The job itself has to be temporary. An H2B limits the worker to things like landscaping and seasonal hotel work. Yes, if you're in a resort area where your restaurant shuts down you can hire workers with H2B visas. But an H2B does not resolve the problem for the unskilled work that immigrants do.

The regulations are complicated for both H2 visas, she points out. "You have to have an employer willing to do it. The employer has to advertise in a newspaper and show there's no qualified U.S. worker. For most employers it's just easier to hire somebody and pay them in cash." In addition to all that, many Mexicans cannot qualify for the H2 visas. Anyone who was caught trying to get into the United States illegally or picked up and deported must wait 10 years before being considered for an H2 visa.

Another reason the H2 visas are unappealing to Latino migrants is made obvious by David Coffey's research in Kentucky. "The Latinos—I call them Hispanics[2]—are no longer transient. They're here. They're not going back. They're community members." That's a good thing, says Coffey, because Bowling Green, a quiet college town with a growing manufacturing base, would cease to function without its Latino workforce. But despite the growing Latino presence in Kentucky, little government support is available to help Latinos assimilate into rural areas of the state. That's due, in part, to the fact that they barely show up on official U.S. census data. Catholic Charities estimates the Kentucky Latino population is seven times the number cited by the census; Coffey figures that's much too low and he estimates it's twenty times the official count. Since so many Latinos in the state are undocumented, census figures are a joke compared with the real population. "The census says Bowling Green has 250," he says about the count back in the year 2000. "We probably have five thousand or so." Another example he offers is the crossroads Kentucky town of Albany, where the census lists only five Latino residents. "You can see 35 on the square," says Coffey, laughing at the absurdity of the official figures.

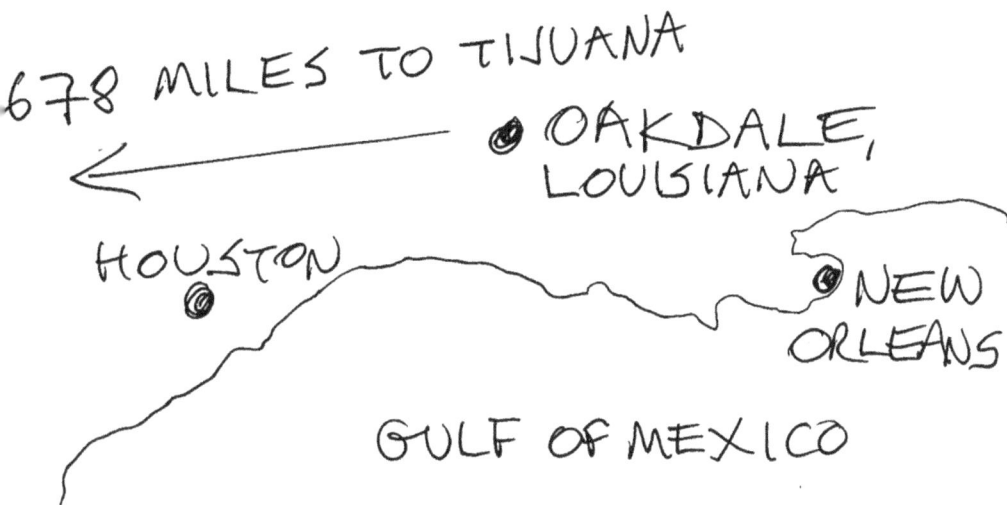

678 MILES TO TIJUANA

← OAKDALE, LOUISIANA

HOUSTON

NEW ORLEANS

GULF OF MEXICO

Chapter 17

DEPORTATION MADE EASIER

In 1986, a new Federal prison was built in Oakdale, Louisiana, specifically to expedite deportation proceedings. Oakdale is a pleasant little city "where plans become realities," its motto proudly claims. "Oakdale is not Paradise," its citizens acknowledge with bizarre candor in a Chamber of Commerce brochure, but "it is a nice place to live." In the mid-1980s the Oakdale economy was struggling. The Chamber of Commerce worked hard to explain why Oakdale is a nice place to live: "Quiet cars rolling on clean, wide streets," ranked second after "Good, gray, serious mockingbirds singing from rooftops" on its list of reasons to consider relocating to a place with "solid, serious citizens going to work in modern, prosperous plants."

The federal Detention Center was an important new plant for Oakdale, providing construction jobs and then permanent employment, initially for some three hundred guards and other workers. This was the first Bureau of Prisons lockup designed and built specifically to hold migrants awaiting deportation. But that was not all. Oakdale was not just a prison. Inside its walls were courtrooms of what was called in more language that sounds more like Newspeak, the Executive Office for Immigration Review. Migrants picked up by Border Patrol sweeps were detained in Oakdale, deep in the rural pinelands of Louisiana, far from the border and far from cities where concentrations of Spanish-speaking lawyers practice. There they waited until their cell doors opened and they were marched before immigration court judges.

In a makeshift office on the sleepy Oakdale main street, shortly after the Oakdale prison started operating, a few lawyers and social workers set up shop and struggled to meet the needs of these dislocated prisoners.

"These people are not criminals," lawyer and Catholic priest Ted Keating told me. Father Keating began helping the inmates when Oakdale opened.

> They have all kinds of needs other than legal. They're basically innocent people who have been taken up off the street and thrown into a large federal penitentiary, and that creates psychological problems and social problems. They've been wrenched away from their support groups and their families, their communities. Many of them have just come across the border and here they are in the middle of an enormous United States prison. That creates its own psychological and social displacement problems.

A mournful freight train whistle blows as he talked about his challenge. At the time the Central American civil wars were raging and many of Keating's clients were seeking political asylum. Ronald Reagan was president, setting the stage for the gross abuses of asylum seekers perpetrated by President Trump.

"These people don't come across the border with elaborately documented cases," Father Keating said.

> They come with the clothes on their back. Somehow it has to be proved that they have an objective, well-founded fear of persecution. To do that they need an attorney. Almost any lawyer looking at the system would

say that they need legal help. Without that, this is a deportation mill. Refugees will be sent back. Their claims will not be fairly handled. Many of them will not even have the opportunity to make that claim.

Even connecting with Keating and his few volunteers was difficult. Inmates—if allowed to use the phone—were required to call collect, to reverse the charges of the phone call, charges that were and still are often excessive, charged by the private phone companies contracted with by prison authorities, companies profiting from prisoners without alternative options for calls to family, friends and lawyers. There were no Spanish-speaking telephone operators in tiny Oakdale. I tried placing a collect call in Spanish from Oakdale, the operator hung up. Keating was convinced the prison was located in isolated Oakdale to make it more difficult for people caught to fight deportation.

Inside the prison, I talked with one of the few bilingual detainees. He interpreted for several of his fellow prisoners, all waiting for their court appearances. "They feel kind of left out of everything because they don't speak the language," he said, referring to the English used in the court proceedings. Few of the guards spoke Spanish. "They don't know what's going on and they don't know the system well enough to know that they have rights as human beings not to be crowded around like animals." The government was flying inmates to Oakdale for a quick court appearance that usually resulted in a bus ride to Houston and another flight south of the border.

Since those days in the 1980s, continuing traffic across the border resulted in the immigration courts only getting busier, and the government is becoming ever more sophisticated at streamlining the court proceedings required for deportation. Abuses of migrants seeking political asylum during the Trump administration included that forced separation of children from their parents and the detention of those children in deplorable conditions: unsanitary, overcrowded cages and ad hoc prisons.[1] Universal outrage was somewhat mitigated when Mexican president Andrés Manuel López Obrador made a Faustian deal with Trump: Families of asylum seekers crowded into temporary camps on the Mexican side of the border during long waits for interviews with U.S. immigration authorities. The result of the bulk of such meetings, if they ever occur: asylum application denied.[2]

"It's much broader, it's much bigger than Oakdale now," said immigration lawyer Barbara Hines not long after the Louisiana facility opened. "The big issue now is video conferencing out of the jails. They just started this in San Antonio." Court proceedings were handled with the inmate in jail far from the judge's San Antonio courtroom.

> It's not just Oakdale. The access issue for immigrants is so overwhelming. I just looked at some statistics. In San Antonio, 80 to 90 percent of people are unrepresented. You can't talk to the people in the jails. They can't call out collect. You can't call in. The only way you can talk to them is to drive a hundred or a hundred and fifty miles to see people. At least we used to at least be able to talk to the clients before their bond hearing when they were brought to the courts in San Antonio. That's been eliminated and everything is now done by video conferencing. So that means that we go to San Antonio and never can talk to the client. The client sits in front of a video screen in Laredo or some other place. The client never comes to court. The judge never sees the real person. There are some really big due process issues, I think, about video conferencing these proceedings. When Oakdale was built, many of us said, "This was built deliberately to get people away from their lawyers." There are very few immigration lawyers in Oakdale.

The new video conferencing policy only exacerbated the lack of due process that I observed in the Oakdale court behind prison walls. As if I were watching an assembly line, I looked and listened as migrants were marched in front of a judge who barely glanced up as he banged his gavel over and over again sending desperate migrants back across the border. Immigration lawyer Hines was lamenting and I was watching the deportation techniques of the Bill Clinton and George W. Bush administrations, abuses perpetrated years before the draconian developments devised by Trump's heartless immigration advisers.

CHICAGO

ST. LOUIS

OWENSBORO, KENTUCKY

TO MEXICO 1,182 MILES

ATLANTA

ATLANTIC OCEAN

Chapter 18

ONE FARMER WORKING BY THE RULES

"They come across in trucks," David Coffey said he learned. "Usually come in eighteen wheelers. The people are in the middle of fish or fruit or ice. We're talking forty to eighty people in a truck." Once these truckloads of human cargo are well north of the border, the freight is transferred to smaller vans that fan out across the country.

They usually drop them off at a truck stop in St. Louis or Memphis. They give them sixty dollars, and then they call for someone to pick them up. Family members. We have one I'm concerned about who should have been here Saturday and he hasn't arrived yet. I don't know what happened. But eventually they get here, regardless of the law.

One of the gringos who signed up for Coffey's language lessons and took the trip down to Mexico to see his laborers' hometown was Joe Elliott, a fourth-generation Kentucky farmer. On a crisp autumn day in late November, the peak of the tobacco production season, he met with my wife Sheila. Elliott is a stocky man; his work pants are cinched up tight against his belly. His striped work shirt shows off a patch announcing Elliotts Farms. He's wearing a windbreaker against the morning chill, and on his head is a camouflage baseball cap courtesy of the South Central Bank.

"Oh, your hands are so cold," his wife Mary Sue is sweet and warm as she shakes a welcome with Sheila. Mexican music is blaring from the tobacco drying barn. There the crop is being sorted by type and color—the richer the golden brown the higher the quality of the leaf. Workers are "stripping the 'baccer," pulling the leaves off the tobacco plant stalks. It is time-consuming hand work. The sorted dried leaves are stacked and prepared for auction. The tobacco season for these workers lasts about four months. One of the Mexican workers stops stripping the leaves to explain that in those four months he'll earn what it would take him two years to make in Mexico. A sign high on the wall advises, "This farm has pride in tobacco." The walk to the farmhouse is paved with heart-shaped stones.

"It's been real good this time," Elliott is pleased with the harvest. His accent is broad Kentucky, "[…] this taahmm." The Elliott farm is 90 acres of tobacco, along with 1,800 acres of corn and soybeans. It's just outside of Owensboro, across the Ohio River from Evansville, Indiana.

Fifteen Mexicans work the place, all in the United States legally on H2A visas. For some of them it's a regular, if seasonal, job. Elliott has been hiring them and bringing them up to Kentucky for several years. It's a business deal that only improved when he began studying Spanish under Coffey's program.

"We been to Mexico," says Elliott. "We seen their problems."

He shows off the concrete bunkhouse he's built for the workers, quarters that meet or exceed the federal standards for H2A workers. "We done insulation. We done it right, all the way around." Beds are separated with shelves and a clothes rack, offering slight privacy enhanced by curtains. The industrial-looking particle board walls are punctuated here and there with ad hoc décor: an image of the Virgin of Guadalupe, for example, alongside a calendar featuring Old Glory blowing in the wind. "After work hours they relax. They go fishing here on the farm ponds."

The Kentucky Housing Authority considers Elliott's operation a model for treating farm workers properly. He received a $30,000 grant from the state to expand the bunkhouse. "We ended up putting a porch on it. That was really the neatest thing."

Joe Elliot bought his farm in 1965. In those days, he hired American hands. No longer. "They not here. They not here to hire."

It's been several years since he's employed American laborers. But Elliott does not join the chorus complaining that the loss of American workers is bad news, or that Americans are turning down the work because it's demeaning, or that Americans are lazy and spoiled.

"They got better jobs. Not a part time labor job, full time. They got benefits. You can work at McDonalds for the same money we're paying here. Anybody who wants to work has got work." But that's not all that's wrecked his native work force. "There's another thing too. People quit having kids." He can't find a local workforce in the contemporary Kentucky rural younger generation.

Without the immigrant labor, Elliott says his farm would be paralyzed. "Yeah, I'd be out of business." There is no consistent local work force to work the 40–50 hours a week needed to bring in the crops. He pulls out a newspaper clipping about "600 illegals" being caught in the United States. Elliott knows stopping the influx is impossible; he sees evidence of that fact throughout Daviess County. "There are six million of those guys in the States," he says, undercounting most estimates. But he says he never liked working with undocumented workers.

"It's really not worth it. Honesty and trying to do something upfront the right way is the right way to do it. I like to work legally."

But problems loom for Elliott's desire to play by the rules.

"The government is either going to change this thing or it's going to force me to go back to undocumented labor. They're not trying to get along with us. With all their paperwork and regulations, they're not trying to help us at all." Elliott decided to hire legal workers after rumors started spreading through Daviess County that the INS was planning raids and would seek fines of $5,000 a day per person for any undocumented workers found working local crops. And he was disgusted with the middlemen he felt forced to deal with to hire workers with stolen or forged papers. "It got so scary that we got out of it. The people that was running the damn thing was so crooked. We was getting guys with visas that belonged to people in Tennessee. It was a whole crooked game." He started using legal workers through the H2A program and in return he embraced a steady supply of reliable workers plus a clear conscience.

Drive a Stick Shift

Joe Elliott tries to teach his neighbors the value of Mexican migrant workers. "The people that's fighting them are breaking their own dinner plate. The biggest issue I see is they're thinking they're going to take their jobs." But Elliott is convinced that is a fatuous line of reasoning. "Down at Fields Packing Company here at their local processing plant, there's 20 percent Mexican people. They do the job." He says Kentucky workers hire on and leave after a few days because

> they don't want to do the work. Purdue chicken farm, same thing. Or Tysons. They all got Mexican people. It could be stopped if the American people wanted to stop it. You don't feed your neighbor's dog unless you want him to be in your yard. If you feed him, he'll come and see you. If you give these Mexican workers the opportunity to work, they want to work and they will take over your job.

But the belief that Mexicans are taking jobs from native-born Kentuckians is not the only factor fueling prejudice against the migrants. "Race is one of them. They just don't want Mexicans here."

Elliott downplays claims that Latino migrants abuse U.S. social services.

> We've had different things—operations with up to $10,000. The Mexicans can't pay it. An operation for appendicitis is $8,000. They can't pay it. They're going to die. What are you going to do? Let 'em die? In Mexico—I saw it when I was down there—you die. You didn't have the money, you die. Here that's just the advantage of being an American.

David Coffey said his research confirmed that abuse of social services is minimal, and he pointed out that even those migrants without documentation who are bold enough to apply for government help are eligible for few programs. Families benefit the most through subsidized school lunches, emergency Medicaid and immunization opportunities. These programs are primarily for young children and pregnant women in need of prenatal care. Social welfare programs for single male migrant farm workers are nominal.

Fear plays a role in fostering negative attitudes toward the foreigners. Farmer Elliott hears the complaints about Mexicans congregating in public places, like the Walmart parking lot. He says his experiences touring Mexico help him understand why his workers like to hang out together.

> You've got to learn the different lifestyles, the different thinking, how they do things. When you learn their culture a little bit, you can understand how they gang up. They're just being friendly. Are the Mexicans, just because they get together, dangerous any more than if you go to some sports bar where they got fifteen TVs and the thing is crammed. Are they dangerous too?

Coffey agreed. "Walmart is the nearest thing to a *mercado*"—a community marketplace in Mexico—"that we have in most areas." He wants the farmers to look at the crowds from the perspective of the laborers themselves. "Perhaps they need to socialize after a week in the fields." Coffey offered the farmers and their families other questions to ponder. "Are they not like the rest of us," he asked,

> or is reality that people of different skin color and a different language fuel our fear and ignorance to invite racism, prejudice and xenophobia? Do they roam in gangs after innocent women or is the reality that they roam in gangs because one member can speak, read or count in English? Are they taking our jobs, or is the reality that their strong backs work hard and long hours at jobs that everyone else is either too lazy to work or that they think is below their dignity?

Whatever the answers of his neighbors, Joe Elliott sees Owensboro changing around him. "They have filled in all the spots that nobody else wants," he says about Mexican migrants. And he favors them over some of the locals he's employed. "We had whiteys," and he laughs at his use of the term, "we had whiteys who could tell you every basketball game in the last ten years: who won, who played, scores. But they couldn't count six 'baccer plants in one pile at any one time. They was thirty workers out of Owensboro here and there wasn't any of 'em could drive a stick shift. Grown men."

H2A workers can only stay in the United States for nine months at a stretch. On the Elliott farm the goal is to finish with the tobacco work by the Christmas holidays. "We work our butt off to make that happen, because we understand that any family man that ain't seen his family for four months, it's time for him to go see his family. That's just how it is. We pay their bus ticket all the way back to their house." Elliott is only required to buy a ticket to the border.

He's heard stories of Mexicans getting drunk weekends in Kentucky and being rolled for their cash or losing their earnings on the bus back to their hometown when Mexican police stop busloads and shake down the passengers. Improved banking opportunities between the United States and Mexico made it easier and cheaper for his workers to ship their money home instead of carrying it back as cash. "We finally got a Mexican store that's wiring most of the money back to Mexico. On Saturday they may have $25,000 in there. They only wire back cash money. They don't accept no checks. The police department, they keep a damn close eye on that store."

La Reina de Mexico is the little Owensboro general store catering to Latinos. "*Tienda, taquería, y carnicería 100% mexicana,*" it advertises under a big Mexican flag over its front door. Store, taco stand, and meat market 100% Mexican. The storefront is a community bulletin board. The front windows are plastered with billboards selling tickets on buses that run directly to northern Mexico cities, money wiring services and Spanish-language music CDs. "*Bienvenido,*" says a flyer taped to a window, "*Aprenda el inglés. ¡Gratis!*" Welcome. Learn English. Free. Another offers a 1997 Plymouth Breeze for $3900, complete with air conditioning and a CD player, with just 66,000 miles on the odometer. And the *carnicería* is promoting its sale price tripe for only $1.59 a pound.

Inside *La Reina de Mexico* the shelves are lined with products from Mexico. *Masa* for tortillas, Charras brand tostadas "The REAL Mexico Flavor," vibrant blue bottles of Fabuloso to clean floors just like at home and tall candles in glass holders decorated with dramatic illustrations of Christ and the Virgin of Guadalupe. On one wall the flags of the United States and Mexico hang side by side, along with a huge sombrero topping some of the stars and stripes.

The lessons of farm work in rural Kentucky were clear to David Coffey. "We've not accepted that we have a labor force that is no longer transient and is doing most of our work. We need to help them assimilate." But at least as important, maybe more important, is the other half of that equation. We need to work on "our assimilating to them. This whole idea of them being illegal—undocumented—scares a lot of people, and we don't know what to do with them."

Meanwhile, an underground and subservient labor force continues to grow. "We have forced most of them to stay here," Coffey pointed out one of the unexpected consequences of post-9/11 border controls.

"Although they can still cross the border and get here, we're forcing them to stay here, and they really want to go home." They fear they either won't be able to get back across the reinforced border, or they can't face the inflated prices *coyotes* now command. "They would love to go home and see their families, see their wives and children, their parents. And have some kind of legal documentation where they could come up here and work, and then go home for the holidays. But since they're illegal, they don't exist."

"Since they're coming anyway," I suggested," why not just allow them free passage?"

"Wouldn't that be wonderful," he said, "and logical."

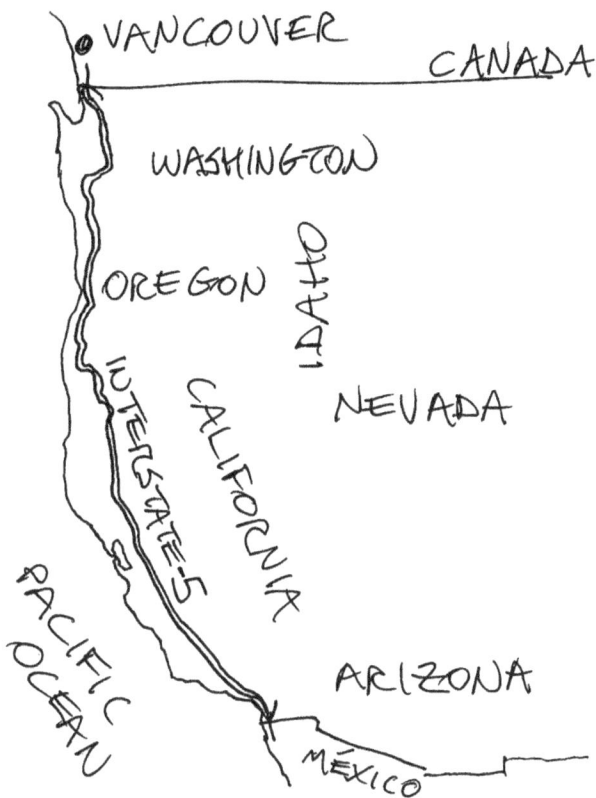

Chapter 19

WHO WANTS THE BORDER CLOSED?

Who are those Americans afraid of immigrants? I've found some of them via the radio, while hosting talk shows. One fascinating program was based on seeking callers from a California audience who were considering leaving the state, moving out permanently. I solicited their opinions, asked them why they felt the California Dream failed them.

I received a steady stream of calls, and letters, after the show aired. One of those was from a trucker named Marty Kemmeries. "I put it to you," Kemmeries wrote, "that you are naïve and uninformed as to the facts about the financial state of our state. I put it to you further, that you will come to the realization that Caucasian America is sick of minorities, foreigners, and deviates." Marty Kemmeries wrote that to me in late 1991. During the 1990s, according to government figures, the undocumented immigrant population in the United States increased by several hundred thousand each year. More migrants without proper papers arrived than left, died or became legal residents.

"Possibly I can enlighten you as to some facts that are staring us in the face," wrote Kemmeries.

You must remember that the immigrants of today are from cultures diametrically opposed to the culture that has arisen with the entrenchment of the Caucasian European settler, who established this country with intelligence and the work ethic.

In the early days of this country there were not the social programs in place (as we have now) to insulate the original settlers from the consequence of laziness, and a lacking of the ability to, or desire to, apply themselves. These now in place programs assure the immigrating Mexican that he can reproduce without personal consequence, or the necessity to support, discipline, or educate his offspring. Look around you at the graffiti, check the arrest records in Fresno County as to the predominate race incarcerated for driving under the influence. Are you aware that food stamps were made available to illegals, who could obtain them without fear of arrest or deportation?

I could elaborate further, but suffice to say that the behavior, birthrate, and cultures of minorities and immigrants are destroying our daily lives with a mosaic of graffiti, foreign language, irresponsible behavior, violence and intimidation. These lately known as people of color are at the same time burdening the taxpayer to the breaking point with their continuing and expanding dependency on the working Californian.

Marty Kemmeries signed his letter, "looking forward to leaving this state, and hoping to find real America," with his name and address and telephone number, adding, "You have just read a letter written to you by a professional trucker, an owner-operator, running intrastate California. If you have any questions or comments, my office is seventy feet up ahead."

A couple of weeks later I aired another talk show, this one dealing specifically with Mexican immigration into California. I quoted from Marty Kemmeries letter, and he wrote back to me. He carefully deconstructed the radio show, critiquing the callers and my conversations with them. Here's an example:

"To another caller you said you believed that those that wanted to assimilate into our society would learn our language. I say that the predominate number of our Hispanic residents do not want to assimilate into our society, but rather would prefer to re-establish California as a Mexican colony. In the event this ever happened, these people would be biting the very hand that feeds them."

Kemmeries then suggested that I write a book "on the minority, immigrant, and deviate, and expound on their social and financial impact on our state and indeed across the nation." If I take on this project, he wrote to me, and decide to write a book about Mexican immigration into the United States, he offered the following as fodder:

Why is Interstate 5 being modified down by San Ysidro to make it safer for illegals to enter at this common spot for border running? These modifications are being done at taxpayers' expense, while there are sections of Interstate 5 that shake and bounce a trucker and his rig all over the road. This year the disgraceful condition of Interstate 5 caused a numbness in my foot, later found to be a pinched nerve in my back, and the constant rough ride shook the inside of the factory stereo in my big truck apart. I also had to replace the steering tires on my big rig twenty thousand miles sooner than normal, just because of the condition of Interstate 5. These big truck tires are $350 each. And yet we spend money to make it safer for Hispanics to violate our borders, this idiotic endeavor supported by our Hispanic lawmakers, interested only in perpetuating the Hispanic here on our shores.

Figure 19.1 A retaining wall north of the border in California on Highway 101 holding back a hillside threatening to slide a blockade of mud across the crucial coastal corridor.

He was referring to the fencing put in place on I-5 in an effort to reduce the number of migrants hit by cars and trucks as they ran across the freeway seeking hiding places and paths around the authorities. Special signs were posted on I-5 showing the silhouette of a desperate family running across the road, erected to warn drivers of the unusual hazards and potential victims on I-5 near the Mexican border (Figure 19.1).

Kemmeries asked me, "How is it that Mexicans can seemingly work for much lower wages than an American?" And then he answered his own question.

The Mexican is used to, and indeed thrives on, living conditions we find unacceptable. Living in garages and tool sheds, and fifteen or twenty people to a house originally designed and constructed to house a family of four, these people can do well on small individual incomes pooled together. Much of this income is sent to Mexico to smuggle still more of their people here. Those that live here soon learn to rely on food stamps, subsidized health care, rent subsidies, welfare, unemployment, and workman's compensation.

Kemmeries urged me to

talk to people in neighborhoods where Mexicans have moved in. You will hear of constant illegal construction to make room for more border runners. You will hear of the raising of fighting cocks and dogs. You will hear of Hispanic girls having babies at very young ages, the birth rate of these children insuring still more income for the Hispanic resident of California.

And Kemmeries told me he was offended by what could be seen from the window of his truck. "Listen as the trucker tells you of constantly seeing Hispanics urinating alongside the highway, making little effort at modesty. This type of behavior is manly to the Hispanic. However, this type of behavior is illegal and deviant, and further it is the type of behavior that embarrasses any male that deems himself intelligent and civilized."

Trucker driver Marty Kemmeries ended his assignment sheet to me with this sweeping charge. "The largest number of Mexicans and Negros [*sic*] lack personal integrity. This is reflected in their daily lives, openly violating common sense and common decency. We need to face the fact that there are intellectual and cultural differences that have made them, and continue to make them, a social and financial burden." Twenty-five years later 2016 presidential candidate Trump and his promised wall must have looked mighty attractive to trucker Kemmeries.

The Trucker's Lament Is False

The 2000 U.S. census alone officially contradicts many of the fears and racist charges of the Marty Kemmeries of the world.

I lived in Sonoma County, California, when he wrote his screed. The local economy is fueled by tourism and the wine industry. Golden hills surround valleys packed with bedroom communities of commuters who struggle daily down Highway 101 toward jobs in Marin County and San Francisco. Sonoma County thrives in good and bad economic times, with low unemployment and a fast-growing Latino community.

According to Census Bureau figures[1] Latinos hold most of the lowest-paying jobs in Sonoma County. In the decades since the census in 1990, few Sonoma County Latinos managed to break into higher-paying managerial jobs and professional careers. By 2015, a fifth of workers in Sonoma County were counted as Latinos in a work force of a quarter million. A vast majority of agricultural workers in the county were Latino. Over half the county's maids were Latino and half of the cooks. And, of course, these percentages are based on official census figures. Many—if not most—of the people who are in the United States illegally are not going to trust census takers who come knocking on their doors. They avoid them or provide them with false information. Consequently, the percentages of Mexicans engaged in these low-paid, unskilled labor jobs is no doubt higher than officially reported.

Half of the Latinos counted by the 2000 census in Sonoma County were foreign born, and most of those immigrated during the 1990s, coming north to take the low-paying jobs left unfilled. Twenty years later the figures reversed and most Latinos living and working in the county were born in the United States.

"The University of Mexico grads don't come to the United States," shrugged George Ortiz after studying the figures back in the 1990s. "It's the ranch hands and the poor guys who are trying to find a job that are coming here in large numbers." Ortiz was president of the California Human Development Corporation, an organization providing support services to Latino immigrants. "They're the latest influx of immigrants, and it takes time to get ahead."

Those Latino workers in Sonoma County, and their counterparts across the United States, hardly posed a threat to Marty Kemmeries and his ilk. "The farmworkers are, I'd say, 90 percent Latino, mostly Mexican," said Ortiz. "Nobody else wants those lousy jobs. They're not taking anything from anybody. On the contrary. They're the volcano that keeps the whole system up."

George Ortiz served on the Mexican government's *Consejo Consultivo*, and was an advisor to former president Fox on issues relating to farmer workers in *El Norte*. Especially irritating to him is the charge that

Mexicans in the United States without proper papers are criminals, are law breakers who have entered the country illegally. "Who's doing the hiring?" he asked. "These guys aren't coming in to vacation or fool around. They're coming to find work and somebody's giving them the work. It's the needy getting jobs from the greedy. Let's talk about economics and how these peasants, these workers, are helping the general economy. They're paying taxes, too. They're contributors."

The restrictions against Mexicans at the U.S. border eventually will disappear, Ortiz was convinced. "It's an economic imperative. We're talking about billions and billions of dollars," he said about trade between the United States and Mexico. "The second largest trading partner with the United States is Mexico. The largest trading partner with California is Mexico. California would be in really bad straits if commerce stopped." He pointed out that money sent home annually by Mexicans working in the United States is Mexico's second-largest source of income after petroleum, estimated at close to $15 billion dollars. "Green is the color that we see most of all. When we have great commerce between ourselves, it brings all kinds of peaceful solutions to all kinds of things, because that's the way it is."

But it isn't just the statistics in Sonoma County that refute the attacks of trucker Marty Kemmeries. The Rand Corporation, the Santa Monica-based think tank, published a study in 2003 that devastates the racist fears of people like Kemmeries. Economist James Smith is the author of the study. He poured over Census figures and supporting documents covering the twentieth century, and tracked the progress of Latino immigrants in comparison with those coming to the United States from Europe. Using education and income as measure, Smith concluded that "across generations, Latinos have done just as well as the Europeans who came in the early part of this century, and in fact slightly better."[2]

"There's a widespread view among both scholars and the general public that the Latino experience has been very different than the European experience," said Smith about his motivation for his work. "That view is just wrong."

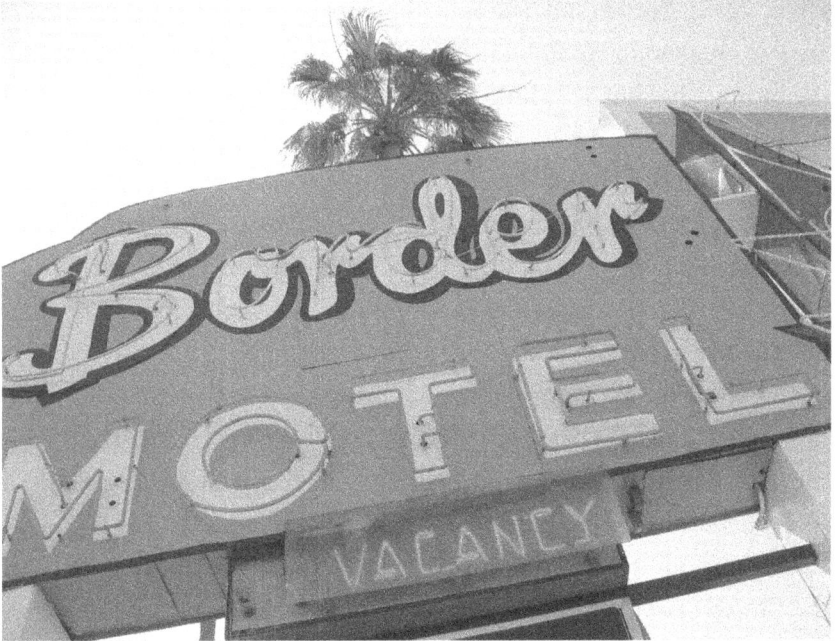

Figure 19.2 The border as business. Modest lodgings like this Calexico motel greet travelers coming across the border from cosmopolitan Mexicali.

Journalist Ruben Navarrette Jr., who frequently writes about Mexican immigrants in his widely circulated newspaper column, lauded Smith's research, using his own family as an example of one that went "from the grape fields to graduate school" after just three generations in the United States.

"Regardless of ethnicity or nationality or economic resources," Navarrette wrote,

immigrants are the same the world over. That's because a big part of what shapes their character is not the country they come from, but the fact that they leave it in the first place, risking whatever they have—including their lives—in search of a better life. Once here, they work hard in any job they can find. They instill in their children an appreciation for education and teach them the value of a dollar.[3]

Deep in Mexico on the Yucatan Peninsula is another example to crush the Marty Kemmeries theories. There, the small city of Peto lost thousands of its young men to Marin County, California, where they made four and five times more an hour than in a 12-hour day back home. "It's necessary," said Felipe Acosta Díaz about the migration north and his four sons who were working in Marin when Marty Kemmeries was driving his truck. "The young are obligated to go to the United States." His neighbor Carlos Ruiz agreed. "Is it any wonder that the boys leave?" he asked. Three of Díaz's sons worked in Marin restaurants, sending back *migradollars* to help support the family. "It's sad and we miss them, but they must go"[4] (Figure 19.2).

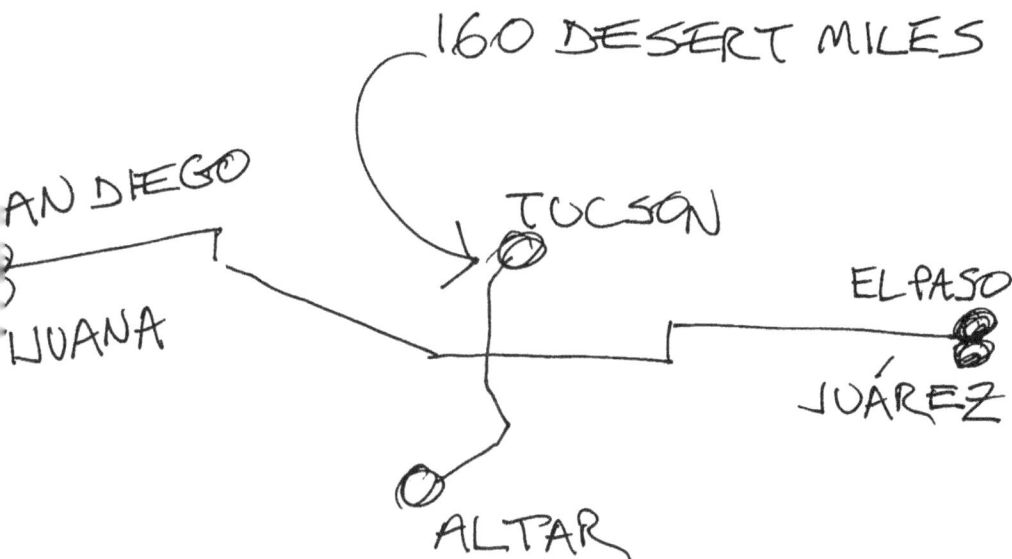

160 DESERT MILES

SAN DIEGO

TIJUANA

TUCSON

EL PASO

JUÁREZ

ALTAR

Chapter 20

BURDEN OR BENEFIT?

A wave of anti-immigrant fervor swept the United States in the 1980s and 1990s. Many of the almost three million undocumented immigrants who had received amnesty and legal status under the 1986 immigration law decided to remain north of the Mexican border. The new rules allowed them to bring their families. Meanwhile, more undocumented workers were coming north. Political refugees headed north across Mexico to escape the civil wars in Central America. "The simple truth is we've lost control of our borders," President Ronald Reagan announced at the time, "and no country can afford that."

A million and a half migrants were being caught each year trying to cross into the United States illegally during that era, most of them Mexicans. Estimates vary regarding the numbers who made it across safely but they obviously were huge. One thing is certain: since the 9/11 attacks, many Mexicans in the United States without proper paperwork were loath to return home, fearing that increased security at the borders would make it more difficult and more expensive to get back to their jobsites—perhaps even impossible.

Not only would free passage for Mexican workers into the United States make it easier to secure the southern border against intruders who may have a more nefarious intent than getting a job, it would also make it possible to begin to account for those Mexicans already in the United States without official approval. If those millions did not fear deportation, many, if not most, would likely feel more comfortable about registering their status and normalizing their residency.

That's the point former Mexican interior secretary Santiago Creel made during a Spring 2003 meeting with U.S. Secretary of State Colin Powell. Creel came out of his meeting with the usual diplomatic platitudes. "What this trip proved," he said, "was that, though both countries had different views on Iraq, we can work together closely and intensely."

But in reality, Mexico's decision to oppose the U.S. war on Iraq only exacerbated frustrations between the two countries that had been building since September 11, 2001. Radio news commentator Paul Harvey mocked Mexico's position against the Iraq invasion by reinforcing anti-Mexican stereotypes during a broadcast to his huge audience. "Vicente Fox drinks water in Mexico every day," announced Harvey with his trademark singsong delivery. Following a distinct Harvey dramatic pause, he offered his punch line, "He can't be worried about a little thing like biological weapons."[1]

After the attacks, hopes on both sides of the border for solutions to the Mexican migration crisis were extinguished as the Bush Administration tried to secure U.S. borders. Creel saw that the two goals were not mutually exclusive.

"I think to a point," he said during his Washington trip, "the U.S. internal security depends on knowing who its people are. And an important part of that population is four million Mexicans. It's not known who they are, where they are, whom they work for. If we're talking about security we have to talk about the security of immigrants as well, giving them documents."[2]

By legalizing a victimless crime, such as migrating north for work, you can, as Creel pointed out, control it. You can also protect the migrant from ludicrously expensive border crossing charges inflicted by predatory *coyotes*. It is less likely employers will take advantage of workers who are in the United States legally. That means fewer cases of inappropriately low paychecks, poor working conditions and forced overtime. Legal workers will be less inclined to keep quiet since they won't fear deportation.

9/11 and the Mexican Border

Early in September of 2001, President Bush announced, "The United States has no more important relationship in the world than our relationship with Mexico." Less than a week later the World Trade Center and the Pentagon were in flames. Washington scratched Mexico off its to-do list. Interior minister Creel expressed the frustration of his government. "Mexico has shown a willingness to work on drugs. Mexico has shown a willingness to work on security. But when Mexico asks the United States to work on migration, we have not seen the same willingness."[3]

The exact number coming north is relatively unimportant. Whether visitors overstay the time limits on their visas, or the desperately poor run across the frontier, hiding along the route like animals, people keep coming for the American Dream. Nothing—not U.S. laws, fences, walls, nor the Border Patrol—stops this migration. Whether one believes in unlimited immigration or tight controls over who and how many people can move to the United States, there is no question that allowing illegal immigration is bad for everybody involved, except for the *coyotes* and exploitive employers.

The Game-Changing 1986 Immigration Law

Congress passed the 1986 immigration law in an attempt to deal with the illegal immigration that had already occurred and to control the flow of migrants in the future. Former Wyoming Senator Alan Simpson was a coauthor of the law, a law that offered amnesty to those already in the United States illegally and provided for penalties against U.S. employers who hired undocumented workers. We talked while his bill was being debated in the Capitol.

"We're not looking for perfection," Simpson acknowledged, "Anybody who is looking at this bill for perfection is off the wall. I don't know whether it will work. But I think it will be the best approach before we try a military presence at our borders." Lawmakers hoped the one-time amnesty for those migrants living in the United States without documentation would encourage Mexicans to return home when their jobs were finished and then return only when there was new work. The reality showed the flaws in the arguments that Mexican immigration is not an assimilating immigration. Many of those granted amnesty not only stayed, they used their new legal status to bring family members into the United States legally, and to leave farm work for better paying and more stable jobs in cities. That exodus opened a labor void filled by new and often undocumented immigration from Mexico. In addition, it was relatively easy for immigrants who did not qualify for the amnesty to generate forged papers that indicated they met the criteria for legal status. Consequently many more Mexicans became legal U.S. residents because of the law than Congress anticipated.

Alan Simpson is another who invokes the Emma Lazarus poem when he talks about immigration. "The Statue of Liberty doesn't say on it, 'Send us everybody you've got, legally or illegally.' That's not what it says."

No, not in those exact words. But what the Emma Lazarus poem says, essentially, is send me everybody in need. "Keep ancient lands, your storied pomp," are the words Lazarus reports the Statue is crying out to the world, a statue she calls Mother of Exiles. Next follows the oft-quoted lines, "Give me your tired, your poor, your huddled masses yearning to breathe free, the wretched refuse of your teeming shore." But less frequently quoted are these closing lines of the poem, "Send these, the homeless, the tempest-tost to me, I lift my lamp beside the golden door!"

The Statue of Liberty herself is an immigrant. Most Americans probably know she was a gift from France, but few must be aware of the fact that she is a hand-me-down. She was originally designed for Port Said, at the entrance to the Suez Canal in Egypt. French sculptor Frédéric-Auguste Bartholdi came up with the idea of placing a woman at that spot to represent progress, or "Egypt carrying the light of Asia," as he put it at the time. But the Egyptian government decided she was too expensive, and the project eventually was diverted to New York harbor.[4]

There Goes the Neighborhood

Plenty of American citizens fear the surge of Mexicans coming north is a threat to their society. "It's getting more in your face," said Gordon Lee Baum, a founder and the CEO of the racist activist group Council of Conservative Citizens (a headline in their newsletter reads, "Non-White Immigration Will Ruin America"). "All of a sudden they see it happening in their community. They wake up one morning like the people at the Alamo and say, 'Where did the Mexicans come from?'"[5] Perhaps Baum, who died in 2015, skipped history class the day the Alamo was taught. The Alamo was first a Spanish mission, then a Mexican fortress. It was the Texas insurgents who occupied it and refused to surrender it back to the Mexicans. The Mexicans were there first. Such details do not infiltrate the Council of Conservative Citizen's mission statement: "The C of CC also stands against the tide of nonwhite, Third World immigrants swamping this country."[6]

In the mid-1980s Immigration and Naturalization Service Director Alan Nelson told me as many as 12 million people were in the United States without official authorization, and that he believed they were taking jobs away from U.S. citizens. Just as so many Mexicans working in the United States are undocumented, so were those statistics waved by Nelson. They were based on guesses and theories, just as such charges of job losses to immigrants are undocumented. Since no one knows for sure how many Mexicans are in the United States without government approval, is it not clear how many, if any, take jobs from workers who are citizens or who have papers authorizing them to work.

But the late free-market economist and longtime University of Maryland professor Julian Simon told me he didn't believe the huge numbers published repeatedly as estimates of the number of Mexicans in the United States without formal paperwork. "The volume of illegal immigration now," he said, back in the mid-1980s, "may be zero. That is, as many illegals may be going home in the average year as are coming." Since the 9/11 attacks, there are no average years. But what may be an apocryphal story sums up the realpolitik of the revolving door at the border ever since President Polk's war seized half of Mexico for the States. Asked what would happen if she were caught crossing into Texas, the maid at a McAllen, Texas, motel is said to have replied simply, "I would be late for work."[7] Comedian Diane Rodriguez used the routine of border crossing in her act during the campaign against Proposition 187 in California. "Oh, the trials and tribulations of American life," she told her audience in a monologue of Latina experiences. "Today I had to get my hair done. I broke a nail and then I got deported again."[8]

The refrain that the United States cannot survive without Mexican labor is familiar, and can be traced throughout the troubled history between the two countries. Back in the 1930s, for example, one Fred H. Bixby was moved to define his industry's need for Mexican workers with this litany of complaints: "If I do not get Mexicans to thin those beets and to hoe those beets, I am through with the beet business. We have no Chinamen. We have not the Japs. The Hindu is worthless, the Filipino is nothing, and the white man will not do the work."[9]

But Julian Simon was not seeing the humor when he said, "The INS has advertised wrong and false information on the subject." His research convinced him that immigrants do take some jobs that would otherwise be held by Americans. "The number, however, is relatively small." Simon was from the camp convinced that immigrants—with papers and otherwise—improve the economy. They open businesses, spend money, pay taxes and often do not use social services because they fear getting caught and deported. Simon was convinced that open borders would not inundate the United States with immigrants. And he had a simple example: "If that were so, how come all of Puerto Rico doesn't move to New York?"

Many of them do, warned George Borjas, a Harvard economics and social policy professor. "The Puerto Rican experience may be instructive," he writes. "Puerto Ricans are American citizens who can move freely within the United States, and the differences in economic opportunities between Puerto Rico and the mainland are quite large. Not surprisingly, about 25 percent of Puerto Rico's population moved to the United States in the last fifty years."[10] Borjas argued that Mexicans do take jobs that U.S. citizens and legal residents would perform if the wages weren't deflated by the availability of desperate illegal laborers.

Of course a counterargument, and a strong one, is that New York doesn't suffer from this influx of Puerto Ricans. It thrives from it.

Rogers, Arkansas, and other chicken-processing cities in northwest Arkansas provide another counterargument. In the early 1990s these plants were hungry for employees because local laborers were rejecting the low wages offered by the chicken industry. Mexicans inundated Rogers, Fayetteville, Springdale, Bentonville, Bella Vista—not only directly from Mexico, but from the southwest of the United States. They filled the jobs at the chicken-packing plants and added vibrancy to the local economy with grocery stores and restaurants, newspapers and video rental shops serving the new Spanish-speaking population.[11] Periodic and highly publicized ICE raids on these plants during the Obama and Trump administrations wreaked havoc on such communities, disrupting business and ripping apart families.

A 2017 study conducted by the National Academy of Sciences is one of the most comprehensive attempts to determine if immigrants cost the United States money or fuel economic growth. The report concludes that "the long-term impact of immigration on the wages and employment of native-born workers overall is very small, and that any negative impacts are most likely to be found for prior immigrants or native-born high school dropouts." Although overall the statistics show "first-generation immigrants are more costly to governments than are the native-born, but the second generation are among the strongest fiscal and economic contributors in the U.S." The study mirrors what a lay observer of immigrant influences in America should conclude: "Immigration has an overall positive impact on long-run economic growth in the U.S."[12]

In a similar study in 2017, the National Academy of Sciences made clear that crucial industries such as agriculture, restaurants and clothing "would not exist on the same scale without immigrant workers." It stated without equivocation, "The vast majority of Americans are enjoying a healthier economy as a result of the increased supply of labor and lower prices that result from immigration."[13]

Statistics are used by all those involved in the immigration controversy, often announced without documentation and impossible to verify or negate. Without accurate figures, it is not possible to ascertain how much undocumented immigrants pay in taxes versus how much they use in the minimal public-funded social services available to them. Both sides in the immigration controversy use statistics convenient for bolstering their arguments.

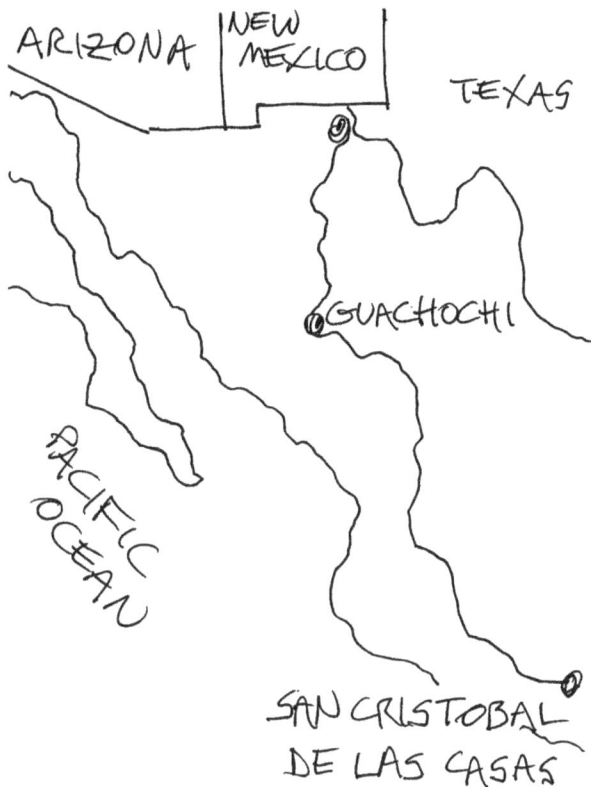

Chapter 21

THE LONG ROAD NORTH FROM CHIAPAS AND CHIHUAHUA

In Mexico's impoverished regions, desperate *campesinos*, peasants, must decide whether to scratch out a marginal income or take a chance with *El Norte*.

To Pancho Villa's Chihuahua

The sprint from the U.S. border at Juárez to Chihuahua is on a high-speed, four-lane toll road, a little more than three hours across the dry lakes and past the dunes and mesas of the Chihuahua Desert. The main avenues of Ciudad Chihuahua look like Los Angeles—it takes another half hour of stop-and-go driving to get through the sprawl of car lots, strip malls and traffic to downtown. Cars, trucks and buses spew out their acrid smog—a choking mix of untreated exhaust and burning oil. Streets, stores and houses suffer from a hodgepodge of L.A.-style glitz with incomplete construction and poor maintenance. Paint peels, windows crack, concrete breaks, rebar waits to reinforce. These are the common denominators of the Third World: incomplete construction and poor maintenance—here in Mexico decorated with its distinctive clashing pastel colors and punctuated by the sound of blaring baa-boom-boom-ba music from car speakers, bars and street corner kiosks.

Pancho Villa's sprawling Chihuahua mansion is now a museum, proudly documenting his attack into New Mexico during the Mexican Revolution.

From Chihuahua, the highway to the Tarahumara Sierra climbs up to the plains cultivated by transplanted Mennonites. The Mennonites immigrated to Mexico during the First World War following conflicts with the U.S. government over their refusal to serve in the military. The Mexican government offered them refuge and land in return for lessons in modern farming techniques. Today the descendants of these immigrants are distinctive in Chihuahua market towns—their fair skin combined with their clothing give them away. The women wear bonnets or scarves that harken back to their northern European roots, but they protect themselves from the harsh Mexican sun with a culture-clashing *sombrero* over their head cloth.

Three hours of climbing brings the traveler to Creel, a strip of shops and hotels along the highway and railroad that prides itself as the jumping-off point for tourists visiting the wilds of the Tarahumara Sierra—its canyons, its railroad ride through the Copper Canyon to the Pacific, the opportunity to meet the remote and indigenous Tarahumara people. The businesses along the main street crank out steak and burritos, dolls and baskets, beer and Coca-Cola. Weekend nights the local teenagers cruise for each other in cars, on horseback, some still strolling on the sidewalks—making eyes at each other and giggling.

Creel is named for Enrique Clay Creel, the businessman and Chihuahua governor who ran the railroad. Creels also ran Chihuahua. At a social function a patriarch of the family—Luis Terrazas—supposedly answered a casual question about his homeland with a dismissive, "I am not from Chihuahua. I own Chihuahua." Santiago Creel, the Mexican interior minister who talked migration crises with the George W. Bush administration, is a descendant of the extended "Chihuahua es mío" Creel-Terrazas clan.

Some Tarahumara women in Creel—dressed in their unique eye-catching costumes (typical: turquoise and red, chartreuse and pink ruffled full skirt with puffed-sleeves blouse, solid colored socks matching one of the colors of the skirt, all topped off with a scarf of some nonmatching print of flowers or paisleys in more bright colors)—send their children up to tourists, peddling colorful woven belts and elegant, intricate basketry. Further up the railroad line from Creel are the luxury resorts of the Copper Canyon, surrounded by the camps of the Tarahumara and the encroaching international lumber harvesters, along with marijuana and opium poppy cultivators who take advantage of isolation to do their business.

The Mexican army patrols the region, charged with protecting cash-fat tourists and with chasing narco-farmers. Hints of the complications caused by the army presence are made evident by the posters dominating the foyer of the small Catholic church on the square in Creel, posters explaining to the Tarahumara their human rights guaranteed by the Mexican Constitution, posters advising the Tarahumara what to do if they are harassed by the army. Posters in the windows of the state government building on the square report a missing 35-year-old man, announce the CD released by a local band, advise citizens to exercise their right to vote, "the key to democracy."

Driving fast, fast, fast across the Sierra, it's almost three hours to Guachochi. It's a spectacular and exhausting trip through canyon wilderness, punctuated by overhanging sheer rock walls towering over the highway—with pieces of rock littering the two-lane blacktop, adjacent to Falling Rocks warning signs. Maguey, piñon and nopal line the route. The lonely road surprises periodically with its decorations of Tarahumara in their colorful costumes appearing seemingly out of nowhere from side canyons. They're toting plastic bags, herding cows or sitting by the side of the road.

Kilometer after kilometer click by with no services: no phones, no gas stations, no Starbucks and nothing on the radio.

Finally a Pemex station looms at the bottom of a hill, its familiar green sign welcoming me to a cold Coca-Cola and a tankful of gasoline. It's shuttered. Out of business. Whoever labeled U.S. 50 across Nevada "the loneliest road in the world" never made the Creel to Guachochi run.

Guachochi is a windswept market town on the edge of the Tarahumara Sierra, dominated by a harsh-looking stone prison and ramshackle single-story houses with rusting corrugated tin roofs. When I got close to Guachochi, I searched the radio dial for evidence of XETAR, the local radio station, and heard only static at 870 AM, its frequency. I saw the telltale transmitter tower on the horizon at the outskirts of town and beat my old rented Chevy over the rutted dirt roads to the site, looking for the studio. Townsfolk directed me to an anonymous-looking house. On the building were two signs: one advising that this was indeed XETAR, *La Voz de la Sierra Tarahumara*, the voice of the Sierra Tarahumara, the other a simple, *Cerrado*. I banged on the closed door. No answer. That's when I went over to *Los Pinos* restaurant and ordered a Coke. I asked the proprietor what was wrong with the radio station. "Technical problems," he told me. I borrowed his phone and called the station. The fellow who answered said no one was available to talk because the station was off the air, and he hung up.

I looked frustrated, I'm sure, and that's when the proprietor suggested I visit his friend across town, Petronilo González. González owned another restaurant in Guachochi, *La Cabaña*, and he worked at XETAR as an announcer and engineer. I found him asleep in front of a TV in his empty restaurant. "*¡Pase, pase!*" he said when I woke him. I sat down and we talked.

The station was off the air, he told me, because a relay had failed and there were no spare parts available in Guachochi. The station is plagued by its old equipment, he said. "We need new equipment, but it is not forthcoming from the government." How important to the community is the station, I asked him, how serious a problem is it that XETAR is off the air? "*Es muy importante,*" he said. It provides many of the Tarahumara with their only source of communication with the outside world. It is, he said, the only radio station within 200 kilometers. I knew that to be true, I had been looking for a radio signal since leaving Creel. "There is no other communication for the indigenous people who do not have money. *No hay nada,*" he said, nothing, no newspapers, no TV, nothing but XETAR for people who live out in these wilds of Chihuahua, the largest Mexican state.

As we talked in *La Cabaña,* President Fox appeared on the TV, praising the pending access to information law in Mexico.

"God willing, we'll find the relay in Chihuahua Monday and we'll be back on the air," Gonzalez told me with confidence as we said good-bye.

No News Is No News

I'm reading the book *A Fortune-Teller Told Me* on this trip, the account by the late journalist Tiziano Terzani of the year he spent without traveling by airplane. Terzani writes,

> There is one aspect of a reporter's job that never ceases to fascinate and disturb me: facts that go unreported do not exist. How many massacres, how many earthquakes happen in the world, how many ships sink, how many volcanoes erupt, and how many people are persecuted, tortured, and killed? Yet if no one is there to see, to write, to take a photograph, it is as if these facts never occurred, this suffering has no importance, no place in history. Because history exists only if someone relates it. It is sad, but such is life; and perhaps it is precisely this idea—the idea that with every little description of a thing observed one can leave a seed in the soil of memory—that keeps me tied to my profession.[1]

Terzani was musing about the critical importance of journalism during a reporting trip to Burma. He could just as well have been writing from the pre-internet journalistic void of Creel and the Tarahumara Sierra. Of course there is a corollary to Terzani's correct remarks. When journalists draw attention to an intriguing remote locale such as Burma and Creel, one common result is not necessarily advantageous, hyper-tourism. Without attention and its following tourism, Creel would not attract Tarahumara from the hinterlands to beg and try to sell trinkets in the streets. What to make of the impact of the tourists with their short pants, loud voices, pricey cameras and one package-tour marga-rita at sunset? Probably, overall the influx of tourist-fueled capital is a healthy thing, and when news reports highlight social problems in pre-viously isolated locales, it might be more difficult for the villains to go unpunished, for the crises to be ignored. Visiting rural Chihuahua and Chiapas, studying Mexico's urban slums and impoverished hinterlands, helps make it clear why so many Mexicans go north.

On to the Zapatistas

San Cristóbal de Las Casas is a slow, two-hour propeller plane ride over the mountains south from Mexico City. As the plane descends toward the airport, the Mayan highlands are close enough to view the poverty of the villages: ramshackle housing, humans as cargo bearers.

San Cristóbal de Las Casas is idyllic Mexico, storybook Mexico. The town square features a two-story gazebo. The evening I first arrived it was filled with the final fiesta of a week of Easter partying, this one dedicated to peace, as hope continued that *Presidente* Fox and *Subcomandante* Marcos would become the "*amigos*" Fox called them, and that the indigenous rights bill pending in the Congress would be passed and prove satisfactory to the Zapatistas. The bill was passed; it was not satisfactory.

A marimba band filled the *zócalo* with a mood suggesting the Buena Vista Social Club. Couples were hugging and kissing, kids were playing, lovely aromas filled the square from the carts of vendors selling snacks.

This is the city Marcos and the Zapatistas took from the Mexican military in the surprise attack in 1994 that continued a conflict that goes back to the Conquest. The Chiapas rebellion was launched on January 1 of that year, the same date that the North American Free Trade Agreement (NAFTA) became operative. Thousands of armed Zapatistas took control of San Cristóbal and several other municipalities in the state, demanding land reform, indigenous autonomy and cultural rights. One of their slogans was "NAFTA is Death!" The Zapatistas' protest and their charismatic leader *Subcomandante* Marcos found some initial enthusiastic support in Mexico and throughout the world. But the Mexican army reacted to the Zapatistas with counterassaults that left at least 145 Zapatistas dead. Demonstrations in Mexico against the military response helped lead to a ceasefire by mid-January. Throughout the 1990s the fragile ceasefire barely held, violated by the army and paramilitary groups who fought—and killed—to disrupt the political efforts of the Zapatistas. After Vicente Fox was elected president, the Mexican Congress passed the indigenous rights law that the Zapatistas called inadequate and the standoff continued.

The second part of San Cristóbal's name honors Las Casas, the first bishop of San Cristóbal and an early activist for indigenous rights who wrote extensively against the oppression perpetrated by the Spanish conquerors, calling the injustices he witnessed sins.

Soon I was twisting up the Chiapas mountains in Onésimo Hidalgo's jeep, heading for San Andrés Larráinzar. Onésimo Hidalgo was the director of the Centro de Investigaciones Económicas y Politícas de Accion Comunitaria, known as CIEPAC (a few years later he was charged with sexual harassment of women CIEPAC colleagues and he left the organization). When we met, Hidalgo proudly labeled CIEPAC as an organization without government, religious or political party connections. We were en route to a most basic and efficient news broadcast, with Hidalgo as newscaster and *campesinos* assembling from villages even further remote than San Andrés Larráinzar as the initial audience. As we worked our way toward the village, claimed by both the Zapatistas and the longtime governing political party in Chiapas as under their jurisdiction, Hidalgo explained CIEPAC's chores.

"We work with the poorest," he said, pointing out that the fighting had devastating effects on the poor indigenous population in the isolated Chiapas highlands. CIEPAC, he told me, is working to help rebuild infrastructure and to try to repair society in newly polarized communities. The long-term goal was to create models for a society based on equal rights in a region where the indigenous people have been treated by the ruling classes as second-class citizens since the days of Bishop Bartolomé de Las Casas.

Hidalgo is a sociologist and a graduate of the National Autonomous University of Chiapas, a Chiapas native. He titles himself an investigator, analyst and popular educator with extensive experience in the *campesino* and indigenous movement. Much of his work was to assemble data from primary sources regarding the Mexican military's presence in Chiapas and the activities of paramilitary groups. Hidalgo traveled to remote enclaves such as San Andrés Larráinzar and met with assembled *campesinos*, listened to them report to him what is going on in their villages and then presented a day-long lecture on current events.

In rural zones such as San Andrés Larrainzar, Hidalgo cited figures of over 70 percent illiteracy. "There are not enough schools," he tells me, "children must work. They are too poor to go to school. They must work to live. There is no time for school." Hidalgo points to a group of little kids by the side of the road. "Look at these *niños*," he says, "they must carry water and wash clothes." They look about five years old. "How can they go to school?" Looking past the colorful costumes of these indigenous children with roots back to the pre-Columbian Mayan the reality is shocking to watch: While leading scattered little herds of goats they struggle alongside the highway with heavy backloads of firewood and other goods slung from a cloth pressed tight against their foreheads.

An open army truck passes us on the highway as we near San Andrés Larrainzar, the locale of the peace talks between the government of President Ernesto Zedillo and the Zapatistas, negotiations that resulted in the 1994 shooting war truce. The truck is filled with uniformed soldiers, guns at the ready. "Look," says Hidalgo, "the government says soldiers are no longer in this region, and there they are." He pulls the jeep into the churchyard and we move to a low classroom building with whitewashed brick walls under a corrugated metal roof where we're greeted by a couple of dozen smiling straw-hatted *campesinos*. There are no women in attendance. The chatter of greeting from the crowd is in Tzotzil. Only half the Chiapas population speaks Spanish. It's been a month since the group last met. Through a Tzotzil translator they report the news to Hidalgo. He listens and takes notes, asking questions. These men, called *catequistas*, are chosen from volunteers in their villages to be the oral news gatherers and reporters under a program organized by the Catholic church. Most take out their notebooks and write in detail as Hidalgo makes his day-long presentation. Once back in their local communities they become teachers before a group assembled from even more remote localities.

Onésimo Hidalgo lectures in front of an old wooden-framed blackboard hanging on nails, using it to scribble detailed notes and charts. "We're going to speak about neoliberalism and Fox," he says, "and what this means to Chiapas and Mexico." Over the next several hours Hidalgo details NAFTA and the connection between Mexico and the European Union. He explains from his perspective Fox's economic policies and the impact of these factors on *campesino* life. He talks about the effects of globalization on family farms and explains "*transgénicos*," genetically modified food. He condemns Monsanto, the purveyor of genetically modified corn seed.[2] It is a remarkably detailed and balanced report. In this primitive-looking remote classroom, these *campesinos* are thoroughly analyzing world trade and its effect on local control. "All this," sums up Hidalgo, "includes the large companies and excludes the poor *campesinos*."

We break for lunch in the churchyard. Lucky for me, it is a *campesino* meal: vegetarian, and I do not need to make up an excuse for rejecting meat. We eat rice, eggs, cabbage, potatoes, beans and tortillas—delicious.

After another hour of lecture, Hidalgo turns the session into the equivalent of a radio talk show, taking questions and stimulating discussion, finally asking this concluding question of the group:

"Why is it important for us to talk?"

And he gets these answers:

"Because it is how information is transferred."

"Because it is important to know what is happening in our country in order to construct a better life."

"Because it is important to have information about what is happening in our country and the world."

Hidalgo tries to convince the *campesinos* in his class to stay in Chiapas and work for change, not head north for jobs in the global economy. It's much the same argument yelled by the vigilantes on the border who advocate ordering the Marines to seal the border. "We're being sacrificed on the altar of globalism," was the chant from Glenn Spencer, the founder of the American Border Patrol—the band of self-appointed border patrollers that operated in Arizona at the time Chris Simcox was active with his Civil Homeland Defense Corps. "You have big corporations," said Spencer, "who want no barriers to the making of their profits."[3]

NAFTA We Don't Hafta!

For years after NAFTA was approved by the United States and Mexico, it was blamed for pushing Mexicans north. NAFTA—and its replacement cousin, the Trump-initiated U.S.-Mexico-Canada Agreement (USMCA)—both call for the free, or at least freer, movement of capital and goods across the North American borders. But not labor. The elimination of the trade barriers that vigilante Glenn Spencer complained about means that U.S. agribusiness can sell corn in Mexico for less, much less, than the subsistence amount of pesos local farmers earned for their crops before open competition from the United States was allowed. Kentucky farmers export much of their white corn to Mexico for the manufacture of tortillas. This corn trafficking is a disaster for the Mexican family farmer. "The prices seem to go down and down each year," reported Tlacuitapa farmer Maurilio Marquez. "If it weren't for my family in California sending money, we wouldn't have any choice but to go north and join them."[4] Mexican government studies reported that soon after the inception of NAFTA, corn prices dropped an astounding 80 percent.[5] The numbers add poignancy to an editorial cartoon that shows a gringo businessman in a big car asking a Mexican farmer with a burro what he'd like to trade. "Places," answers the Mexican. Proponents of NAFTA and the USMCA continue to say that in the long term, Mexico and most Mexicans will thrive because of the increased trade with the United States, even if the family farms never recover.

But it isn't only the farmer in Mexico who suffered from the effects of NAFTA, effects that don't change with the updated USMCA. Businesses seeking U.S. investment fired workers in attempts to improve their profit margins and appear more inviting. More workers lost jobs when U.S.-owned factories operating on the Mexican side of the border slowed production during the recession beginning in 2001. A decade after NAFTA was signed the average wage at these border plants was all but unchanged at just over four dollars. Not four dollars an hour, but four dollars a day. At that time a gallon of milk in Tijuana cost about three dollars.[6] When the USMCA was negotiated more than another decade later, the income and costs ratio barely changed. These kinds of numbers can make a border crossing look quite seductive, especially to workers already living right on the borderline.

The gross difference between most personal incomes in the United States and those in Mexico forces migration north. NAFTA promoters promised the agreement would result in a reduction in this disparity between wages paid in one of the world's largest economies and those paid in its Third World neighbor. In fact the opposite occurred, and the wage gap increased over 10 percent during the first ten years of NAFTA—a prime factor seducing companies to move their American factories south of the border. Even many of those Mexicans who try to deal with the wage inequity by crossing the border face a down-wardly mobile lifestyle. "Recent moves in California to prevent illegal immigrants from receiving driver's licenses and medical care have been a depressing sign that conditions for Mexican immigrants in this country are getting worse," wrote Columbia University economics professor and

Nobel Prize laureate Joseph Stiglitz in a critical appraisal of NAFTA on its tenth anniversary.[7] And although driver's licenses and medical care became available to undocumented immigrants in California and some of the other States, gross inequities persist along and across the border.

Nonetheless and obviously, most Mexicans do not migrate north. I joined a Guadalajara talk show host to talk borders. We took calls from her audience, asking listeners why they did not want to move to *el otro lado*. The radio station switchboard filled quickly: "It's too violent up there." "I love my hometown." "There's prejudice against Mexicans." "I'd miss my family and friends." "I don't make much money here, but I make enough. And this is home."

Politics and the Pulpit

On another trip up to San Andrés Larrainzar, I met with the parish priest, who spoke freely of the difficulties he experienced trying to continue his work under the jurisdiction of the new Chiapas bishop. José de Jesús Landín García (known locally by his nickname Chuy) receives me in his modest office. He's wearing jeans, a T-shirt and his warm engaging smile. We talk just prior to Sunday Mass. He acknowledges violating the desires of the new bishop by making himself available for interviews with the foreign press. The bishop wants all information disseminated from the centralized control of the church authority. But Chuy says expressing his opinion regarding local conditions is an integral aspect of his work as a priest.

Chuy uses his pulpit and the bully pulpit of his position as priest to report the news as he sees it, and he preaches the same sermon as Onésimo Hidalgo: globalization is adding to the crisis for Chiapas *campesinos*, severe social and economic problems persist. The bishop wants to send him to Rome to study. Chuy is resisting such reassignment, which he is convinced is designed to silence him. In his office are stacks of political literature.

The congregation gathers in the churchyard. Men in their traditional garb: pointed straw hats adorned with multicolored ribbons with colored pom-poms trailing over white headcloths, gray serape-like suits tied with a red sash over white shirts with red sleeves. Women in dark blue cotton skirts with white blouses embroidered in wild colors with complementary sashes—often carrying one or two babies wrapped in white.

Inside, the church is decorated with blue and white banners illustrated with images of doves. Elaborate assemblages of candles, flowers, peacock feathers, figures and paintings of saints are surrounded with pots filled with burning incense. Mirrors hang from the necks of the figures, perhaps to reflect any evil in the parishioner so that it doesn't enter the saint, but the origin and purpose of many such rituals are no longer known for sure, they're simply repeated. The sanctuary fills with the incense smoke. The women sit on the pine needles covering the floor and chat, breastfeed, tend the incense while the prayers drone from the altar. The men stand.

"Peace is a gift of God, but it is also something we have a responsibility to build together," says Chuy as part of the service.

On one wall, the Virgin of Guadalupe looks out from a tiled altar in a frame featuring flashing Christmas-tree lights. Behind the main altar are glass-covered cases lit by fluorescent tubes and filled with figures of the Virgin Mary and Christ. Recorded popular music from the Sunday market outside drifts into the church, competing with the service.

The mainstream mass media in Chiapas and the world report improvement in Chiapas since the peace talks, or report nothing at all. But Chuy says problems continue and must be addressed. As I leave San Andrés Larrainzar, a drunken man lies across the road as if dead. Sunday is market day, church day and drinking day. Potent *pox* (pronounced posh)—distilled from fermented corn, sugar cane and wheat bran—is a popular knockout that also is used for indigenous ceremonies.

Massacre Memorial

On the 22nd day of every month there is a memorial service in Acteal, another Chiapas highlands community, commemorating the massacre perpetrated by paramilitaries in the village on December 22, 1997. The memorial service is both a religious event and a news report, another example of the Mexican oral tradition for reporting news.

In a packed open-air chapel under an orange plastic tent roof, I join the congregation as Father Pedro Arriaga—in a long speech—announces the news. He reiterates the story of the massacre. He reports that justice is unfinished regarding finding the perpetrators and holding them accountable for their horrific crimes. He points out that the massacre is an example of the crises caused in Chiapas by globalization. He identifies Plan Puebla Panamá—the Central America-Mexico economic cooperation plan that includes controversial infrastructure development such as the proposal to build a land bridge across Mexico to compete with the Panama Canal—as an unjust sop to capitalists.

Simple wooden crosses decorated with colorful ribbons adorn the dais. An indigenous music group plays: trumpet, drums, harp and violin. An elder chants a droning prayer while the congregation kneels on the dirt floor covered with pine needles. A picture of the Virgin of Guadalupe hangs below a bell on a pole. Incense burns, Calla lily blossoms peek from plastic buckets—one of the buckets is red and features the Coca-Cola logo.

The chanter drones on. One of the visiting priests on the dais pulls a camera out of his robe and snaps a picture. The droning continues and the chanter's eyes glaze. Periodically the assembled priests prostrate themselves.

A local Chiapas parish priest, Father Marcello, the first Tzotzil priest, begins the homily. He says he has two goals with the Mass. One is to come together as a community for a traditional religious meeting. The other is a remembrance of the massacre and a concern for the future. He says a good pastor makes clear what is needed in a community. And then he announces his news story, "It is very dangerous when one's enemies are quiet because you don't know when or where an enemy will attack." He is referring to the day's news—or lack of news—in Chiapas. "Here attack is not theoretical," he says. Then he warns, "There is more danger when you cannot hear the shooting. So it is imperative to be attentive." In a void of credible traditional news media, this is a credible newscast. "Jesus is a good shepherd who can protect sheep from wolves," preaches Father Marcello, adding as an explanation of his activist role, "priests and nuns—like Jesus—must take care of the sheep God gave them."

The names and ages of all the massacre victims are recited: 15 children, 21 women, 9 men.

An electrified band alternates tunes with the traditionalist musicians. A couple dozen members of the congregation parade in a clockwise circle around the altar and give an offering: corn and beans in shallow baskets, flowers, a poster about human rights in the Dominican Republic, a new book about the former Chiapas bishop Don Samuel Ruíz.

Following the Mass I am invited to a communal lunch of eggs and tortillas with coffee. The combination of poverty and violence makes it easy to understand what motivates these *campesinos* to trek north; the warmth of their community makes it just as easy to understand their homesickness once they cross the border.

Not far down the highway from Acteal, in the last main city before the Guatemala border, Comitán, a local commercial radio station was blasting pop tunes from loudspeakers in the *zócalo*. A small group of teenagers gathered to listen, an ice cream vendor provided them with refreshment from his cart. At a video arcade, teenagers are sweating on the Dance Dance Revolution machine, working out to the latest hits from *El Norte*. In front of the arcade's open doors, out on the sidewalk, little kids mimic the dance steps of their teenage elders, learning rituals of the global pop community (Figure 21.1).

Millions of desperate people seeking relief from poverty and a 2,000-mile land border inviting them to cross over with one step from the Third to the First World guarantees that there will be trouble on the U.S.–Mexico border unless and until a fair day's work earns a fair day's pay on both sides—no matter the status of Trump's wall fantasy.

My amigo Víctor Reyes is a journalist and a translator in Marin County, California. He writes regularly about the life of Mexicans living in Marin and Sonoma Counties. Over the years he's been my Spanish-language *maestro*. We often talk about the border crisis and the migration from Mexico. Victor is one of the fortunate migrants. Born in Puebla into

Figure 21.1 A smoke break up against a wall in Varadero. Cuba.

a middle-class family and educated at the university there, he could choose to come north for a visit legally, and eventually he chose to stay, again legally. But he sympathizes readily with *campesinos* struggling to cross the border and decode life in the United States.

Victor appreciates the fact that he's living not just the American Dream, but also the California Dream. Life for him in Marin County is free of the prejudice many Mexicans face throughout the 50 states that are their diaspora. Mexicans and things Mexican are well appreciated in Marin County. But he insists he's only around for the convenience, that he's still invested south of the border. We argue about his attitude.

"Are you an American or a Mexican?" I ask him.

"I'm a Mexican," he says without hesitation.

"But you're an American citizen now."

"So what? I'm a Mexican citizen too. I'm an American citizen because I could remain being a Mexican citizen. That's just a piece of paper. That means nothing."

"You're a Mexican in your heart?"

Oh, absolutely. I couldn't be an American. I know how to be here. I know how to relate to Americans. But I cannot be American, give me a break. I can't. It's an identity. You cannot change your identity. You are who you are. That's the tragedy of the second generation of immigrants who don't know who they are. I know a lot of folks like that, very intelligent people. They struggle because they don't speak Spanish very well. They know how to become Americans, but everybody calls them Latinos. They have no defined identity.

My father suffered none of Victor's inner conflicts about living in one place and belonging to another. He was an American as soon as he passed through Ellis Island, an American by choice who didn't pine for the Old World. Distance may well play a role in the difference between the assimilating immigration from Europe and the commuting migrations from Mexico. It was not feasible in those days before easy air travel to move regularly back and forth between Middle Europe and New York. Coming to America usually meant a one-way commitment. The proximity of Sinaloa to California, Veracruz to Kentucky, Sonora to Arizona means Mexicans can taste and test the United States knowing they can go home *mañana*. But that opportunity to stay in close touch with the homeland does not mean Mexicans don't assimilate into the American mainstream. Many do, of course, and do so without losing contact with their native land.

Directly along the border, from Tijuana to Brownsville, are Mexicans and Americans who deal with this mélange of cultures that Victor still fights. They've created the borderlands culture. "Nothing is sacred," is how Daniel Rivera, a deejay who calls himself Tolo, explains border life. "Every day, new people come to Tijuana with new traditions, languages and religions. All the icons arrive. If you don't like one, you discard it for another. There is no nationalist pressure. You don't know where your Mexican authenticity ends and your Gringo influence begins."[8] He's describing the American ideal: the melting pot.

A Mexican who has lived most of his adult life in California approached identity poetically in an interview with a *San Francisco Chronicle* reporter. "If a *nopal* is planted here or there," said Ramón Mezquita, "it's still a *nopal*."[9] Or, as Víctor Reyes wrote in his newspaper column after we talked about his identity struggle, "*Soy mexicano simplemente porque no puedo ser otra cosa*."[10] I am Mexican simply because I am unable to be anything else. Nonetheless, even as he argues against it, Victor knows he's melting into the American pot. In emails to me now he refers to himself as "your *seudo gringo amigo*," and "*el gringo nuevo*," and "*mexigringo*, or vice versa."

UNIVERSITY OF OREGON
EUGENE

CENTRO FOX
GUANAJUATO

Chapter 22

NO AMIGOS IN THE WHITE HOUSE

Toward the end of 2003, President Bush assembled members of his cabinet, along with a carefully picked collection of Latinos, in the East Room for the announcement of his plan to deal with undocumented immigration. During his short speech he initially placated those frustrated by the inequities of U.S. immigration policy. He identified the crisis honestly and correctly.

"As a nation that values immigration and depends on immigration, we should have immigration laws that work and make us proud," Bush said, looking ahead to the November 2004 elections and the huge bloc of Latino and other immigrant voters. "Yet today," he acknowledged, "we do not. Instead we see many employers turning to the illegal labor market. We see millions of hardworking men and women condemned to fear and insecurity in a massive undocumented economy. Illegal entry across our borders makes more difficult the urgent task of securing the homeland. The system is not working."

Compare that compassionate speech (Bush identified himself as a "compassionate conservative") with Trump's 2015 rant against Mexico and Mexicans when he announced his candidacy for president: "They are not our friend, believe me. They're bringing drugs. They're bringing crime. They're rapists. And some," he added with the caveat of a demagogue seeking to hide behind plausible deniability, "I assume are good people."

President Bush had succinctly assessed and summed up the problem. But his proposed solution was vague and filled with traps for immigrants working in the United States. The Bush plan was not another amnesty for workers who have been contributing for years to the American economy and culture. Nor was it a plan for the free flow of people across the U.S.-Mexico frontier. The Bush plan was a guest worker proposal, with all the inherent benefits such programs reap for employers, and all the discrimination they heap on employees. And, with the European model for guest workers in mind, makes clear that such programs leave a legacy of social problems for future generations.

"I propose," the President said, "a new temporary worker program that will match willing foreign workers with willing American employers when no Americans can be found to fill the jobs."

That statement means that foreign workers would not, under Bush's proposal, be invited to enter the U.S. labor pool. They would be restricted to those jobs that employers would deem impossible to fill with American workers. Such a system is a double threat. Not only is the foreign worker reduced to a second-class status, the American worker is subjected to job offers designed for him or her to refuse because they are such poor offers, allowing the employer to plead the need for foreign replacements.

Next Bush explained, "This program will offer legal status as temporary workers to the millions of undocumented men and women now employed in the United States and to those in foreign countries who seek to participate in the program and have been offered employment here."

This broad "offer" from the president of the United States to people—that they might end a life underground and their worry about deportation—cruelly sent out false hope to millions. As vaguely defined, the president's proposal offered legal status only for three years at a time, and only as long as the foreigner was working only for the employer whose offer of a job allowed him or her to stay in or come to the United States. That fact alone skews the dynamic of the boss–worker relationship perversely in favor of the boss.

"Don't like it?" yells the boss at the recalcitrant worker. "I'll fire you and call the *Migra* to send you back to Mexico." Under the president's plan, the worker would have no right to stay in the United States under such circumstances and would be forced to go back underground or back across the border. And of course, although the president's plan referred to "foreigners," it was designed primarily to deal with Mexican workers and the ease with which they slipped across the U.S.-Mexico border. And what about all of those desperate workers who had no deal with a specific employer? What would encourage them to stay in Mexico rather than jump the border? Nothing. And what about the wives and husbands? There was no provision for maintaining family unity. So much for fostering family values.

"The legal status granted by this program will last three years and will be renewable," announced the president as he explained his deal, "but it will have an end."

How different such harsh language—"it will have an end"—is from the embracing welcome on the base of the Statue of Liberty. This proposal was no invitation for assimilation into the American dream. And it carried a nasty threat.

"Participants who do not remain employed, who do not follow the rules of the program or who break the law," said President Bush, "will not be eligible for continued participation and will be required to return to their home."

Immigrants develop acute street smarts quickly, otherwise they could not survive. This is especially true of undocumented immigrants who constantly fear deportation. What motivation could there be to sign up for a program so weighted against them unless they enjoyed a fine relationship with an employer? The slightest digression in the workplace, the slightest misstep in public and ICE knows exactly who they are and where to find them. It sounds remarkably close to a variation of an old American immigration tradition, indentured servitude. Assessed in this harsh light, living underground as an undocumented worker seems as if it may be a much better deal for many workers, especially casual workers, day-by-day unskilled laborers.

"Employers must not hire undocumented aliens or temporary workers whose legal status has expired," Bush proclaimed about his proposed program.

Well and good to say with authority from the East Room. But impossible to enforce. Employers readily hire undocumented workers. There continues to be little policing of the workplace for such violations. Not only that, if the papers are false, as long as the employer can credibly deny knowing they are fakes, it is only the worker who is liable for prosecution. Besides, the law includes a giant loophole for agribusiness. Growers and ranchers are exempt from penalties if they hire laborers indirectly through labor contractors, and consequently slippery contractors provide undocumented workers to agribusiness.

The U.S. economy would collapse if employers had no workers and many would have no workers if they had no undocumented workers. But law enforcement is moot regarding documentation when you easily can buy a fraudulent Green Card in Bowling Green, Kentucky. Employers are not trained to detect counterfeit Green Cards. Even if they were, they would have little motivation to exercise that training. They can just smile and tell the cops and their neighbors that they checked. They thought the guys in the fields or the kitchens were in the States legally.

In case anyone thought that the Bush proposal was a welcome to join the American dream and not just a device to obtain cheap labor, the president stated, "This program expects temporary workers to return permanently to their home countries after their period of work in the United States has expired."

It couldn't be said any clearer than that unless Bush said, "Come here. Work cheap. Go home."

Aside from the crassness of the Bush foreign labor proposal, the European experience shows that guest worker programs are not tidy. Generations later Germany is still trying to deal with its Turkish minority, workers who were invited to fuel the post-war economic miracle yet were treated as legal and social second-class citizens. After the Berlin Wall fell, the united Germany was forced to deal not only with Turks, but also with guest workers brought into East Germany, some sixty thousand socialist brothers from North Vietnam. When the East German economy collapsed, their jobs disappeared. United Germany made cash deals to get rid of the Vietnamese. Germany provided Vietnam with $140 million in development aid. In return, Vietnam agreed to repatriate some forty thousand workers. No one asked the displaced workers for their opinions.[1]

The Bush plan was designed to accomplish three basic goals for the U.S. economy: exploit labor, control labor and send labor home. And it was designed to achieve those goals while gaining Bush votes from immigrants among whom it generated false hopes of residency for friends and family. The Bush guest worker proposal was a variation on a variety of other proposals offered by concerned lawmakers in Congress. None appreciated the obvious: it's impossible to prevent unauthorized immigration from Mexico.

Woody Guthrie posed the still-unanswered germane questions when he wrote his agonizing song "Deportee" after a planeload of Mexican workers sent south crashed in California. "Is this the best way we can grow our big orchards?" he asked. "Is this the best way we can grow our good fruit? To fall like dry leaves to rot on my topsoil, and be called by no name except deportees?"

Critics were quick to vilify the Bush plan. "A guest worker bill isn't enough," said Katherine Culliton, speaking as a lawyer for the Mexican American Legal Defense Fund. "It doesn't provide equal worker rights, family unity or a path to citizenship. Unless this plan is changed, it will produce a permanent underclass."[2]

"Look, our immigration policy has to show some consistency," insisted former Congressman Luis Gutierrez after the Bush speech.[3] The Democrat from Illinois provided a stark example of what he considers unfair about U.S. priorities, pointing out that just as those who favor the laws that provide immediate legalization of refugees from Cuba

> would find it unacceptable for all Cuban-Americans to return to Cuba after Fidel Castro is no longer there, we should find it unacceptable that Mexicans that have come to this country that have worked hard, pay their taxes, want to be Americans, fight in our wars should have to return to their country. Have their children here and then return to their country. Work here and then return to their country. No, America's immigration policy has always been blessed with one thing: that if you work hard and pay your taxes and you show good moral character, we accept you genuinely and completely into our great American society.

The flurry of Washington interest in border problems dissipated quickly. A couple of weeks after Bush made his proposal in the East Room, he held forth in the Capitol, delivering his third State of the Union message. Buried in rhetoric about Iraq, his war on terror, and the "sanctity of marriage" was a single short paragraph reiterating his vague immigration proposal.

The continuing limbo for the migrants from Mexico brings to mind the lyrics of another troubadour, Willie Nelson, who sings in *Across the Borderland*, "When you reach the broken-promise land, every dream slips through your hand." The mournful refrain concludes like a sorry summary of stillborn immigration reform proposals, "You've paid the price to come so far, just to wind up where you are. And you're still just across the borderline."

Bush's Legacy of Scammers

A sad result of the president's speech was not only to raise the hopes of immigrants in the United States without papers. While the applause from the assembled Cabinet members and invited guests was filling the East Room, scam artists were busy figuring out how to turn the Bush proposals into hustles. Lawyers, and others posing as experts, offered their services to migrants, suggesting they could help Mexicans apply for legalization under Bush's program. Problem was, of course, that Bush was just musing, suggesting, brainstorming, electioneering. Only Congress can change the law. Nonetheless, typical was an ad in the *Diario de Juárez* offering, "Guest workers under the immigration reform by Fox-Bush. First consultation free."

Watch out, warned the Texas attorney general.

Jesus Sandoval, the El Paso lawyer who placed the ad, insisted his motives were pure. "I'm advising people for them to prepare," he explained. But the attorney general's office was convinced that nefarious actors were expecting to make money from desperate migrants, particularly susceptible because of the vast differences in American and Mexican political cultures. Arturo Vázquez, a lawyer working both sides of the border, said the official look of Bush's speech led to misunderstandings that opened the door to con artists. "In Mexico when the President says something, it's law," he explained. "So Mexicans think it's a done deal."[4]

Problems were created far north of the border, too. The *Denver Post* reported that so-called immigration counselors operating out of storefronts in predominantly Mexican neighborhoods were selling advice on how to get the visas suggested by President Bush. More aggressive predators were going door-to-door offering to help migrants get the new visas. "The fraud appeared immediately," announced the frustrated acting Mexican consul in Denver, Juana Roberto Gonzalez. His office produced a television advertising campaign warning of the hoaxes.[5]

One George W. Bush policy for immigrants guaranteed immediate citizenship. During the Iraq war, some thirty thousand U.S. troops were foreigners, including Mexican David Cuervo, a Texas resident who emigrated from Tampico. He died in Baghdad, victim of a bomb attack two days after Christmas 2003 and two days after he called his mother to tell her he missed the smell of his favorite American food, the Whataburger. Mike Villasenor and Cuervo were classmates in school in Texas. Villasenor told a local newspaper in the Rio Grande Valley that he missed his friend. "He was so proud," he remembered. "For a Mexican national, he had a lot of pride in America."[6] U.S. Army Private David Cuervo is buried in Texas, as an American. Under an executive order the president signed in 2002, any immigrant who joins the U.S. military and is killed in combat is eligible for immediate posthumous citizenship.

Foreigners interested in legal U.S. residency can skip the long line if they offer the government enough money. In 1990, Congress passed a little-known law designed to encourage immigration by rich investors. The Investor Visa Program reserves up to ten thousand Green Cards a year for investors and their immediate families. Applicants must agree to invest at least a couple of million dollars in a U.S. business, an investment that will generate jobs.

U.S. citizenship is for sale to high-enough bidders: your money or your life.

Build the Wall!

Fast forward a generation and any George W. Bush immigration reform plan is a distant memory. President Obama presided over a record number of deportations during his eight years in the White House, which earned Obama the moniker of Deporter-in-Chief. President Trump rode to his Electoral College victory at least in part based on his inflammatory nativist and racist rhetoric, braying about Mexicans as "… bringing drugs … bringing crime. … rapists," and squawking perpetually about the wall he failed to build after four years in office. "I want nothing to do with Mexico other than to build an impenetrable WALL and stop them from ripping off U.S."

Such prejudicial rhetoric continued as the 2020 presidential campaign trail headed toward the November election. Trump called the Covid-19 pandemic "the Chinese virus" and "Kung flu" with the same vitriol he exerted against Mexicans. His administration instituted unprecedented travel restrictions in response to the disease. Those controls were best-practices border policy for attempting to contain spread of the virus. They were an example of the types of temporary international and intranational borders with the potential for good. The urgent Covid-19 crisis orders that limited cross-border movement are night-and-day different from border-control policies designed to lock Mexican laborers, students, tourists and families seeking reunification out of a fortress America (Figure 22.1).

As the disease continued to kill in the absence of a coordinated national strategy to contain it, heartless Trump administration rules kept captured undocumented migrants confined in Covid-19 petri dishes of spreading infection. By mid-2020, under the cover of the pandemic, it used an emergency Centers for Disease Control and Prevention directive to expel tens of thousands of migrants—including children and asylum seekers—immediately upon their arrival on American soil. Prior to the implementation of the pandemic-rationalized ruling, most such migrants would have been housed in the United States while their cases were adjudicated. Customs and Border Protection was proud of its instant deportations, telling the public its agents were able to "process and return, in under two hours, 96 percent of those subject to the Order, dramatically reducing human contact, the risk of spread, and the strain on U.S. healthcare facilities, helping the United States avert a public health disaster."[7]

Not true. Pandemic mismanagement by the Trump administration exacerbated a public health disaster regardless of migration from Mexico.

Toward the end of 2017, when prototypes of Trump's wall were on display just north of Tijuana, I arranged with the Border Patrol to cross into the exclusion zone surrounding the monoliths for a close-up inspection (Figure 22.2).

Figure 22.1 The severe and serpentine borderline wall separating Fortress America from the Global South at Tijuana.

I stay at the Holiday Inn Express at Otay Mesa—the closest hotel room to the massive display. I wander down to breakfast just another anonymous hotel occupant. Fox News was screaming from a huge TV screen. The desk clerks are speaking with each other—in Spanish of course, the mother tongue for so many hotel workers from coast to coast and border to border. And a *Dia de las Muertes* altar decorates the lobby—it's almost Halloween.

As is my journalistic wont, I check out my fellow diners: With whom was I sharing breakfast? I see well-worn work clothes, beards and tattoos. And as I listen, the chatter makes it clear that the drawls I hear between mouthfuls of eggs and slugs of coffee are coming from workers who just finished one of the wall models.

"You think it'll ever get built?" I ask a guy sharing my table who seems—as he answers packing-up-and-moving-out questions from the others—to be the foreman.

"I dunno," he opines from under his wide-brimmed straw hat. A blue work shirt covers his sprawling midsection and a Yosemite Sam moustache decorates his face. "But it sure would be good for the economy."

Figure 22.2 With prototypes for Trump's wall as a backdrop, a family walks along the borderline on the Tijuana side. Note the little girl riding on the bike: Her angelic face illustrates the front cover of *Up Against the Wall*.

At least it would be for his personal economy and that of the company he works for: KWR Construction, one of the six construction firms building the soaring sample walls.

"If this fence is inevitable," announced KWR Construction, "it might as well be built well and by us." The company is headquartered in the Arizona border city Sierra Vista, just down the highway from Tombstone. "It should provide jobs to our workers who actually belong to these same border communities and care about the communities. All of us can make lemonade out of what some call a lemon." From breaking ground to the finished product, Yosemite Sam and his crew built their section in six days.

What happens next? Testing. Evaluation. Decision. And if KWR is not picked for the job, what happens to their prototype (and the others)? The mock-ups are just north of the actual borderline.

"Demo 'em," my tablemate replies. How? He suggests cut through the rebar and the concrete at the base, attach a line at the top and just pull the thing down. Other KWR workers add their musings.

"I hate to brag, but we did a great job," says one worker.

Their wall is made of galvanized steel with a transparent feature that allows those on each side to see the Other. It would be bad press, suggests another, to destroy what costs so much. Half a million taxpayer dollars were budgeted for each prototype.

"Maybe leave it as a monument," offers still another.

While we talk, Fox News broadcasts with it calls an "exclusive" interview with President Trump. He looms large in the Holiday Inn breakfast room, yet he's ignored—his volume low. The jocular talk turns to the long drive across the desert home.

"Watch the speed limit with that trailer!"

"Eighty-five, right?"

Congress denied President Trump the billions of dollars he sought for his wall so he declared border chaos a national emergency and raided the Pentagon treasury, diverting funds from previously budgeted military affairs in order to keep his masquerade in the headlines. As the 2020 presidential election campaign intensified, legal challenges to spending Defense Department dollars on the wall headed toward the Supreme Court. At the same time, construction on enough miles of Trump's wall allowed the incumbent to gloat that his 2016 promise to seal the border was an ongoing—if delayed—success. The campaign hoped loud wall talk would drag public attention from the administration's failed Covid-19 strategies and the resulting collapse of the economy. Reality is a tough customer. Although Trump bragged about 220 miles of "the most powerful and comprehensive border wall structure anywhere in the world" as election day neared only three of those miles were new construction. The rest was repair and replacement.[8] And of course, despite Trump's promise that he would send the wall bill south of the border, Mexico didn't pay a *centavo* toward the billions of dollars his administration spent.

The Trump-era wall construction was mocked shortly after crews hung up their hard hats on a highly publicized and supposedly impregnable slab. Marauders from the south side deftly poked man-sized holes in it with Sawzalls.[9] Whether ladders or Sawzalls are the tools, the false sense of security created by billions spent on the wall must be augmented with more tax-payer dollars spent on sensors, spotlights, drones and phalanxes of border patrol officers in order to perpetuate the charade of migration control.

Presidente Fox on the Border

My travels contemplating walls, borders, migration and identity took me traipsing around all the world's continents save Antarctica. As I was wrapping up my research and reporting for *Up Against the Wall*, I took a jaunt south of the border to Guanajuato to meet with Vicente Fox. He welcomed me to his family's *hacienda*—now a luxurious hotel—where we lounged at the patio bar enjoying cold drinks and wall talk.

"Trump thinks he's right," Fox frowned, "separating the world of the poor from a world of progress." But, he said, Trump misses the fact that both worlds need each other. "There's a vanguard with dreams that moved the world to where we are today in education, science, economy and philosophy." He took a modest sip from his bottle of beer. "But this vanguard must be linked with the rear guard. If we leave the rear guard behind walls," he said, we all fail. He cited the General Motors (GM) plant just a few kilometers down the highway. GM, he said, is a vanguard but it needs its thousands of Mexican rear-guard workers to build cars and trucks. It's important to note a snag in the example: GM left thousands out of work in Michigan. We both sipped our beers. "Walls don't work," he mused, "but you cannot just open borders." Of course. My call to open the U.S. border to Mexicans who want to come north requires controls such as the United States exerts on the Canadian border. But no Trump massive wall.

"They built the huge Great Wall of China to prevent their enemies from conquering them," noted Fox (from behind the wall of the hacienda that protected his grandfather from Pancho Villa). "And the Mongols jumped the wall." We tossed more stories and opinions back and forth. Fox thought back on his presidency and defended NAFTA, insisting free trade helps develop the Mexican economy. "There's no extreme poverty anymore." To paraphrase another president, Bill Clinton, that depends, of course, on what the meaning of "extreme" is.

We talked religion: "We all believe in love," said Fox. We talked independence from England and Spain: Washington up north and Hidalgo in Guanajuato. We talked economic equity and personal security: without them we all seek panic rooms. We talked migration: his poor boyhood friends who trekked north. "This passion, this force that takes you to walk though deserts, to risk your life. You might die, you might be stopped at the border and sent back. Yet you go, you go, you go." And, of course, we kept talking walls: "If you're hungry, you jump the wall."

EPILOGUE: A PRACTICAL BLUEPRINT FOR NORMALIZING THE BORDER

There are no real national borders any longer. From the incursions of "wetbacks" pulling themselves out of the north bank of the Rio Grande to the global business conducted by international conglomerates, people have transcended the artificial constructs of national borders—even as the scores of new national border walls appeared around the world since the Berlin Wall fell.

Communication plays a key role in punching through the walls built by those who try to control migration. Radio magically proves uncontainable, spreading Mexico into the United States and vice versa. The Internet virtually destroys the remnants of borders. What's left—especially along the Mexico-United States line—is, aside from the deadly games being played out during these last days of the border, a nominal irritation for the truly motivated. Despite the heavy-handed efforts of the U.S. government, people prove they move as they always have, particularly when they are motivated by financial or family needs. From Jericho to Tijuana, walls fall.

So what are the possible solutions to the border crisis?

More enforcement and barriers along the border? Unworkable, no matter the "Build the wall!" ranting bellows of President Trump and his ardent followers. Neither the funds nor the pragmatic desire exists for such an attempted solution even though Trump manipulated the federal budget to raid the Defense Department for enough cash to construct nominal samples of his dream wall—his chimeric campaign promise. Anyone who has ever eaten in a restaurant, happened on a construction site or watched field hands at work knows how much the United States depends on Mexican labor.

Opening the border to the passage of vetted Mexicans who wish to come north is the only reasonable and long-term solution to our Mexican border wars. Open the border to Mexicans who are coming north no matter what we do, people we want and need, no matter how much we may say otherwise. Once Mexicans travel north when they wish in the same manner Canadians travel south, the real bad guys can no longer hide in their shadows. Once Mexicans travel north freely, the logistics for dealing in a civilized and controlled manner with migrants who come north from south of Mexico will become much more manageable. Over time Mexicans and we will learn to blend, not collide. And once Mexicans can again travel north with no more restrictions than a clean record and a valid ID, the U.S. government will know that the people in the tunnels and jumping the fences and running across the desert are not honest and honorable Mexicans fueling the U.S. economy.

There is no question that the U.S. southern border will be more secure if law-abiding Mexicans are allowed to pass when they so desire. Once Mexicans no longer feel the need to sneak north, most undoubtedly will be happy to register with American authorities and carry whatever documents the United States requires for them to move between the two countries via official ports of entry. After that change occurs, the Border Patrol and other U.S. government agencies will be facing a trickle instead of a tsunami of illegal border crossers. With their advanced detection equipment and huge staff, the Border Patrol will then be well prepared to detain and deport most of those who will try to cross into the United States illegally. Because of such a new neighbor-friendly policy, U.S. authorities will no longer be chasing Mexican workers needed and wanted in the north. They can pursue unwanted—and potentially dangerous—border violators. Gangsters and drug traffickers, terrorists and spies seeking to infiltrate U.S. borders will be left alone in the spotlight without the protection offered them by the cover and chaos of desperate, motivated Mexicans violating the border.

But there is more. Almost overnight the status of millions of Mexicans vis-à-vis the United States will change. No longer wanted as criminals, they will be wanted and invited guests. By making Mexicans feel officially welcome and protected by police and society instead of afraid of being caught without valid documents, most Mexicans will become willing and active participants in helping to keep those who endanger the United States out of the country.

Whether we actively work to make this policy happen or just allow events to overwhelm us, now or later the artificial line separating Mexico from the United States (so much of which is, of course, Mexico's former territory) will disappear.

Mexico in My Dreams

As I made clear with the notation of my father's passage through Ellis Island, I am prejudiced to favor immigrants. Especially after the borderlands horrors and tragedies perpetrated by the Trump administration it remains obvious to me that welcoming Mexicans who wish to come north to work and study and play is the pragmatic solution to the crises along our border. But I'm not just prejudiced to favor immigrants; I'm prejudiced to favor Mexico and Mexicans. Perhaps it comes from growing up in California. I was surrounded by the food, the music, the costumes, the language of Mexico. ¡And, *por supuesto*, Mexicans! I appreciate the influence of Mexico and Mexicans on my culture. I savor Mexican evenings like one in San Cristóbal de Las Casas when I ended a workday with a colleague listening to a guitarist at a local jazz club.

As we said good night, and I strolled toward my hotel, in the distance I began to hear the comforting sound of a marimba band. The melodies grew louder and I followed the music, straying from my path to the hotel.

There on Avenida Cristóbal Colón, a full marimba band—six marimbistas, a bass player and a drummer—were set up in the street, playing Chiapas classics under the glowing street lights. The bassist cautiously moved aside when the periodic late-night taxi cruised by. The traffic lights seemed to flash in time with the music.

I leaned against a nearby shop wall listening: all older men, playing for themselves—and me. The magical rattle of the marimba reverberating against the pastel walls of the stucco buildings lining the narrow streets: the Mexico of my dreams.

All I needed was my girl to dance with me on the gleaming paving stones.

NOTES

Foreword by Former president of Mexico Vicente Fox

1 https://www.youtube.com/watch?v=vtk_zcbVAeE.

Chapter 1 UP AGAINST THE WALL (EXPLETIVE)

1 Raskin's warm poem "Ode to Bread" hangs on my kitchen wall and his send-up of the academy, "More Academic," includes the spot-on line: "I have a better Ph.D. than you, from / A more prestigious school."

2 http://spectatorarchive.library.columbia.edu/?a=d&d=cs19681211-02.2.5&srpos=1&e=------en-20--1--txt-txIN-that+we+should+be+out+fighting%2c+rather+than+just+sitting+watching+a+play.

3 *Jet*, July 17, 1969, "LeRoi Jones 'Not Guilty' in Newark Riot Retrial," p. 5.

4 Jones changed his name to Amiri Baraka in the mid-1960s. His *New York Times* obituary calls the surname Bantuized Arabic for "blessed." Other interpretations cite Baraka as "blessed prince." https://www.nytimes.com/2014/01/10/arts/amiri-baraka-polarizing-poet-and-playwright-dies-at-79.html.

5 Charles Reilly, ed., *Conversations with Amiri Baraka*, Jackson: University Press of Mississippi, 1994, p. 253.

6 Ron Perlstein, *Nixonland: The Rise of a President and the Fracturing of America*, New York: Simon & Schuster, 2010, p. 238.

7 Jonathon Green, *Dictionary of Slang*, London: Cassell, 1998, p. 1246.

8 Eric Partridge, *A Dictionary of Slang and Unconventional English*, New York: Routledge, 2006.

9 Robert Stone (dir.), "Guerilla: The Taking of Patty Hearst," Hudson Valley, NY: Robert Stone Productions, 2005.

10 Jean-Paul Sartre, *The Wall*, New York: New Directions, 1975, p. 8.

11 http://christojeanneclaude.net/mobile/projects?p=running-fence.

12 Frances Stonor Saunders, "Where on Earth Are You?," *London Review of Books* Vol. 8, No. 5, March 3, 2016.

Chapter 2 ILLEGAL ALIEN OR CLEVER NEW AMERICAN

1 Juana María's name is changed for this book, and I've excised the name of her new hometown from her story.

2   *Cholo(a)* is a Mexican term originally used to describe a person of mixed Spanish and Indian heritage. On the north side of the border it's been used as a derogatory identifier for Latino street gang members, and often implies the specific attire favored by the subculture.

3   Mexicans use many different terms for the United States including *El Norte*, the North. *Gringolandia* is another. *Gringolandia* tends to be used disparagingly, whereas *El Norte* is simply an identifier. And the United States is often just referred to as *el otro lado*, the other side.

4   Juana María still said INS, using the acronym for the Immigration and Naturalization Service. The new nomenclature of the Department of Homeland Security Immigration and Customs Enforcement had not replaced her jargon. She didn't refer to the INS with the Spanglish slang word *Migra*.

5   The Border Action Network report "Justice on the Line" can be seen at their website, www.resistmiltarization.org.

Chapter 3 STILL LIFE ON THE BORDER

1   Raul Llamas, "Border Town Marks 5th Migrant Day," *Miami Herald*, September 8, 2003, international edition.

2   Ginger Thompson, "In Border Town, Migrant Crackdown Rankles," *New York Times*, June 5, 2003.

3   Michael Marizco, "Sonoran Priest's Shelter Helps Cut Desert's Human Toll," *Arizona Daily Star*, December 26, 2003.

4   John Reed, *Insurgent Mexico*, New York: International Publishers, 2002, p. 245.

5   Mary Harris, "This Border Town Mayor Wanted More Roads. What He Got Was Razor Wire," *Slate*, February 12, 2019, https://slate.com/news-and-politics/2019/02/trump-border-wall-nogales-arizona-razor-wire.html.

6   Joel Millman, "On Trips to Mexico, Some Americans Bring Back Mexicans," *Wall Street Journal*, November 17, 2003.

Chapter 4 ON GUARD

1   Gregory Gross, "Battle at the Border," *San Diego Union Tribune*, August 21, 1997.

2   https://www.pewresearch.org/hispanic/2012/04/23/ii-migration-between-the-u-s-and-mexico/.

3   Mary Jo McConahay, "Human Smuggling Deaths," *Dissident Voice*, May 20, 2003.

4   Joseph Torres, "Nearly 1,200 Perish in Three Years Attempting to Cross Border," *Hispanic Link Weekly Report*, August 18, 1997.

5   Bob Moser, "Samaritans in the Desert," *Nation*, May 26, 2003.

6   Testimony of Representative Silvestre Reyes to the House Subcommittee on Immigration and Claims, February 25, 1999. Reyes was calling for more funds to pay for more Border Patrol personnel.

7   Marjorie Valbrun, "At the Frontier of Irony, Border Patrol Ranks Swell With Hispanics," *Wall Street Journal*, October 22, 1998.

8   Louis Freeberg, "Clinton and Dole's Dueling Immigration Ads," *San Francisco Chronicle*, July 7, 1996.

9   Ken Ellingwood, "Border Patrol Agent Kills Immigrant," *Los Angeles Times*, September 28, 1998.

10   Ken Ellingwood, "Agent Shoots Man in Second Border Killing," *Los Angeles Times*, September 29, 1998.

11   Martin Kasindorf, "Texas Death Puts Focus on Military's Role in Drug War," *USA Today*, June 10, 1997.

12   Robert Draper, "Soldiers of Misfortune," *Texas Monthly*, August 1997.

13   S. C. Gwynne, "Border Skirmish: A Teen's Death Forces the Military to Question Its Role in Fighting Drugs," *Time Magazine*, August 25, 1997.

14   Howe Verhovek, "After Marine on Patrol Kills a Teen-Ager, a Texas Border Village Wonders Why," *New York Times*, June 29, 1997.

15   Rep. Tancredo (Colo.). "Securing American Borders," *Congressional Record* (March 6, 2003), H1657.

16   https://twitter.com/i/events/1092831071241007104?lang=en (accessed June 30, 2020).

17   Adam Woodward, interview, January 2020.

18   Michael Janofsky, "Immigrants Flood Border in Arizona, Angering Ranchers," *New York Times*, June 18, 2000.

19   Morris Thompson, "Crackdown Forces More Migrants into Desert Crossings," *Santa Rosa Press Democrat*, July 29, 2000.

20   Janofsky, "Immigrants Flood Border in Arizona."

21   Kevin Johnson, "50 More Immigration Agents to Fight Smugglers in Phoenix," *USA Today*, November 11, 2003.

22   National Public Radio, December 1, 2003.

Chapter 5 DEATH ALONG FOR THE RIDE

1   Kate Zernike and Ginger Thompson, "Deaths of Immigrants Uncover Makeshift World of Smuggling," *New York Times*, June 29, 2003.

2   In 2007, a few years after he left the sheriff's office to become the Victoria County public defender's chief of staff, the former sheriff was arrested, charged with aggravated sexual assault of a teenage boy and criminal solicitation with a handgun of a minor. A plea deal reduced the charges to aggravated perjury and Ratcliff was sentenced to 10 years' probation.

3   Kevin Sullivan and Mary Jordan, "7 Days of Desperation along Mexican Border," *Washington Post*, May 25, 2003.

Chapter 7 WHAT IS A BORDER?

1   Michael Specter, "10 Years Later, Through Fear, Chernobyl Still Kills in Belarus," *New York Times*, March 31, 1996.

Chapter 8 FAILED BORDERS

1 William Truni, "Kids Going It Alone," *Barcelona Metropolitan*, June 2003.

2 Graham Tutthill, "Refugees Died Fighting for Air," *Dover Mercury*, June 29, 2000.

3 "Let's Hear It for Dover!" *Express*, June 29, 2000.

4 Gershom Gorenberg, "The One-Fence Solution," *New York Times*, August 3, 2003.

5 *National Geographic* magazine, January 2004.

6 Michele Kambas, "Cyprus Dividing Line Opened for Day Trips," *Washington Post*, April 24, 2003.

7 Alastair Jamieson, "Far-Right Mayor Hails Success of Hungary-Serbia Border Fence," NBC News, May 2, 2018, https://www.nbcnews.com/news/world/far-right-mayor-hails-success-hungary-serbia-border-fence-n868676.

8 Refugee interview, March 22, 2017.

9 Rosa Flores, CNN, January 26, 2019.

Chapter 9 U.S. ANNEXATION OF HALF OF MEXICO

1 *Economist*, August 16, 2003.

2 Carol Christensen and Thomas, *The U.S.-Mexican War*, San Francisco, CA: Bay Books, 1998, p. 41.

3 *New York Morning News*, August 13, 1845, cited in Frederick Merk, *Manifest Destiny and Mission in American History*, New York: Alfred A. Knopf, 1963, p. 25.

4 Carol Christensen and Thomas, *The U.S.-Mexican War*, San Francisco, CA; Bay Books, 1998, p. 19.

5 Carol Christensen and Thomas, *The U.S.-Mexican War*, San Francisco, CA: Bay Books, 1998, p. 43.

6 Eugene Irving McCormac, *James K. Polk, a Political Biography*, New York: Russell & Russell, 1965, p. 373.

7 Ibid., p. 381.

8 *National Intelligencer*, August 5, 1845, cited in Eugene Irving McCormac, *James K. Polk, a Political Biography*, New York: Russell & Russell, 1965, p. 377.

9 From the June 10, 1847 edition of the *Chronicle*, under the title "Rough and Ready," quoted in the book *Chronicle of the Gringos, the US Army in the Mexican War, 1846–1848: Accounts of Eyewitnesses & Combatants*, edited by George Winston Smith and Charles Judah, Albuquerque: University of New Mexico Press, 1968, p. 12.

10 Carol Christensen and Thomas, *The U.S.-Mexican War*, San Francisco, CA: Bay Books, 1998, p. 62.

11 James K. Polk, *Polk: The Diary of a President 1845–1849*, edited by Allan Nevins, New York: Capricorn Books, 1968, p. 83.

12 Polk's message to Congress was delivered on May 11, 1846.

13 From President Paredes proclamation of what he called a "defensive war" on April 26, 1846, cited in Eugene Irving McCormac, *James K. Polk, a Political Biography*, New York: Russell & Russell, 1965, p. 413.

14 *New York Morning News*, July 7, 1845, cited in Frederick Merk, *Manifest Destiny and Mission in American History*, New York: Alfred A. Knopf, 1963, p. 50.

15 The *New York Sun*, November 20, 1847, cited in Frederick Merk, *Manifest Destiny and Mission in American History*, New York: Alfred A. Knopf, 1963, p. 122.

16 James K. Polk, *The Diary of a President*, edited by Allen Nevins, New York: Longmans, Greens, 1952.

17 Carol Christensen and Thomas, *The U.S.-Mexican War*, Bay Books, San Francisco, 1998, p. 101.

18 Christensen, Carol and Thomas, *The U.S.-Mexican War*, San Francisco, CA: Bay Books, 1998, p. 111.

19 From a letter Belton wrote to his wife and son quoted in *Chronicle of the Gringos, the US Army in the Mexican War, 1846–1848: Accounts of Eyewitnesses & Combatants*, edited by George Winston Smith and Charles Judah, Albuquerque: University of New Mexico Press, 1968, p. 191.

20 Ibid., p. 192.

21 John Ross, *The Annexation of Mexico*, Monroe, ME: Common Courage Press, 1998, p. 68.

22 May 29, 2000, at the Memorial Day service at Arlington National Cemetery.

23 Elijah Wald, *Narocorrido: A Journey into the Music of Drugs, Guns, and Guerillas*, New York: HarperCollins, 2001, p. 35.

24 "La Tumba del Mojado" is on the Los Tigres del Norte collection *Internacionalmente Norteños*, released by Fonovisa.

25 "El Deportado" is collected on *Corridos & Tragedias de la Frontera*, released by Arhoolie/Folklyric.

26 John Ross died in 2011 at Lake Pátzcuaro in Mexico.

27 "Los Mandados" was written by Jorge Lerma and can be found on the Fernandez compilation CD, *Los 15 Grandes Exitos*, released in 1990 on CBS Discos.

28 Tortilla Industry Association market research study, "The State of the Tortilla Industry Survey: 2002." The study concluded 32 percent of U.S. bread sales are in the tortilla category, just 2 percent below white bread, the nation's most popular breadstuff.

29 Glan Collins, "Developing a Taste for 'Gringo Food,'" *International Herald Tribune*, January 1, 1997.

30 Simon Romero, "Mexican Wealth Gives Texas City A New Vitality," *New York Times*, June 14, 2003.

Chapter 10 EARLY BORDER CONTROL

1 *The New Columbia Encyclopedia*, New York: Columbia University Press, 1975, p. 540.

2 *An Immigrant Nation: United States Regulation of Immigration, 1798–1991* Pub. Date 6/18/1991 Ch. 5: "Amendments and Reform in the late 20th century," p. 23.

3 Jasmine Aguilera, "Citizens Facing Deportation Isn't New. Here's What Happened When the U.S. Removed Mexican-Americans in the 1930s," *Time* magazine, August 2, 2019.

4   Leo Grebler, *Mexican Immigration to the United States: The Record and Its Implications*, Oakland, CA: University of California, 1965, pp. 25–26.

5   Congressional Record, Immigration from Countries of the Western Hemisphere, House Committee on Immigration and Naturalization, Seventieth Congress, First Session, 1928, pp. 7–10.

6   "Says 400,000 Aliens Are Here Illegally," *New York Times*, January 5, 1931.

7   Gardner Jackson, "Doak the Deportation Chief," *Nation*, March 18, 1931, p. 295.

8   U.S. Commerce Department, Census Bureau, Sixteenth Census of the United States, 1940.

9   Fred L. Koestler, "Operation Wetback," Texas State Historical Society, 2010, https://tshaonline.org/handbook/online/articles/pqo01.

10 John O. West, *Mexican-American Folklore*, Little Rock, AR: August House, 1988, p. 36.

11 Elijah Wald, *Narocorrido: A Journey into the Music of Drugs, Guns, and Guerillas*, New York: HarperCollins, 2001, p. 176. The song "La Discriminación" can be found on the Los Norteños de Ojinaga album *Corridos Pa' Mi Pueblo*, Vol. II.

12 Boye Lafayette De Mente, *Dictionary of Mexican Cultural Code Words*, Chicago, IL: NTC Publishing, 1996, p. 123.

13 David Dorado Romo, "Crossing the Line," *Los Angeles Times*, February 27, 2006.

14 Jenifer Hanrahan, "Braceros Seek Justice," *San Diego Union-Tribune*, November 26, 1999.

15 Juliana Barbassa, "Former Braceros Oppose Bush Plan," Associated Press dispatch, January 2004.

16 *Wetbacks* was released in 1956, directed and produced by Hank McCune.

17 Kelly St. John, "San Quentin Prison Was His Art School," *San Francisco Chronicle*, July 27, 2003.

Chapter 12 THE VIGILANTE MOVEMENT

1   William Drozdiak, "German Town Admits Role in Firebombing of Immigrant Hostel," *Washington Post*, February 13, 1997.

2   From www.americanpatrol.org.

3   Julie Watson, "Arizonans Watch Line in Sand: Armed Civilians Enforcing U.S. Border," Associated Press dispatch, February 10, 2003.

4   Ray Borane, "Do You Hire Illegal Immigrants?," *New York Times*, August 30, 1999.

5   In fact, "illegal aliens" fails the politically correct test. A person cannot be illegal. One can commit an illegal act. But no one is illegal.

6   "Police Beat," *Bisbee Observer*, February 13, 2003.

7   Megan Cassidy, "Chris Simcox Sentenced to 19.5 Years," *Arizona Republic*, July 11, 2016.

8   Stephen Lemons, "Ex-Minuteman Chris Simcox Guilty of Molestation, Victim's Mother Hopes He 'Meets Karma in Prison'" *Phoenix New Times*, June 9, 2016.

9   Roberto Rodriguez and Patrisia Gonzales, "Auntie Immigration," *San Francisco Chronicle*, August 29, 1994.

Chapter 13 AMERICANS PARTY SOUTH, MEXICANS STRUGGLE NORTH

1   Rafael Carranza, "Tohono O'odham Historic Sites at Risk as Border Wall Construction Advances in Arizona," *Arizona Republic*, January 20, 2020.

2   "Border Wall", Northern Jaguar Project, https://www.northernjaguarproject.org/northern-jaguar-reserve/threats-and-opportunities/border-wall/.

Chapter 14 THE POROUS, SHIFTING BORDER

1   *How to Handle an Accident in Mexico* is printed and distributed by the insurance company Seguros Comercial América.

2   *Tourist Guide Tijuana*, published by the Fondo Mixto de Promocion Turistica de Tijuana, 2001.

3   Carl Franz, "Traveler's Update," in *The People's Guide to Mexico* (Digital version), Open Library, PDF, p. 522.

4   Sandra Dibble, "Man Says Mexican Police Robbed Him," *San Diego Union*, January 1, 2004.

5   Sandra Dibble, "More Women in US Say They Were Raped by Tijuana Cops," *San Diego Union Tribune*, December 19, 2003.

6   Committee to Protect Journalists, https://cpj.org/americas/mexico/.

7   Carlos Fuentes, *The Crystal Frontier*, New York: Farrar, Straus and Giroux, 1997, p. 252.

8   *Reforma* was founded with a policy that bans all bribes. Reporters are forbidden from taking anything from sources on penalty of being fired. They are required to pay for everything associated with their news gathering work, even a cheap coffee and sandwich during a lunch meeting.

9   Tom Miller, *On the Border: Portraits of America's Southwestern Frontier*, New York: Harper, 1981.

10   Jill Kramer, *Pacific Sun*, May 29–June 4, 2002.

11   Cecilia M. Vega, "Tensions Persist at RP School," *Santa Rosa Press-Democrat*, January 31, 2004.

12   "The O'Reilly Factor," Fox News Network, February 6, 2003.

13   www.michaelsavage.com (2003).

Chapter 15 ILLEGAL AMERICANS

1   Diane Schiller, "Illegal Immigration Sometimes Goes South," *San Antonio Express-News*, October 19, 2003.

2   Rick Lyman, "Gun Charges and Trouble South of the Border," *New York Times*, October 23, 1998.

3   Tim Weiner, "Busy as Sin in Mexico, Tending to Straying Sheep," *New York Times*, May 12, 2003.

Chapter 16 ON THE KENTUCKY-MEXICO BORDER

1   Mark Stevenson, "Border Patrol's Trap, Transplant Program Works," Associated Press dispatch, September 27, 2003.

2   Hispanic is the term used by the federal government for Mexicans and other Latin Americans in the United States. Latino is the identity preferred by the people themselves

according to Coffey's research, and indicates some Indian blood. In recent years Latinx has been a popular alternative for those seeking a gender-neutral term. Chicano has been used to identify ethnic Mexicans born in the United States, and dates from the early 1900s.

Chapter 17 DEPORTATION MADE EASIER

1   Human Rights Watch testimony before U.S . House, https://www.hrw.org/news/2019/07/11/written-testimony-kids-cages-inhumane-treatment-border#9,23ß.

2   https://www.washingtonpost.com/world/national-security/deal-with-mexico-paves-way-for-asylum-overhaul-at-us-border/2018/11/24/87b9570a-ef74-11e8-9236-bb94154151d2_story.html.

Chapter 19 WHO WANTS THE BORDER CLOSED?

1   Cecilia M. Vega, *Santa Rosa Press Democrat*, June 2, 2003.

2   Associated Press dispatch.

3   Ruben Navarrette Jr., "Latino Immigrants Have Done Just Fine in Pursuing Dreams," *Los Angeles Times*, May 28, 2003.

4   Ellen Hale, "Mexicans Look to San Rafael for New Lives," *Marin Independent Journal*, September 4, 1994.

Chapter 20 BURDEN OR BENEFIT?

1   "Paul Harvey News and Comment," ABC Radio Network, October 28, 2003.

2   Gerry Hadden, NPR broadcast "Morning Edition," May, 2003.

3   Ginger Thompson and Tom Weiner, "Mexico Struggles for the Attentions of a Preoccupied U.S.," *New York Times*, October 13, 2002.

4   Anthony Humphreys and Siona Jenkins, *Egypt*, Melbourne: Lonely Planet Publications, 2002, p. 257.

5   Deborah Kong, "Anti-Migrant Backlash Brews across U.S.," Associated Press dispatch, August 4, 2001.

6   SPLC, "Council of Conservative Citizens," https://www.splcenter.org/fighting-hate/extremist-files/group/council-conservative-citizens.

7   Associated Press dispatch, July 3, 1994.

8   Roberto Rodriguez and Patrisia Gonzales, "Auntie Immigration," *Francisco Chronicle*, August 29, 1994.

9   Dr. Jorge L. Chenea, "Ethnic Prejudice and Anti-Immigrant Policies in Times of Economic Stress: Mexican Repatriation from the United States, 1929–1939," *East Wind/West Wind*, Winter 1996, p. 11.

10 George J. Borjas, "Mexico's One-Way Remedy," *New York Times*, July 18, 2000.

11 "El barrio de Fayetteville," *Economist*, September 19, 1998, p. 39.

12 James P. Smith and Barry Edmonston, eds., *The Economic and Fiscal Consequences of Immigration*, Washington, DC: National Academy Press, 2017.

13   *The New Americans: Economic, Demographic, and Fiscal Effects of Immigration*, Washington, DC: National Academy Press, 1997.

Chapter 21   THE LONG ROAD NORTH FROM CHIAPAS AND CHIHUAHUA

1   Tiziano Terzani, *A Fortune-Teller Told Me*, New York: Harmony Books, 1997, pp. 46–7.

2   By early 2004, the Commission for Environmental Cooperation, a unit of NAFTA, warned that genetically modified (GM) corn was contaminating Mexican native varieties and threatening the survival of some sixty types of native corn, despite a ban on the GM seed imposed by the Mexican government in 1998. GM feed corn is not banned and is likely used by some farmers as a cheap alternative for seed.

3   Dan Baum, "On the Border," *Los Angeles Times Magazine*, March 16, 2003.

4   Robert Collier, "NAFTA Gives Mexicans New Reasons to Leave Home," *San Francisco Chronicle*, October 15, 1998.

5   Richard Brand, "Many of Mexico's Poorest Forced to Leave Homes to Work on US Farms," *Miami Herald*, November 14, 2003.

6   David Bacon, *The Children of NAFTA*, Berkeley: University of California Press, 2004, p. 35.

7   Joseph Stiglitz, "The Broken Promise of NAFTA," *San Francisco Chronicle*, January 6, 2004.

8   Anne-Marie O'Connor, "Emergence of a Hybrid Culture," *Los Angeles Times*, April 29, 1997.

9   Robert Collier, "Family Ties across the Divide," *San Francisco Chronicle*, October 15, 1998.

10   Víctor Reyes, "¿Mexicano, gringo o qué?" *Point Reyes* (CA) *Light*, February 12, 2004.

Chapter 22   NO AMIGOS IN THE WHITE HOUSE

1   Associated Press dispatch, October 18, 1995.

2   Nina Bernstein, "Immigrants Are Divided on Bush Proposal," *New York Times*, January 8, 2004.

3   "Newshour with Jim Lehrer," PBS, January 8, 2004.

4   Louie Gilot, "Bush's Migrant Plan Brings Scams," *El Paso Times*, January 16, 2004.

5   Michael Riley, "Guest Worker Scams Arise," *Denver Post,* January 16, 2004.

6   Bud Kennedy, "Salute to Pvt. David Cuervo, Mexican Immigrant Killed in Iraq," *Fort Worth Star-Telegram,* January 12, 2004.

7   CBS News, "U.S. Ramps Up Mass Expulsions of Migrants as Border Crossings Rise," June 13, 2020.

8   Michal D. Shear and Zolan Kanno-Youngs, "In Arizona, Trump Boasts about His Wall and Repeats Unfounded Predictions of Voter Fraud," *New York Times*, June 24, 2020.

9   Nick Miroff, "Smugglers Sawing through Trump's Wall," *Washington Post*, November 3, 2019.

ACKNOWLEDGMENT

While I was finishing my research for *Up Against the Wall*, Barbra Streisand released an album titled *Walls*. "We would have that better day," she sang, "if all the walls came tumbling down." Nice, I thought. And since we're both probing the same territory, maybe it would be a good idea to ask her if she would like to write a blurb for the book. So I asked one of my researchers, University of Oregon journalism masters student Laurie Galbraith, to get in touch with Barbra's handlers. Doggedly, Laurie tackled the task. A few weeks later, she returned to my office and crooned, "Getting to Barbra Streisand's manager was meaner than second skimmings."

"What?" was my natural response.

"Getting to Barbra Streisand's manager was meaner than second skimmings," she repeated. I asked for a translation. Turns out Laurie grew up across the road from a dairy farm. Her family bought milk fresh out of the cows. She used cheese cloth to skim the cream off the top of the milk, an easy task. But to make sure all cream possible was separated from the milk, she would make another pass. And that pass was harder work because it is a challenge to pull more cream off the top—a tough chore because there is so little cream left. Hence the fresh cow's milk jargon: meaner than second skimmings. So a thank you to Laurie for seeking a Barbra blurb and for the entrée to farm talk.

We all cross borders. Our reasons vary. Crossing borders is both my job and my advocation. I seek borders because I want to experience what's on the other side. I fancy myself a long-distance flâneur.

I've been reporting and studying borders, walls, migration and identity as a journalist and an academic since those days when my high school buddies and I were turned back north by the *federales* in Baja

California—so a tip of the *sombrero* to Mark Allen and Chris Slattery (and our reliable old VW bug). My initial formal forays into Mexico took place working as an NBC News correspondent when I often covered borders and immigration. Thanks to my NBC boss those many years ago, Jim Farley, for the assignments. I am indebted to *Penthouse* magazine editor (at the original *Penthouse*) Peter Bloch and the National Geographic Society for further news reporting assignments about Mexican-American relations.

I studied Mexico, Mexican immigration and Mexican-American relations while working as a consulting researcher for Internews, and I thank the David and Lucile Packard Foundation for the grant that funded my Internews Mexico project. Project manager at Internews, Deborah Mendelsohn, worked with me on developing contacts in Mexico and I thank her for her companionship and assistance during our time South of the Border together. My colleague Pedro Enrique Armendares was gracious sharing his Mexico-based sources with me. Veronica Melgoza opened crucial *puertos* in Chiapas, sharing her contacts with critical newsmakers there. I'm most grateful to Carmen Landa who, from the media relations department of the U.S. Embassy in Mexico City, introduced me to a long list of important sources. I appreciate the efforts of Dean Graber who, when he was project manager at the Knight Center for Journalism in the Americas at the University of Texas in Austin, assisted me reconstructing some notes I lost in Veracruz.

Thanks to my longtime friends and colleagues Bob Simmons, Terry Phillips and George Papagiannis for help with interviews in Texas, California and at the Capitol in Washington, respectively, and to my wife, Sheila Swan Laufer, for help with interviews in Kentucky (and, of course, for everything!). Journalist Alisa Roth forwarded important border and immigration background material to me. Writer Alex Roth offered valued commentary on early manuscript drafts as did actor and theater arts professor Dov Hassan. My old friend (since Kindergarten!) Dr. Tom Steinberg introduced me to a player in the popularization of "up against the wall, motherfucker," a meeting that aided my work on the etymology of the phrase. My friend Milan Melvin, who became a Mexican late in his life, saved valuable Mexican newspaper clippings for me. My comrade-in-arms at the University of Oregon, photojournalist extraordinaire Dan Morrison, manipulated my snapshots into publishable form. *Köszönön* to Michael Laufer for securing the Laufer family Ellis Island records and thanks to Tal Morris for his creative studio work on the Internews Mexico project audio report and on my RIAS Berlin Commission-funded radio documentary "Border Wars"—reporting from both helped fuel the book.

Thanks to my researcher University of Oregon media studies doctoral student Christopher St. Louis who skillfully orchestrated my visit with the Border Patrol to the Trump wall prototypes at Otay Mesa and to my researcher University of Oregon media studies doctoral student Rajeev Ravisankar for believe-it-or-not success probing Ripley's Believe It or Not archives, to Eric Goode for introducing me to the Northern Jaguar Project on the border in Arizona, to my student Khyle Claeys for the use of his interview with a Marine assigned to border duty and to my student Derek Maiolo for access to his reporting from Manitoba—work he accomplished as a student research fellow of the University of Oregon–UNESCO Institute for Intercultural Dialogue and Conflict-sensitive Reporting. An *abrazo fuerte* to Tim DuRoche at WorldOregon for the introduction to Presidente Fox.

Gracias to my friends Eleni and Markos Kounalakis who offered me use of their Barcelona pied-à-terre as an oasis in the ur-Mexico, a place where I luxuriously labored over the early manuscript free from routine distractions.

An *abrazo grande* to Ivan R. Dee. He and his eponymous house published my book *Wetback Nation* in 2004, and on its skeleton *Up Against the Wall* builds. Ivan Dee was a *sueno* for an editor who kept careful watch to make sure my words were not laden with *manteca*. With its sensational title, *Wetback Nation* led to a bizarre promotional experience: debating immigration policy on Fox TV with its soon-to-be disgraced-and-fired talk show host Bill O'Reilly. I won the debate.

Which brings me to Anthem Press. Thanks to Anthem's Elle Bloomberg who first suggested the house for my work and to its acquisitions editor Megan Greiving who midwifed it with such care, grace and good humor. Anthem publisher Tej P.S. Sood and I hashed out details over a long lunch in Seattle, a luncheon rich enough not only to agree that we wanted to do business together but also to establish what promises to be a lasting professional friendship. And hearty appreciation to the Anthem Press production team for the extraordinary copyediting, interior design and cover design work.

I am fortunate to be represented by the extraordinary literary agency MacKenzie Wolf. Thanks to Gillian MacKenzie for long championing *Up Against the Wall* and to Kirsten Wolf and Renée Jarvis for working out the publishing details.

Por supuesto I thank the scores of Mexicans and Americans who agreed to talk with me and share their life histories on both sides of the border. I appreciate their confidence that I would treat their stories with fairness, even when I disagreed with their points of view. And speaking of Americans, we're all Americans here in Mexico and the good ol' U.S. of A. and on down to Tierra del Fuego. But on both sides of the border we've become accustomed to using the identifier "American" to mean gringos. I so use it in this book while remaining aware of course that Mexicans are Americans too.

I am privileged to hold the James Wallace Chair in Journalism at the University of Oregon, endowed by the *U.S. News & World Report* foreign correspondent and Oregon alumnus James Wallace and his wife Haya. His datelines ranged from Moscow to Peking to Saigon, from Havana (Fidel Castro reportedly expelled him from Cuba for his reporting) to capitals throughout Latin America. Unfortunately I never had the opportunity to meet Wallace, but from everything I've learned about him, I wager we would have enjoyed each other's company—especially sitting at a saloon in San Cristobal de las Casas, Tijuana or most any Mexican *pueblo* in between, nursing tequila and tonics, trading tales about being on the road in search of the next story.

ABOUT THE AUTHOR

Journalist Peter Laufer reports on borders, identity and migration along with the relationships between humans and other animals. He is the James Wallace Chair Professor of Journalism at the University of Oregon School of Journalism and Communication and received the James Polk Award, among many other prizes and awards, for his journalism.

INDEX

Note: **Bold** page numbers indicates figure pages.

COLOPHON

The main text of *Up Against the Wall* is set in Adobe Text Pro and the subtitle text is Minion Pro. Both were designed by Robert Slimbach. They harken back to classical moveable typefaces and are easy to read in print or on screen. The chapter titles typography is Woodford Bourne, a face designed by Paulo Goode. Goode based it on the type he noticed on Cork, Ireland, facades of buildings that identified them as Woodford, Bourne & Co. "I had long admired these distinctive stone cast letters," he writes, "and jumped at the opportunity to interpret this genuine 19th century grotesque." The table of contents is DIN Alternative; DIN Schrift is used for chapter section headlines. They are derived from what type designer and DIN expert Albert-Jan Pool calls a "model for lettering" created in 1931. DIN 1451 Mittelschrift originally served railway and highway signage. It is a sans-serif face with a heritage dating back to the early 20th century and was created for easy identification of German railroad cars. DIN is the abbreviation of Deutsche Industrie-Norm (German Industrial Standard). The DIN faces used in this book are based on 1980 revisions by typographer Adolf Gropp. Hand lettering that notes place names on the chapter head illustrations is the author's design, developed by him for its legibility when his barely decipherable cursive ossified during third grade.